BEYOND AVERAGE

BEYOND AVERAGE

DEVELOPING YOURSELF THROUGH
THE 20X PRINCIPLE

Robert Hamilton Owens

American Ghost Media, LLC
Santa Monica, CA

BEYOND AVERAGE
Developing Yourself
Through The 20X Principle

Published by
American Ghost Media, LLC
Santa Monica, CA 90405
www.AmericanGhostMedia.com

Book Design By David Pisarra
Cover Photo By
Nathaniel Taylor
Nathaniel Taylor Photography
https://www.photonate.net

Copyright © 2019 Robert Hamilton Owens

All Rights Reserved. No part of this book may be reproduced, scanned or distributed in any printed or electronic form without the prior written permission of the author. Please do not participate in or encourage piracy of copyrighted materials in violation of the author's rights.

Printed in the United States of America

November 2019
First Edition
1 3 5 7 9 10 8 6 4 2

ISBN 9780999467251 Hard Cover
ISBN 9780999467268 Soft Cover

"The Most Interesting Triathlete in the world."
– Triathlete magazine

Some of Robert Owens' Adventures

1. Adopted at 3 months old.
2. Rode his tricycle to elementary school at 4 years old with his cowboy hat, boots and guns on. Mother called police on a possible kidnapping. Police found him 4 hours later at school with his sister.
3. At 6, dove out of the side door of a moving milk truck, but missed the front yard grass. Wasn't supposed to ride in the milk truck. Landed in the street. Didn't get caught.
4. Started Beach Lifeguarding for the City of San Clemente at 15 1/2 when the legal age was 16.
5. At 16 started parachuting without parents knowing.
6. At 18 traveled to Europe to ski on a one way ticket.
7. At 18 worked for a ski film business traveling around the U.S. showing a ski film at ski resorts and ski towns in his van.
8. At 19 worked on the "floor" on the Pacific Coast Stock Exchange in downtown L.A. as a Specialist Clerk.
9. Rowed Crew at Orange Coast College for 2 years: 1970 and 1971.
10. At 23 tried out and became a USAF Pararescueman.
11. At 26 broke his right wrist playing rugby against the University of Arkansas.
12. At 27 broke his left leg playing rugby against University of Kansas.
13. At 28 in 1980 finished first Ironman in Honolulu in Year 3.
14. Smuggled literature into the Soviet Union and Eastern Europe and political documents out in the late 70s and early 80s.
15. Smuggled literature and other things in Asia in the late 90s through 2008.
16. Did a family skydive to celebrate 50th birthday in 2000.
17. Sailed from Askalon Israel to Crete in 2000. Had to "May Day" twice in storm.
18. Sailed across the Atlantic in 22 days from the Canary Islands to the US Virgin Islands in 2001.
19. Jumped from, at the time, the world's highest bungee jump of 111 meters or 364 feet in 2005 at Victoria Falls Africa.
20. Did "Angel Walking" down the face of a 25 story office tower in Sydney in 2006.

21. Dove with great white sharks twice in South Africa in 2005 and 2006.
22. Completed 10 Ironmans Triathlons between 2000 and 2016.
23. Was asked to be a member of the "Adventurers Club of LA" in 2012.
24. In 2014 was hit by a car head on preparing for Ironman.

And the adventures continue…

To Get Something You've Never Had,

You Have to Do Something

You've Never Done.

———————

Everything you dream or desire

lies outside your comfortability.

MY MAIN THOUGHT

WHAT IF....

I could pull this off.
I NEED to BE OBSESSED
w/ BEING GREAT !
THERE CAN BE NO
          DOUBT
I must BE DRIVEN !

MY MOTIVATION CARDS

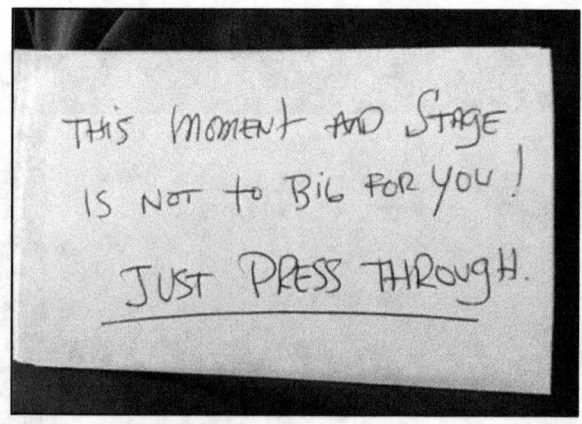

MY MOTIVATION CARDS

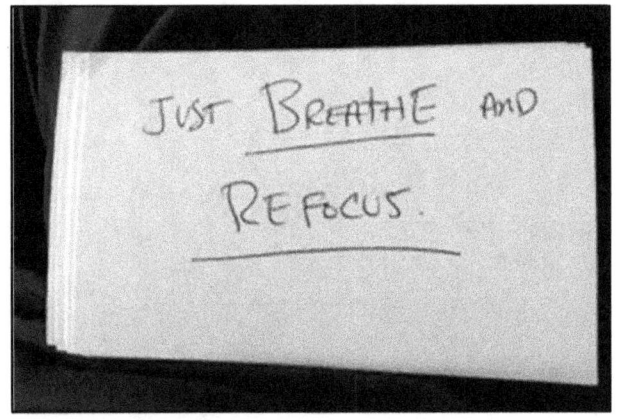

Table of Contents

ACKNOWLEDGEMENTS	i
FOREWORD	v
INTRODUCTION	1
PROLOGUE	5
INTRODUCTION	19
CHAPTER 1	31
The Journey: 1951-2019:	31
"Overcoming Average"	31
CHAPTER 2	53
Air Force Pararescue: Learning to Save Lives.	53
Starting with my own.	53
CHAPTER 3	75
After Pararescue:	75
1980 IRONMAN: Year 3	75
CHAPTER 4	93
My IRONMAN Comeback at 50.	93
CHAPTER 5	101
Making A Plan To Get Stronger.	101
CHAPTER 6	127
Greece Part 1	127
CHAPTER 7	141
Greece Part 2	141
Chapter 8	165
The Quest Run	165
CHAPTER 9	185
Training For Kokoro	185
CHAPTER 10	197

Kokoro	197
CHAPTER 11	235
Post Kokoro	235
CHAPTER 12	245
Training For 12th IRONMAN - Mexico	245
CHAPTER 13	253
12th IRONMAN Mexico	253
Race Day	253
CHAPTER 14	285
The World Marathon Challenge - The 777	285
Final Thoughts:	371

ACKNOWLEDGEMENTS

I am a man mostly richly blessed. Throughout my life I have had people help me, guide me, mentor me, support me, and love me. The list is long of those who deserve my thanks. I don't have the space here to thank everyone individually, so I will start with a Thank You for all those who have helped me get to where I am in my life.

As the year of challenges is now over, I am happy to thank the following people who helped me make it all possible, and to then carry the message forward into this book.

1st: My wife Sandy. She loves me and puts up with me. She always encourages me to live my dreams.

2nd: My Mom. No matter what happened to me or what stupid thing I did she always encouraged me and believed in me. I remember the day that she told me that I was special and I would do something great with my life. It changed me.

3rd: My Son Matt Owens. It was so good to have you there at Kokoro. It was a once in a lifetime experience for both of us! Thanks for staying up filming 50 straight hours.

4th: Water Polo and Swim Coaches Jon Urbanchek and Howard Terry at Anaheim High School. You taught me that hard work can beat better talent. You taught me to be scrappy. You taught me never give up.

5th: Albie Pearson. He was my first pastor. He was the American League Rookie of the Year in 1958 and made the American League All-Star team in 1963. He didn't pastor me. He coached me and benched me often. He changed my life as a punk 20 year old kid.

6th: Air Force "Indoc" Commandant Master Sergeant TJ Bruce. He brought me into Manhood. He developed me along with my surviving classmates and many PJ Indoc classes. Thank you for developing all of us.

Hooyah!

7th: Garry Lewry . One of my PJ classmates and good friends. You are a good man and a good friend.

8th: Air Force BA Prep Superintendent and Pararescuemen Chief Master Sergeant Josh Smith. For bringing me back into the Air Force Training world. It's been wonderful. Thanks.

As well, thank you to current BA Prep Superintendent Master Sergeant Dean Criswell who took over for Josh. It has been fun working with you.

8th: Author John Maxwell. He taught me about Leadership. It changed my life. John always believed I could do more and become more.

9th: Dr. Edwin Lewis Cole. He mentored me for 20 years. Because of him, I've taught and mentored in over 30 Nations. He was a Father Figure to me.

10th: Michael Jordan. For his drive to be the best. He inspired me and convicted me for years. Game 6 against Salt Lake City in 1998 rocked me. Again I learned that great players and people rise up in the most difficult moments and achieve greatness!

11th: Kobe Bryant. For his memorable workout ethic. Reading about Kobe in the LA times regularly inspired me. Watching him play was just icing on the cake. I had no excuses when reading about his workouts.

12th: Retired Navy SEAL Commander Mark Divine and Founder of SEALFIT. He modeled a Warrior ethos that challenged me in my 60s to press into new areas of my life. He encouraged all of us that the 20X Principle was for any age. The 20X Principle is that there is 20 times more potential in you than you have ever allowed anyone to bring out of you.

13th: Tim Grover. For your Book "Relentless". It was life to me as I trained for 3 years for SEALFIT's Kokoro. I have read and reread it many times.

14th: Tom Bilyeu. For your inspiring YouTube interviews with outstanding people. I've watched you interview David Goggins, Tim Grover, James Lawrence, Mark Divine and others, over and over. They inspired me tremendously.

15th: David Goggins. I want to thank you for your videos that are posted on YouTube as well as for the interviews you've given. I believe I've listened to everything that is posted on you or by you. You've inspired me for over 5 years with your focus and intensity. I often imagine myself trying to live with that same intensity and focus from 63-66 years old. Especially training for SEALFIT's Kokoro and the 777, I listened to you daily before my workouts.

16th: Tom Brady. For being the role model on excellence and demonstrating so clearly that one chooses how one ages.

17th: Jon Gruden When you regularly told the collegiate quarterbacks "there can be no doubt" it really resonated with me. I was reliable viewer of your ESPN show.

18th Jill – our intrepid server at our "office" – Applebees.

19th: David Pisarra. For guiding me in writing these two books. He thought I was crazy to write these books with my thumbs on an iPhone.

FOREWORD

Robert Owens is the fittest and mentally toughest guy in the world over 65. Period. Training and completing SEALFIT's fifty hour non-stop Kokoro Camp is a major feat even for young studs who want to be Navy SEALs. Yet Robert did it with distinction... then went on to complete four other major feats of endurance in the same year. Impressive. However, his message, which I back, is that this is achievable by anyone with the goal to get physically and mentally fit for life.

In fact, lifetime fitness and mental toughness are what I teach in my books, training programs and discuss on my Unbeatable Mind Podcast, where Robert was one of the more popular guests.

If you are over 55 and reading this book, please don't just be impressed by Robert's accomplishments... as impressive as they are. Rather, I encourage you to use his insight and example to get strong, fit and mentally tough yourself. It is NEVER too late to start training... in fact why not start today, and then chip away at it daily with micro-goals and an unbeatable mind. You will be well on your way in just a short time.

Know that 75 is the new 55 these days and longevity research says we can live well past 100. Why not be physically and mentally fit and enjoy the extra time in these bodies of ours? A daily training plan, proper fueling and sleep will re-define what it means to age well. Robert is leading the way for us, and I intend to follow his lead to continue training until the last day.

Another thing to consider is how the younger generations seem to be getting weaker in our culture. You can help put a stop to their weakness by being a great role model for what's possible, to help them see a new norm for health and wellness.

So, I implore you to stop being common, thinking that you can't do what Robert is doing. Get off your butt to move that body and enjoy the benefits of aging like a champ. You CAN do it... one day at a time.

Refuse to be average. Be uncommon. Do today what others won't, so you can do tomorrow what others can't. Step up to your full potential whatever your age, and be an impeccable role model for others.

I believe in you... and I know Robert does too. Both of us need your help in making our country, and the world, healthier, stronger and more compassionate.

See you in training... hooyah!

Mark Divine
Retired Navy SEAL Commander
Founder, SEALFIT, Unbeatable Mind, Kokoro Yoga
New York Times Best Selling author:
    Unbeatable Mind
    The Way of the SEAL
    8 Weeks to SEALFIT
    Kokoro Yoga

> "Remember Robert, It's 80% mental and 20% physical. Time is irrelevant – stay in the moment."
> – Mark Divine

INTRODUCTION

I am honored that you would consider reading this book or listen to it as an audiobook. I hope it encourages you to think about how much real untapped and undeveloped potential is in you, your kids, grandkids and your friends.

As you may or may not know, in my early twenties I was a U.S. Air Force Pararescueman. One day while I was doing a rescue in Alaska I had a life changing experience. Our search and rescue helicopter team had found a missing Army Major's body parts on the side of a mountain. I was lowered down on a "penetrator", I gathered over the next hour scattered pieces of his head and brain and untwisted his broken body from his large metal backpack frame. He had a broken neck, a broken back and two twisted broken legs. He had slipped off a cliff. Then I put the guy in a body bag. We then hoisted him up into the chopper and returned him to his distraught and grieving wife and children.

After getting him out of the helicopter and getting the body bag onto a gurney, I pushed his pieces towards his wife and kids who were on the tarmac awaiting his return. It was a miserable few minutes.

As I approached the family, I heard a unique and distinct voice in my head. It spoke a number of things to me. Not long thereafter, I left the Air Force and started delivering vehicles that were made for smuggling to the Port of Houston. Later, I would pick them up in Amsterdam and along with some teammates smuggle Christian literature into the former Soviet Union and Eastern European countries. Then we would smuggle out political documents exposing Helsinki Peace Accords violations by the Russians. The Russians were building SS-22 ballistic missiles and equipping them with banned nuclear warheads in secret "non-existent" cities in central Russia. This was during the Carter Administration and the Cold War. I did this off and on for a number of years. I also enrolled at Oral Roberts University and after two and a half years earned a BA Degree in Theology. After graduation, I started a nondenominational church at the University of Nevada-Reno. I was the senior pastor there for 25 years working with students, athletes and families. I flew over 4 million miles around the world doing business consulting and leadership training to businesspeople. I have spoken in churches in 30 Nations. This includes 12 trips to China and 10 trips to Russia and 15 trips to Africa.

Let me say at the onset however that this book is not a Christian book. I am not trying to convert or evangelize to anyone. You will not hear Jesus's name mentioned except when guys are getting crushed by Air Force or Retired Navy SEAL instructors for being out of shape and mentally weak. The candidates, while talking to Jesus and any other deity who might deliver them from their situation and pain, were also dropping f- bombs at God or at one another for messing up.

Please note: Throughout this book and especially in the opening chapter entitled "Hour 44", is some explicit cussing and some timely F-bombs. Air Force Pararescue Instructors and Navy SEAL Instructors have colorful language. I felt that deleting the strong language used at me and my class would not give a real depiction of the experience and situation.

You can skip over that chapter if it offends you or you can read about the real world that I live and thrive in. I want to be real and have a book that is real.

The goal of this book is purely to encourage people to know that they have more potential in them than they have ever thought. It isn't a new idea but one that is true and timeless.

Whether you are in your grammar school years or your teens, 20s, 30s, 40s, 50s, 60s, 70s, 80s or 90s you need to know you can do more and be more than you ever dreamed of.

For example: When many other elderly quit believing they can change their physical circumstances, my father wanted to stay fit and as strong as he could be at 92. I moved home to be with him and put him on an exercise program as he was becoming frail. He became stronger, regained his balance and stopped needing help to get out of his favorite chair till he passed at 101. By 100 he needed a walker but he still could get out of his chair unassisted which gave him a daily win. At 100 years old he was doing three sets of 20 air squats a day using his cane for balance. And he was stretching. He was so happy. Many other seniors marveled at his physical condition. Why do I mention this? Because there is more potential in us at any age if we desire to work for it.

I have a deep passion to encourage people. I want people to experience WINS daily. I enjoy helping people become overcomers and winners. I also try to help people break out of mental and physical ruts in their daily lives.

Why? Because teachers, coaches, parents, mentors have encouraged me, challenged me and changed my life by their belief in me. Often I didn't have belief in me but I believed in their belief in me. Their encouragement and belief in me carried me often.

Therefore, whoever you are, I want to encourage you. "Your Best Days Could Be Ahead!" I hope you will continue to ask people to challenge you to break out of your self-imposed mental and physical ruts.

You don't need to be like me. Just be yourself and what your God has called you to be and do. But know this fact: There is more potential in you than you realize.

Throughout this book I refer often to other authors and motivational individuals like Tim Grover, the man who coached Michael Jordan to greatness. For two years I've watched hours upon hours of David Goggins' videos, read his books and listened to him on podcasts, his language can be difficult to take at times, but his message is clear and important.

I've read the following books that have been instrumental in getting me through my 3 years of training, and finally my year of challenges:

My nightstand library.

Unbeatable Mind
Mark Divine

The Way of the SEAL
Mark Divine

Relentless
Tim Grover

Can't Hurt Me
David Goggins

How Bad Do You Want It?
Matt Fitzgerald

The videos I relied upon were by Tom Bilyeu and Inside Quest with Tim Grover, James Lawrence, Mark Divine and Joe De Sena. I watched them over and over to extract every bit of inspiration and motivation I could from them.

I hope you find these tools useful in your quest for greatness.

Robert Hamilton Owens

PROLOGUE

Hour 44

I was lightheaded and shivering severely. It was super damp. I was really cold. We were doing push-ups and bear crawl repeats on our muddy dirt and gravel PT "Grinder." The instructors continually sprayed us down with hoses while the temperatures hovered in the high 40s. They just kept yelling at us, "What the fuck is wrong with you guys? Why can't you do things right? You fucking can't stay together and do what we tell you. It isn't complicated. Just do what we fucking say, or it's going to get worse. What the fuck is wrong with you? We've been telling you how we want you to do this for over forty one fucking hours. What the fuck don't you get?"

The first 40 hours had been really difficult. I was sort of amazed I was still there. Half the class was gone by the first twelve hours. I was glad to have made it the first three hours. It had been brutal. In the very beginning when we were made to crawl through the gravel and dirt dry stream bed I knew I was in trouble. They wanted the skin to come off your elbows and knees. They wanted to get our attention by having us crawl through thorns and ants. They wanted us terrorized in the first 10 minutes. I, like others, had felt in over my head and crushed, more than once in the first hour.

Guys started puking on the hill sprint repeats and quitting quickly.

Now we had been up all night for the second night in row. I was mentally numb.

The previous six hours, we had been going all night, in and out of the cold Pacific Ocean doing beach PT. "Wet and Sandy's" had become in a twisted way sort of "fun." They had us be "Sugar cookies" over and over all night. Sugar cookies are where you get in the ocean and are told to roll in the sand until every bit of you is coved in sand. Then you do sprints or beach PT for a while then go back in the ocean. Why were we told that we had to go back into the ocean? Because they said we could never get something right. Someone ALWAYS had skin showing as a Sugar Cookie or had screwed up a drill. If that happened, the whole class had to pay. How? By running, or by doing burpees, soft sand crabs, or bear crawl races while being a sugar cookie in the faint moonlight. I really wondered if I could cover every inch of my body in sand including my eyelids. It became a unique challenge. Your swim buddy was to make sure you did what they said and didn't screw up. We did hundreds of lunges in the soft sand along with wind sprints back to our lunges starting point.

And I had survived "The Steps."

There was a set of steps leading from the beach up the cliff to a park and houses. At the end of our second three hour beach experience and our second beach physical training (PT), I had been the last one to finish the lunges because I was the slowest and the oldest. I learned I was older than the other oldest guy in the class by fifteen years. That didn't rock me. Why? Because I loved being the oldest guy to ever attempt Kokoro. I wanted that record, especially as an Air Force guy who was in a Navy world. But it was costly. I thought for sure that I would be dropped from the class for being slow in the runs and bear crawls. However for some reason, they never dropped me. Later they told me that as long as I made the strength standards tests and the first 24 hours they wouldn't kick me out or drop me in the second 24 hours. Some of the instructors then said, "Let's just see if he quits or we can get him to quit in the second 24 hours!"

There were probably 75 to 100 concrete steps in sets of ten that went up the side of this cliff. Maybe overall the distance to be covered was fifty yards. There was a single bulb street light at the bottom, one in the middle, and one at the top. Just enough light in pitch dark of 3 a.m. where you could see the moisture in the air and a little light.

John was about 24 or so, and had been one of my coaches at SEALFIT during my two and a half years of preparation for Kokoro. I liked him back then. He now told me to get down on my hands and knees and bear crawl backwards up the stairs. And he yelled, "Don't let your fucking knees touch the steps, Owens!"

When I trained at SEALFIT he'd been a pretty nice guy. At Kokoro, he had turned into sadistic asshole. He was mean, demeaning, caustic and cold. To think that we had ever talked and smiled together during those two and a half years of morning Crossfit workouts seemed impossible. He had become such a young punk. Who the hell was he to treat me like this? I was 40 years older than him. He hadn't accomplished anything in his stupid young life. He was a want-to-be and a nothing. Yet he acted like he was God. I couldn't believe it. I didn't think I would ever want to speak with him again after this Kokoro experience. He just kept telling me when I was doing my lunges, and now at the stairs, that I was a fucking loser and too fucking old to even be there. And that I was embarrassing myself. Often I heard, "Just fucking quit, Owens." He kept saying to me "What the fuck, Owens? Can't you do better than that? Why are you again the last fucking guy doing this? What the fuck is wrong with you?" Then he'd shake his head in disgust and go yell at somebody else for a while but I knew he'd be back. One time he said, "And you were a fucking PJ?" meaning Air Force Pararescueman. He played his part really well.

I couldn't do the stairs the way he demanded. I tried and didn't have the strength to keep my knees from falling down on the stairs. It was like crawling backwards upwards holding a plank. Or like doing slow mountain climbers backwards up a hill. It was all core and thighs.

Back in the three day SEALFIT Leadership Academy, Mark Divine had made us do a mid-day 40-50 minute "plank" exercise in the heat to show us we could do it. But this was so different.

I thought for sure I was going to be dropped. I could do them slowly only if my knees were allowed to touch the concrete steps. They touched and I got yelled at but I kept going. They didn't drop me. Why? I was baffled.

Soon my wet sandy t-shirt was heavy with sand and sweat, and it slid off my back and down over my shoulders and over my head. The t-shirt came down past my elbows. It was wild. My freezing ocean experience had turned into a sweat rolling down my forehead and off the tip of my nose experience. I couldn't see anything but the inside of my t-shirt. But all I needed to do was lift my left arm back to the next step then my right arm. Do the backwards push-up and then lift my right leg up to the next step then my left. It became all slow painful rhythm. 1-2-3-4.... another

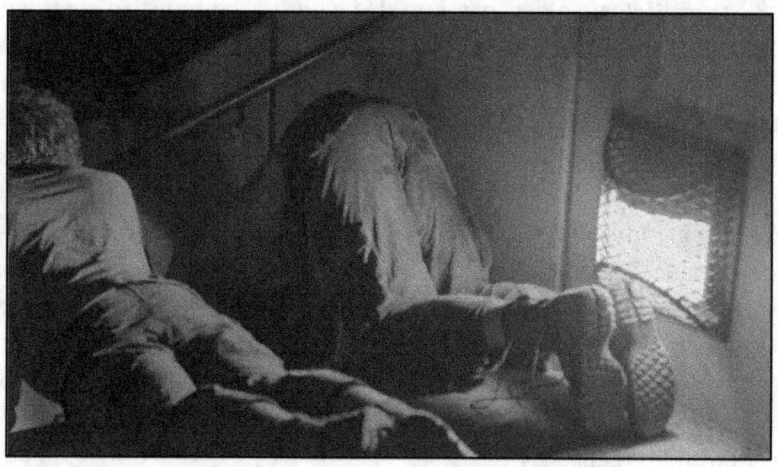

At the top of the stairs, going up backwards on my hands and feet.

step. The sweat was dripping off my nose consistently even though it was a cold 3 a.m.

One of my teammates, who had finished, came back down the stairs to encourage me. "You are doing good, Mr. Owens. You're the man! Keep going. You can do this. You only have 35 more to do!" Then he grabbed my wet, sandy, heavy t-shirt and pulled it back off my head and again pulled it back to a normal place where it belonged on my back.

Coach John yelled, "What the fuck you doing, QTip? Leave his fucking shirt alone. Don't you help him at all." Then my shirt slid back down over my head and face. It was dark in there.

Somehow I pressed through, upwards and backwards twenty steps.

It had been over an hour since I started my backward upward push-ups. Now my classmates were hollering for me. "You can do it, Mr.

Owens! You've got it! Keep going!"

They probably were enjoying the long rest I was giving them.

Finally, just before I was at the top, this kid called QTip for his bushy blond ball of hair, came back down next to me to encourage me again. He knew he'd get in trouble for it but it was worth it to him.

This time the instructors allowed it. Then he yelled back to the team, "Hey, you guys, Mr. Owens has abs!" They all started laughing. What they didn't know was that my abs were severely spasming. They ached and were locked up. But as long as I had great abs for a moment it was great. I even laughed. When I finally got to the top I could see again and my classmates celebrated. Most high fived me and said, "Good job, Mr. Owens. You did it! We knew you would."

Then the instructor Rob did the unbelievable in the dark. Instead of yelling at me for being the last guy and slow, he just stared at me and broke his tough guy character and leaked a slow small smile.

"Owens...... you're a BEAST!"

As he smiled his encouraging smile, it was a perfect moment for me. My whole body came alive with adrenaline and fresh energy. One word of encouragement in forty plus hours was so helpful. Thank God instructor John wasn't there to ruin the moment. I said to Rob, "Thanks Coach."

And then that moment was gone. I lived on the thought of that moment for the final nine hours. I wasn't an embarrassment or a loser. I was, for a moment in my life at Kokoro, a BEAST.

I could do this thing.

We were told again by one of the instructors that we were behind schedule "because Owens took so fucking long. Get in the vans." It was time to drive back to the Grinder.

We endured the one hour drive back to the Grinder with those stupid, wet, sandy clothes on, and the heater in the vans turned on high. Why? To challenge us to stay awake in the heated van. Of course, there were major penalties assessed to anyone and the whole group of guys in the van, if one guy fell asleep. Brutal. Guys fell asleep. Penalties were given.

We were on the Grinder before sunrise. I was back mentally just trying to get through the next evolution or test. We were dropped off outside of the Vale Lake campground and ran back to the Grinder in our area of the campground in silence. Pretty quickly, I had to get back into the horse trough of ice and water with another guy. It was hard to get both of us in but my legs were up by his ears and his by mine. We were crotch to crotch. We just stared at each other as the ice and water sloshed out. When the instructor felt we had reacted properly he told us to get out "and don't splash or lose any of my fucking water." Then we went back on the muddy Grinder doing the push-ups and exercises with the others. It was pre-dawn dark. The only lights on the Grinder were three truck headlights.

My thoughts were, "Just stay in the moment and do what you are told. It won't kill you. They won't kill you. This won't kill you. Enjoy it by not letting them see any mental weakness..."

Then at hour 43, still in the dark, they told us to get our stuff and get ready to run to our next evolution or test. We grabbed our one gallon jug of water, backpack with the 20 pound sandbag in it, and my "weapon" and jogged in silence to the large pool on the property. They had us do some bear crawls and push-ups around the pool deck as they sprayed us down. We were so cold that the pictures show the steam coming off our bodies, as well as from the pool. We were told to go by twos and wash the mud off our clothes in an outdoor cold pool shower. We took off our boots and lined them up "perfectly." We were going swimming before sunrise. They wanted no mud or dirt in the pool.

From the first light of day we began pool PT and swimming laps. Fortunately, the water is my strong suit but having to do races in our t-shirts, fatigues and socks was a challenge. I had to race somewhat handicapped because they wanted me to be as fatigued as the others. I had to start the races late and catch a guy or something. Coach Rob made sure I wasn't slacking. I acted tired but was really recovering from that last previous six hours at the beach. By now my hands and toes were blue white numb. I looked at my fingers when they didn't move and thought, "They don't work anymore. Be careful with them and use my palms more." After 2 hours of pool PT we were told that we would receive a warm breakfast. It was nice thought. I guess.

Coach Jones didn't like the way my swim buddy Grant Langham was smiling when he said "What the fuck are you two smiling about? So you can enjoy breakfast more, go stick your face in the mud."

Hour 44 of 50 non-stop hours. I am in the mudface on the right eating

"Yes Coach!" I loved it. If he thought that was going to get to me, he was mistaken. Nothing on the outside will get to me. No mud, no pee, no puke, no crap, nothing on the outside can get me. It all washes off. Mud was nothing. It is all a game.

I ran over to the puddle of mud in the grass, because you never walk anywhere and got down on my hands and knees and stuck my whole face in it. Up to my ears. It wasn't the first time I had mud on my face and likely not the last. But this was fun mud. We had "un-fun" mud on us every time we did Grinder PT. Coach Jones thought he'd get to me, but I loved it. I rolled my face around in it until it was up my nose and in my hair. Then I stood up and lifted my face up and I wiped the mud out of my eye sockets. I was relishing the moment. I looked at the coach and blew the mud boogers out of my nose towards him for effect and stared at him with a smile on my face. I said to Coach Jones "Thank you Coach. I love the mud. Now what do you want me to do?"

"Get your breakfast" he said.

They said we would receive a hot meal for the first time in forty two plus hours. Sounded great to everyone. It was another mental test. Fortunately, I had asked enough questions before Kokoro to learn that they wanted to see if we were undisciplined in our emotions and give in to the temptation of comfort of a nice large hot meal. The next test after breakfast was designed to get us to puke up the breakfast. The warning I received from the guys I trained with was, "Don't eat too much. You'll pay if you do. They love to watch guys puke their breakfast."

For the breakfast at sunup, we got our hot eggs and bacon and I think pancakes with syrup on Styrofoam plates. We were told to sit down back to back with your swim buddy on a very cold, very wet and muddy tall grass lawn. I ate my bacon and eggs but that was it. I didn't want to puke anything heavy. All was good until about five minutes into sitting when my wet back began to spasm from that L shape sitting position. It began to really hurt and tighten up. On the other hand, the sun was almost where we could see it which gave us hope. We had made it through the second night. However, that early morning time was the coldest part of the night. Some of my fingers were now frost bitten. Six of my toes were frost bitten too.

I didn't get full feeling in my fingers back for two months after Kokoro. The skin peeled off my fingers and toes a week later from being cold blistered.

When my back locked up, I didn't know what to do. I had never had back problems before. I didn't know what to do as I couldn't get up. Grant, the guy next to me with the muddy face said, "You OK?" And I said "No, my back is spasming. I've got to get up and out of this wet grass and straighten my back. But I didn't want to show weakness. They could pounce on it. Finally I caved in and called the medic over. He said, "What's up Owens?" I said, "My back is spasming. I can't get up. I'm losing my back. I need some help."

He helped me up but I could barely stand. I thought "Oh no this could be it." Dave Crandall, the SEALFIT lawyer I had trained with had his back go out on him during log PT on the second night, in and out of the Pacific. He had to quit. He came back later in another class and made it, but hearing talk about his back going out unnerved me. I thought "Oh God, I've got to make it. I only have five or six hours left. I've got to make it."

The medic, who was a Hawaiian Army Medic known as "K" called out to instructor Scott Jones, "We have a medical with Owens. I'm going to take him over by the restrooms and put him under some of our metal blankets and see if I can warm him up." Coach Jones said "OK." "K" had me lay down on a cold piece of concrete entryway to the pool restrooms. I didn't know what was worse.... being in the cold, wet, muddy grass or laying on this really cold concrete slab. He tore open the small bag that carried the small metal blanket and put it around my stomach and my back and up to my neck. And he tucked the excess under my body. He said, "Stay here and see if you can warm up."

I thought, "This is so stupid. He's laid me on a cold piece of concrete that is colder than the grass I was on." It was radiating coldness up into my body. I thought, "How in the world am I going to get warm lying on this concrete?" So I laid there and just shook while my teeth were going nuts. And then I had a special moment.

My face was facing the east and the sun began to come up from behind the tall trees. As the sun hit the metal blanket I began to get warmer little bit by little bit. It was one of those moments that happen in the movies. When all is slipping away, something unexpectedly happens which turns the situation around. I just knew that the higher the sun got, the more hope I had of getting warmer.

"K" came back and checked on me and asked how I was doing. I said "OK." I just can't move my back." He said "OK. Keep getting warmer" and he left.

Then about three or four minutes later instructor Coach Rob came over. He had been a hard-ass on everybody. In an unusually kind and unexpected voice, Coach Rob asked me how I was doing. Shivering, I said "I'm good. I just can't unlock my back."

He kneeled down on one knee and began to bend me and stretch me. He began to push, pull and twist me to see if he could get my back to loosen up. Then he said to me "Stay there and get warm. I'll be back in five minutes."

The sun was getting higher and the blanket was working. Even though the concrete was ice cold underneath me, somehow with the blanket tucked underneath me, my body was getting warmer. A few minutes later both the medic and Coach Ord came over. They both

BEYOND AVERAGE

looked at me when the medic said "Owens I'm sorry, but you're done. I can't let you go back in and continue anymore. You've done great so far but I medically cannot let you continue. I am going to medical you out. I'm sorry."

I said back to him, "There's no way in hell you're taking me out of this. I'm six hours away from finishing. I'm not quitting and you're not taking me out. Got it?" I said to coach Rob "What do I gotta do?" And he said "You got to get up and get back with your team or you will be disqualified."

I asked him "How much time do I have?" And he replied, "I'll go find out. I'll be right back." K, the hard-ass medic just stared at me. He was and is a good guy. But he didn't want to be responsible for me, probably because he knew what was coming up next and I didn't. He said "OK, Owens. We'll see. But I'm warning you, you should not continue. You've done good. Just take that as a win and stop." I said, "Are you kidding me? No way. I stared him in the eyes with whatever hard core stare I could give and said, "I am not quitting and you are not dropping me. I'm going to finish even if it kills me. Understand?" He smiled and shook his head.

Coach Ord came back over and said "You have two minutes to get up and get back with your team." I said "OK." And just about then, I heard my team off in the distance, and out of sight, begin to call my name. "Owens.... Owens.... Owens.... Owens...... Owens... Owens.... Come back Owens..... Come back Owens..... Come back Owens…"

I looked at Coach Ord, and said "What's that? Who told them to do that?" He said, "Your team's calling for you. They need you and they want you back. You're the old man of the group. They respect you, and look up to you. They've watched you the whole time. I didn't tell them to do that. They are trying to encourage you."

I got tears in my eyes and said, "Coach, stand me up. He extended his hand and I grabbed it and he pulled me up to where I could stand. I couldn't move much, but I could stand. He said "Move around. You got a one minute to get back in with your team. And so I stretched a bit, and then ran back on the wet, muddy grass to where the guys were doing the next test or evolution. Sure enough. They were having guys do wind sprints and relay races on full stomachs. Some of the guys were doing log rolling races in the wet muddy grass. As I came into view, the guys started cheering for me. It was a moment I'll never forget.

I ran up to Coach Jones and said, "I'm back." He had his black hat on with his sunglasses on at 6:30 or 7:00 in the morning. He said to me, "Owens, how are you doing?" I said "Fine, Coach, thank you."

He said, "How is your back? I said, "Good, Coach." And then with a sadistic funny smile and chuckle, he said "Good. I want you to run and give me sixteen fast nonstop somersaults in a row to see how your back is. GO!" They always want to exploit a perceived physical and mental weakness.

I thought to myself, "This is f...ing unbelievable. My back has gone out, I'm 66 years old, and he's going to have me go run in the tall, wet, grass and mud, and do 16 nonstop somersaults while he yells at me." I thought "You can do it. Think this through and figure this out to save your back. Show no fear or weakness. This test will pass. It is the last morning. Five hours to go. OK let's do 'em." And I did.

After the last one I got up and stood at attention facing Coach Jones. I was dizzy but not close to puking. Then I ran back to Coach Jones. He was staring in my eyes for any signs of anything, and said "How do you feel Owens?" I said "Great, Coach. They were a lot of fun. Thank you. How many this time?" He said "Do them again." So I did. Coach Jones was loving this.

I ran back to him and said, "More Coach?" He said, "No. You like them too much. You need to wipe that fucking smile off your face. I never want to see that smile again. Do you understand me?" I said "Yes, Coach."

He just shook his head with a smile and said "I want you on the grass, and I want you to act like a log with your arms straight above you, your hands clasped together and I want you to roll fast. These two guys are going to get on the ground and roll and try to catch you. If they catch you, you are going to give me 20 burpees. If they don't catch you they have to do 20 burpees. Got it Owens?" I said "Yes Coach. Let the games begin."

Only after the third time did a guy finally catch me in this big, wide, grassy lawn area. I rolled fast enough to stay away from the 18 - 50 year-olds. I loved the challenge of beating the younger men. They couldn't catch me at 66. Even though I was getting really dizzy I didn't puke. There was a way to keep things compartmentalized.

Finally I couldn't roll straight. The coaches loved it. They kept yelling, "What the fuck is wrong with you guys. Can't you catch a fucking 66-year OLD MAN! Catch him!"

So we did it again and again. Off to the side you could see some other guys puking. They had eaten too much to the joy of the instructors. I never gave them the satisfaction of puking. It was so gratifying. They thought I would break and quit with those somersaults and then the log rolling. I loved it.

I would not be called a "fucking loser or embarrassment" again. I was going to live up to my name. I was going to be a BEAST. I had heard what a loser I was for 44 hours. The 20X Principle was alive and living in me.

That began the last six hours as the sun came up. It was about 6 a.m. We had survived non-stop 44 hours. We just had to make it until noon.

Then it got worse.

> In the next chapter I'd like to give you a little background on how this all started…

USAF Pararescue Flag and Motto.

INTRODUCTION

Imagine what you could do, and who you could become if you knew how to really focus on something you really wanted.
Years ago I learned three insights or truths:
1)   I learned in high school that if I wanted something with enough passion, I would pay any price to attain it. And I mean any price. That revelation changed my world and changed my life. I also observed in myself, that if I wasn't captured by it, I was usually lazy and unmotivated. Therefore, I lived a lot of my life being average or less. Few things ever really captured me.

2)   I learned over the past 50 years most people don't want to pay the price to accomplish their dreams. It would cost too much in relational, emotional, situational, financial and pain. Excuses are easier.

3)   I also know this, in all of us there is another person inside who wants to live. It's the person who dreams, gets excited at possibilities and wants to attempt amazing things. The founder of SEALFIT.com, Navy SEAL Commander Mark Divine calls it the 20X Principle. Meaning, there is 20 times more potential inside you than you've ever allowed to come out or be developed. That 20X person usually does not get a chance to live. You haven't learned how to retrain your mind to think positively and correctly. You stay stuck, defeated and are just existing.

So from those three insights and truths I learned this: When your "Why" isn't strong enough or when your "Why" wavers, a voice inside all of us says, "Be realistic. Relax. Who do you think you are? You're too old or too young, too fat or too skinny. You aren't smart enough or gifted like others. Or the voice says, "It takes money to do that and you don't have it." Or the voices say, "People from your family don't do this", or your ethnic background yells at you to stay like all of them.

When you listen to those voices your world stays small.

I've been living with those thoughts and those voices in my head all my life. Sometimes my "Why" was super strong and I'd do anything to attain the goal. I wouldn't let anything stop me. People watched me and said, "Wow, that kid or guy is really focused. He's really intense and intent on getting it." And whatever it was, I got it.

Other times, I'd stay for weeks, months and years in that "average" place. I always wanted something, but not enough to change my daily world, my habits, my friends, my schedule and my thoughts to attain it.

This book is about the 20X Principle: There is 20 times more talent and potential in you than you realize. It lies dormant in you, waiting to be realized and released.

With that thought in mind, I also know that life can be complicated. None of our lives are simple. My life hasn't been simple.

Childhood can be confusing. So can the teenage years and even our adult lives. But I've noticed that many people who have complicated and painful lives do strange and amazing things. Oftentimes legendary people use pain as a focus to develop their "Why." They use their "Why" as a diversion from their daily circumstances. As their "Why" becomes stronger, they become stronger. They change.

I grew up with a number of issues that were challenging.

I had a lot of rejection in my life, as well as insecurity, embarrassment and shame. As a young man, I wanted approval and acceptance. I wanted love. I wanted to be a part of something significant and on a team.

I struggled a lot, like many people.

I also noticed that my struggles disappeared whenever I found a "Why" that was bigger than all of them. The "Why" made my struggles insignificant. They didn't matter anymore. They became exposed as excuses. I became amazed how creative I became to find a way to win. "Average" disappeared.

With that understanding about myself and that mindset, I began to break out of Average and Existing, into Focused and Overcoming in different areas of my life and in different stages of my life.

There were the teen years with those issues; then the 20s, which posed new unique challenges and struggles. Then the 30s. Then the 40s and the 50s. Now I am in my 60s and there are new unique struggles and challenges to face. The goal is to find my "Why" in each of them. My father lost his "Why" when my Mom died at 91 and he was 92. They had known each other since junior high and had been married for 65 years. From that point on he pretty much just existed.

In each of those stages, your "Why" can and will adjust or change. Many call it "Finding Your Purpose" or "Having a Purpose".

People ask me all the time when I am speaking or training athletes and military personnel, "How in the world did you do what you did last year to celebrate your 66th birthday? That's unbelievable!"

The answer is simple and also profound. When your "Why" is strong enough, you can do just about anything. Nike used the famous slogan, "Just do it." It sounds so simple, but it is so difficult. But you CAN do it. You need to know in the depths of your being, that the 20X Principle lives in you and in all of us. For some of us older people, the great news is that it even lives in seniors!

As I was facing my mid 60s I embarked on a three year personal experiment. I'd been a relatively good athlete when I was young, and then even a better athlete in the Air Force as a Pararescueman. At 27, I left the Air Force and took on my new biggest challenge. I trained and finished year three of the IRONMAN triathlon in Honolulu in 1980. It was a significant achievement for me. It was written up in Sports Illustrated at the time as "The Toughest Endurance Race in the World." There were one hundred of us. There were no aero bars, no helmets, we wore baseball caps. The next year it was moved to Kona Hawaii.

From age 30 to 50 I'd stayed in relatively good shape and finished a number of endurance races while raising five kids. When I turned 50, my oldest son told me that I was REALLY OLD now and so I decided to make my IRONMAN come back. I liked being in really good IRONMAN level shape. So much so, that I enjoyed staying in that type of shape year round.

I found that many of my most creative ideas and problem-solving times came while I was working out, or right afterwards. Working out really works for me, mentally and professionally. It became spiritual, emotional and mental therapy for me.

Each year after turning 50 I would try to do an IRONMAN to see if I was still in good enough shape to do it. I missed a few due to injuries, but would always come back the next year to see if I could do another one. I didn't consider myself a triathlete but just a guy who got in really good shape who could swim 2.4 miles, ride a bike 112 miles and run a marathon in one day, once a year. That meant I didn't ride a bike before the race, and only started swimming a month before the IRONMAN every year.

So at 63, I'd finished 11 IRONMAN triathlons. I had a lingering question: Can seniors can get stronger and fitter while they are getting older? And the bigger question was: I wanted to know if I could become an exceptional aerobic athlete and an anaerobic athlete at the same time? An aerobic athlete is like a distance runner or distance swimmer. Get your heart rate in a certain place and go all day. An anaerobic athlete is like a sprinter or CrossFit games athlete where you repeatedly spike your heart rate and are out of breath. Then you have to recover quickly to do another event that would spike your heart and cause you to be gasping for air. Both are athletes. Just different kinds. Both are in the Olympics. Very few athletes are both. Very few athletes are really strong and fit like Crossfit Athletes. And even fewer athletes at any age can do anaerobic events non-stop for 24 or 50 hours straight.

Here's an interesting thought: The only men in the world that I've found that can be, and are asked to be, aerobic and anaerobic athletes are Navy SEALS and Army, Marine, and Air Force Special Operations men. I believe we may be getting some women in their ranks now, in the Army. Special Ops guys have to be physically and mentally strong enough to handle the quick in and out firefight and issues found in the engagement, but they also have to be trained to go on for days at a time with no sleep if needed.

When I watch videos of senior athletes, they usually are excelling in one sport or event. But I wanted to test myself the way a decathlete has to train for many events, or like a Crossfit athlete who has to become strong in a number of events. I wanted to see if that 20X Principle was still in a 63 year old.

Some of you may remember Jack LaLanne and other fitness experts. For years, they have told seniors, "You don't have to be frail and weak as you age." However, Jack did not tell us how good of shape we could get in. I had occasionally watched YouTube videos of senior athletes and they were doing tremendous things. Watching them, challenged me to see if I could do a bigger experiment. It would be a super challenging experiment.

I also had a couple other thoughts in my mind. First, my father was forced to retire at 60. Most of his generation was told to retire at 60 as well. "Take your pension and go play golf or something." Actually, the mindset was "You're done. It is time for you to move on." He didn't like it. He went on and worked for a while but not like before he turned 60. The culture didn't encourage it.

He said to me at 95 years old, "Son, stay relevant. After 60, people begin to write you off if you let them. They think you're getting old. And younger people stop talking to you. Often you start to tell the same old stories over and over and people don't want to hear them anymore. It means you don't have new stories. When you reach 60 you need new stories and a new purpose. If I'd known at 60 when I retired from being a judge that I'd make it to 95, I'd have started another career. Ages 60 to 90 can be your best times! But my generation like others was put out to pasture to play golf and die after 60. You know better. It doesn't have to be that way for you and your generation. You are aging better than any of the previous generations. You're living healthier and you'll live longer."

Then he said, "By 60 you know who you are pretty much. You've made your mistakes and you know your strengths and your weaknesses. Life needs to be seen this way: 0 to 30, 30 to 60 and now 60 to 90. Now dream your new dreams and accomplish new things. Use all those experiences and let them help you. You need a new business plan for 60 to 90. Stay healthy so you can enjoy 60 to 90. And don't give all your money to the doctors and the pharmacies! Stay in shape and stay healthy. You worked too hard all your life to not be able to enjoy 60 to 90. Have a plan!"

I took his wisdom to heart and began to make a new business plan for 60 to 90. Staying healthy and physically fit is one of those goals. And I've set micro-goals to get to 90. I want to stay relevant and in the game. I don't want to be written off as old. Not yet.

BEYOND AVERAGE

A fun story: Jerry West, the great NBA star and general manager was being interviewed on Colin Cowherd's FOX radio program recently about how Jerry liked being 80. And Jerry responded, "I am so fortunate. Every day I get out of bed and I have a purpose. I help basketball players and basketball teams. I'm excited every day when I get up because I have something to do and I have a purpose. I hope it goes on like this for a long time. Most people my age have lost their purpose. They are just existing. I am so fortunate."

I listened to him and just smiled. I'm gonna try to be like him till I'm 90. Maybe then I'll write a new business plan from 90 to 100.

With that, I needed fun, challenging new goals. I want to have mental goals as well as physical goals. I do my best in life when I am focused on a goal. It keeps me regimented and mentally alert. I eat better, sleep better, and feel better when I'm working on my goals. However attaining the goal is only part of the goal. The journey towards the goal is what enriches my life. All the focus, the discipline, and sacrifice all combine to make attaining the goal even sweeter. Sometimes when I'm helping others with their goals I feel like I should probably be paying them for allowing me to do this, because it is so fun for me.

When I don't have goals, I tend to wander and lose my way. For whatever reason, I am wired to thrive on goals and challenges. So for fun, I began to dream, after my 11th IRONMAN, of doing some events or races that most younger men and women wouldn't dare to attempt. They had to be wild and captivating. They needed to be audacious and epic. It would even be greater fun if they could be legendary.

A friend of mine, Chuck Patterson, who is an extreme surfing and skiing athlete, once said to me, "Hey Robert, Live Legendary. Anyone can be average."

I loved it.

I am not a LeBron, Kobe, David Goggins or Tom Brady. I am a nobody in the world of athletics. I am an outlier. An old athlete that still has some game in him. I just didn't know how much.

But I wanted to know.

When I watch TV or listen to professional athletes talk, there's something inside me that says "I can do some great things too." There are many of us out there. We sit in front of the TV and remember earlier years. We remember our dreams and ambitions. We remember our victories and we still remember with pain, our defeats. We still love winners and losers. We pay money to go watch people win, and people lose. We still try to win at things. Often we still lose. At 63 I still wanted a bigger moment in my life. I had had some great ones but I wanted my moment, My Super Bowl, my Olympics.

So, why did I decide on all five? Because it was insane. It was stupid.. It was probably nearly impossible at any age! Everyone told me it was impossible and not to try. It would be my personal Super Bowl moment except mine had 5 quarters. Like in the movie Braveheart, I wanted to paint my face and take on the impossible. I wanted my

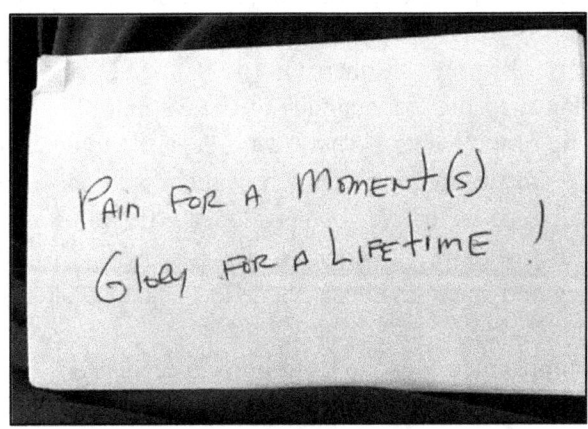

One of my motivational cards I carried with me. I'd say these words over, and over, and over, and over to sear them into my brain.

moment to face incredible odds and plant my spear and plant my flag in the ground and say "I did it! I've won" Like Tom Brady being too old to continue to play quarterback. Not only does he play but he continues to win Super Bowls in the face of critics and disbelief! Attempting these 5 endurance events in 7 months would give me one of those "I'm alive against all odds moments" which few people get to experience. Just getting past Kokoro was monumental. Nobody else at 66 will probably ever do it! But I hope many will!

I thought and pictured in my mind meeting LeBron, Kobe, David Goggins or Tom Brady. They're all champions. They've all defied the odds. They have all had great comebacks that keep people amazed. They remind us of what a totally focused person can accomplish. If I ever met them, maybe they may even say to me "Wow, that's amazing! That is crazy! How did you do that? And you were 66? And I'd just smile and say, "I wanted to have moments like you've had. I want to be a champion sometime in my life. Dreaming this at 63 and accomplishing it at 65-66 means it isn't too late to do significant challenges. I wanted to defy the odds once more in my life just as you have." They'd get it. And many of you get it.

Four months after it was over, the founder of Spartan Games Joe De Sena said to his co-hosts on his Spartan Games Podcast from Dodger Stadium after my interview, "Robert Owens is a BAD ASS! He is 66 years old and knocked out 7 marathons in 7 days on 7 Continents and this is like the tip of the iceberg. That wasn't even the toughest thing he has done. There are twenty year olds who couldn't do half of what he does. If you want to be incredible you need to learn from this guy."

If ever there was a sweet moment, it was hearing him of all people say that. My flag and spear had been planted as I had envisioned. Bring on the young studs.

Those accomplishments lead to the following accolades:
- Triathlete magazine: "Robert Owens Is The Fittest 66 Year Old In The World!"
- 24 Hour Fitness online magazine: "Robert Owens Is Probably The Fittest 66 Year Old You Will Ever Meet!"
- SEALFIT's Unbeatable Mind Podcast: "Robert Owens The Fittest 66 Year Old In The World Talks About Growing And Getting Stronger At Any Age. Then Mark Divine Rephrased The Statement To Say Robert Owens Is The Fittest And Mentally Toughest 66 Year Old In The World. Joe De Sena then agrees
- Endurance Sports and Fitness magazine: Robert Owens Talks About Competing Through The Ages.
- Navy SEAL And USAF Pararescue Guys Call The Experiences EPIC And LEGENDARY.

The fun part is this: We seniors are supposed to clap for the younger generations. OK, I am happy to do so. It would also be fun if younger people clapped for us seniors as well. I want them to not only clap for us, but not write us off as irrelevant. I want them to be amazed by us.

During my daily training, many would ask me why I was pushing myself so hard. I loved the look in their eyes when they would hear what I was planning to do. Most younger people and the older ones didn't know what to say. Usually they just stared at me with that weird disbelief smile, and a 'disbelieving caught off guard' giggle. It was priceless. I'd often tell them real slowly to get the most effect. They'd say, "Really! You? When?...... Why? There's no way. How old are you again?" Then I'd quietly smile. They'd say, "How are you going to do that?" I'd give them some answer to end the conversation because you can't really explain it. And I didn't fully know.

The truth is: You attempt to do this through developing physical strength, deep unshakable and immovable confidence while developing mental toughness. All three are separate crafts that work together. Those things don't come overnight. It's like anything else. If it takes 10,000 hours to be a concert pianist or 10,000 hours to become a spelling bee champion or Olympic gymnast, it also takes a lot of time to develop the mental understanding and physical ability to do something like this.

If you're going to be great at something you have to the spend time developing your craft. I believe I've been developing my craft since high school. Now it's going to be time to put all my experiences into one great seven month period.

I also knew that in a SEALFIT's Kokoro, a 40 year old man had recently finished and while kissing his wife and kids he had a heart attack and died. I didn't tell my wife that. I knew that in most classes, less than half or that starters finished. The event was physically exhausting but even more so it would be a brutal mental beat down. I hadn't been through something like that since Air Force Pararescue training in my 20s. But I had been through it and done well in it. It was still in me to be tapped into. Most others didn't have that in their bank account.

It was going to take Seven Training Truths that I had learned over the 50 years of choosing to do challenging stuff to pull these five events off:

1. Research.
2. Strategy.
3. Count the Cost: relationally, socially, emotionally, financially and physically.
4. Change Friends, Change Schedules, Change Locations.
5. Find Role Models and Train with Role Models.
6. Ask for Accountability.
7. Start and Adjust.

All these events just didn't appear. They happened as I began to work on my strength and fitness experiment at 63. As in life, once the ball is rolling, things begin to find you. I joined the Eternity Crossfit Box in San Juan Capistrano. Immediately, my world changed and expanded. I went in to become a stronger conditioned IRONMAN. Pretty soon I stumbled onto the other four challenging Events. They captured me or called out to me.

When I heard that SEALFIT's Kokoro was "The Toughest Civilian Training in the World" it brought chills to me as I remembered the IRONMAN being advertised in 1979 as "The Toughest Endurance Event in the World." I did it then, and now this Kokoro would be my next great challenge. I knew doing seven marathons in seven days on seven continents was ridiculous. Especially for a non-runner. I make running look hard. The moment I heard each one I was captured. Within a minute there was no turning back. It has always been that way. It made perfect sense to me. Once you get in that kind of shape, you might as well utilize it and get the most out of it you can. I knew I maybe would never be in that kind of shape again. Therefore the game was on and I got really excited. I was 63 and I got to start all over again. I felt like a kid. No one thought it could be done or should be attempted at any age. I didn't get support from anyone except Sandy. And it came reluctantly. I was alone! I felt like Jerry West. I had a purpose and an impossible goal to attain.

My last thought here is this. Your "Why" has to be so intense, so out of balance that you would rather die trying, than live without it.

Balanced people don't usually do great things. Unbalanced people do great things and legendary things. After they have accomplished it, the balanced people clap for them and ask them to come speak and go on TV programs.

Then the unbalanced person can go back to being balanced and tell their story. You've got to learn to pay a price to break out of your rut to become great at something. You can't be balanced all the time. And you can't take balanced people with you, they will drag you down with their skepticism. You have to pay the cost.

I've heard these statements for years:
- Average people don't understand Overcoming people.
- Overcoming people don't have a lot of close friends that are average. They live in different worlds.
- Look at your friends. You will see you. Birds of a feather and all that…

On my three year challenge, only my wife Sandy went with me. She flexed with me in every area even though she didn't understand it.

Here's how we did it.

Next up is my foundation in working hard in sports, harder than I ever thought possible…

BEYOND AVERAGE

I was one of four seniors on our high school swim team, Coach Terry on the left, Coach Urbanchek on the right.
I'm next to Coach Terry on the left.

CHAPTER 1

The Journey: 1951-2019:
"Overcoming Average"

I was too small for football in junior high. I tried baseball and basketball but they weren't a fit. Other students were bigger, faster, stronger and more athletic. Plus, I carried mental baggage into junior high from elementary school.

My parents adopted me when I was three months old from a place called The Children's Home Society which was attached to St. Joseph's Catholic Hospital in Orange California. I have a sister who was also adopted four years earlier from the Children's Home Society. My mom couldn't have children and my parents wanted a girl and a boy.

Back then, during and after the Korean War, there were a lot of babies looking for homes. Men came home from war and had relationships. I am so glad that back then abortion wasn't as prevalent as it is today because I probably wouldn't be here. I was someone's mistake but I was allowed to live. Gratefully, whoever she was, released me at birth to this Catholic charity. My sister says it wasn't an orphanage. I never really asked my mom much about it. I guess it was just a holding tank for babies until they were adopted or put someplace else.

Today I would've probably been classified as a special needs kid. When I was born somehow my legs bent in and touched at the knees when I tried to walk. I also had flat feet that bowed inward. I guess you would call that being knocked kneed and severely flat footed.

I am so grateful that my parents picked a baby boy that was going to need some rehab. Prior to first grade, my parents took me to a podiatrist who recommended I wear corrective shoes, actually corrective boots with metal rods in them, until my feet and my knees straightened out.

Some of my earliest memories were when I was in first grade and all the kids on the playground were playing kickball and I wasn't allowed to play. Actually I probably could have played however I had these dark brown stiff leather corrective boots on that made it really hard to run. I remember a few times when the kids were choosing up teams and I was the last kid to be picked. Often kids said to the teacher, as they chose teams "Do we have to take him?" It hurt and I was embarrassed.

That set the tone for grammar school. I spent a lot of time playing tether ball alone where you stand on the playground and hit the ball that's attached to a rope around the post.

If I was a good boy or if it was a Friday where I had not gotten in trouble during the week, I was allowed to wear my white Chuck Taylor Converse high tops which was a big deal. I remember always thinking Fridays would be a great days because I could try to run and play with the rest of the kids.

Another memory that I vividly recall was when one of my childhood friends asked me if I knew that I was a mistake? And that I was unwanted. It was in third grade. I can remember the exact place in our street where we were standing and what he was wearing. Some moments we never forget.

I didn't know what to say, so I went home and asked my mom if I was a mistake. She asked me, "Who said that?" She was furious. My parents were good friends with his parents. She told me to go back and tell him that "I wasn't a mistake. My parents picked me. His parents got stuck with him!"

I remember the look on his face and the joy I felt after those words came out of my mouth.

He didn't say a word, he just turned around and went home. Funny. We were friends all the way through high school.

DAD

My adopting father was a Stanford graduate and an academic guy. I don't think he ever got a B in his life, even through Stanford Undergrad and Stanford Law School. He wasn't into sports much. Later I was to find out that he was a MENSA qualifier. That means he was a genius.

He loved me and was a great dad. We were just wired entirely differently.

My mom was a Physical Education Major out of UCLA and received her Master's in Physical Education from Wellesley College in Massachusetts. My parents were best friends since junior high. She encouraged me as a kid to find something that I liked and could be good at. She helped me try many different sports.

I really liked Little League but they only put me in the game in the last inning of every game. That was because the rules said that every kid on the team had to play in every game. They had to play me. I only played one position and that was right field. I was always put in the game in the seventh inning. Everyone knew that the safest place to put a non-athlete kid was in right field because the ball was never hit there. I played there for three years.

Mom took me to the Sammy Lee swim school when I was in diapers. I loved it. They had a special round portable pool in the parking lot near the regular swim team pool. It was just for babies and little kids. I took to the water like a fish.

One set of my grandparents lived in Laguna Beach which meant I was introduced to the ocean early on. By junior high, I was skim boarding, boogie boarding, and surfing. Anything that had to do with the water seemed to come easy for me.

I did pretty well in school until about sixth grade. That's when my mom contracted lupus. She became deathly sick. There isn't a cure for lupus, and back then there were few treatment options. Soon, she lost forty pounds and became bedridden and hospitalized. I went from A's and B's in first through fifth grades to D's and F's in sixth and seventh grades.

She was my rock. She was my best friend. Soon, I began to get in all kinds of trouble at school as I begin to act out my inner pain. Most of the teachers knew of my mom's situation and were patient with me. Wonderfully, a few male teachers started to encourage me and believe in me. They knew I was a mess inside and that my mom was in bad shape.

It was 1962, President Kennedy was in office and soon to be shot, people were digging bomb shelters, and America was preparing for a nuclear war with the Soviet Union. It was an intense time in the world and in my home.

I didn't do well in junior high, and it was a tough time on our family. I had a seventh grade counselor named Mr. Smokov who worked with me daily. I spent a lot of time in his office as I was kicked out of my seventh grade classes 36 times. Each time I had to go to his office. Often I'd break down and cry as I was just hurting. And to this day I remember the day that Mr. Smokov cried with me in his small office. He wore a Mister Rogers sweater and as he cried with me he told me I was a good boy and going to make it. I have never forgotten that moment because I held on to his words. I had an eighth grade history teacher by the name of Don Kennedy who was great. He spent time encouraging me and reminding me I had a great future as I struggled to pass his class. He promised me that if I did my homework he would take me with his wife on winter Saturdays snow skiing in our local mountains. My grades came up and I learned to ski. He was a hero to me.

By the time I was in eighth grade, I'd been sexually assaulted twice by boys. Once in grammar school which I never told anyone about until I told my mom at about age 40. The second experience was in junior high at a Boy Scout summer camp out. I was a Star Scout. My dad knew most of the fathers of the boys that had assaulted me in their "older boy" tent. I fought my way out of that tent.

My father was a judge in town. I lived in a world of TV programs like "Fathers Knows Best" and "My Three Sons." They typified my upbringing.

I remember being in our den and embarrassingly crying with my mom when my father walked in and asked what happened at Scout Camp. When I shared with him, his face got very red and he became very stern and then made this comment, "I'm sorry son. Boys will be boys." He then turned around and walked out of the room. It was never brought up again at least with me. I never went back to Boy Scouts. My father was on the County Board of Directors for Boy Scouts. He was an Eagle Scout in High School as I had hoped to be. This is the first time I have said this publicly in my life. I am 67. Maybe it will help Scout Masters and some kids somewhere.

Those two experiences left me with unresolved issues. I never learned to process through them, but I did begin to drink a lot in 9th grade.

The big turning point for me was when I entered tenth grade at our high school. A kid named Greg Bunker, who was a water polo player, and swimmer and a beach lifeguard, urged me to try out for our high school Swim Team and Water Polo Team. We had a three year high school and I was an incoming freshman. The coach was Jon Urbanchek, who was a Hungarian Olympic water polo player and swimmer. He had been on the 1956 Hungarian Olympic team at the Olympic games in Sydney, Australia. He sought asylum in United States after the Russians invaded Hungary during the Sydney Olympic games. He had been in the United States for a few years and didn't speak much understandable English. But he found a way to communicate. Our high school had offered him a job.

Jon's Assistant was a nice, strict and fun man named Howard Terry. They made a great team in handling our "B" freshman team, our junior varsity and our varsity team. In total, we had approximately thirty to forty guys swimming each year.

When Jon saw me, he was kind to me but he didn't think much of me as a swimmer. And I understood why. All the good incoming swimmers came from younger AAU (Amateur Athletic Union) age group swim programs. Some came into high school already competing for six and seven years. A few were nationally ranked and were headed for university scholarships. Here I was starting in tenth grade.

But I remember him saying in 10th grade in his barely understandable English, "If you work hard you could be a good water polo player and maybe get us a point in swimming." Points in swim meets are based on how well you did, 1st place got five points, 2nd place received three points and a point for 3rd place. I quickly had a dream of earning one point on the "B" Team. Somewhere within me, I desperately wanted to get a point.

Coach Urbanchek and Mr. Terry had enough confidence in me to encourage me that I could do well and make a difference if I worked hard. Because of their encouragement I put my face down in the water and began to learn how to swim like a real swimmer.

Looking back, that was all I needed. I wanted a place to fit in and be accepted.

So for the next three years I worked hard and learned to work hard. Just so you understand "working hard" was at an Olympic level, Jon was an Olympian. He set a standard of what was going to be expected and how hard we should work. We did what he said.

Jon ultimately left Anaheim high school after developing our program into a nationally ranked high school Program that produced many All Americans and two Olympians: Greg and Doug Arth. I think my junior year we had five All American swimmers.

He left Anaheim high school to take the Long Beach State swimming and water polo job in Long Beach California. And from there, he became the University of Michigan Head Swim Coach and as the U.S. Olympic Swim Coach. He is the swimming grandfather to Michael Phelps and others. Jon Urbanchek is in the U.S. Swimming Hall of Fame and is still coaching today for USA Swimming at 83, here in Southern California.

He is a legend. And I was so fortunate to have been coached by him and Mr. Terry for those three years. They fathered us and developed us.

So when I say we worked hard, we worked until we were exhausted. Up to three daily workouts: 6:30 a.m., 1:30 p.m., after our last class and the best and most committed came back for the 6:30 p.m. workout.

Often we swam 5000 to 6000 yards a day. Mileage was everything back then. We loved to win in water polo and in swimming so we worked hard. Our varsity, junior varsity and the "B" team won a lot.

I wasn't the All American swimmer or water polo player like some of the others but I learned to work hard and loved it. Many of the high schools had good talent but we out worked them. As I expected, I was average in this group. Occasionally in 10th grade I'd score a goal in water polo. I started getting a point here and a point there on the B team in swimming. I was thrilled. Every time I got out of the pool the crowd clapped, and sometimes even stood up in our outdoor swim stadium and gave us a standing ovation. It was exhilarating. I lived to work hard and to win. I had found a place to fit and get better.

My mom, who was now out of the hospital, even though she was still sick with lupus, never missed one of my water polo games or swim meets in three years. Sadly, my father never came to one of my swim meets or water polo games in those three high school years. He was busy post World War II building his career and providing for our family. There were hardly ever fathers at our games or swim meets in those days. He was part of the "Greatest Generation" that lost out on their children's childhood.

When I graduated from high school, I was still average in our swim program. I had made varsity in both water polo and swimming, but there were much better swimmers in our high school than me. I graduated with a 2.0 grade point average which only came because you could not compete in athletics unless you kept a 2.0 average or above. My coaches made sure that I kept at least a 2.0 average.

As I think back on those years, there was nothing I did that was above average. I was even average in my size. I graduated from high school at 5'11" and about 155 pounds. And sadly, I felt average and insignificant. So I drank a lot and did stupid, fun stuff. Maybe that is like a lot of kids. The pretty girls all liked the popular guys. I wasn't popular or hot. I asked girls out who said no.

Occasionally one might say yes. But usually they weren't the ones I really wanted.

And I knew I had father-son issues. We never really saw eye to eye and I could never compete with his intellect. My sister got straight A's but I struggled to get C's. He loved me but had a legitimate desire that I be more academic minded. His world was academics and law. He had been in the FBI during WWII chasing German subversives around the U.S. and Texas. Then he enlisted in the Army in 1944 "to do more for the war effort." The Army made him a Prosecuting Attorney in The Japanese War Crimes Trials in Manila in 1946-47.

If you asked my dad what he did in the War Crimes Trials he usually wouldn't say much of anything. But if I pressed him, once in a while he said "We hung them."

LIFEGUARD – MY FIRST BIG WIN

During high school, many of the water polo players were ocean beach lifeguards. The tryouts were hard since the college water polo and swimmers tried out too. There were 40-60 guys trying out for 10-15 positions each year.

You had to be 16 to be hired by the city. However, after sophomore year, I wanted to see if I could compete even though I was only 15 1/2. I was a beach guy with a surfing background in junior high. I had been body surfing since I was a boy. I felt like I could compete with the older guys because I hung out with older guys. So I decided to try out anyway.

My father, (the ultimate rule follower), asked me why I would try out if the rules said that no lifeguards would be hired until they turned 16. I said that I wanted to be a guard and thought the experience would be good for the following year's tryouts. He didn't get it.

My mom on the other hand said, "If you want to try, go down and try out if they let you. See what happens. You may be right and learn something for next year."

We probably had half the water polo and swim team working as beach lifeguards in the summer. Being paid to look at girls all day wasn't a bad deal. Plus you could surf before and after work. The guys all chose different cities to work for, and the guys that I was closest to worked for the City of San Clemente, which paid $3.65 an hour.

San Clemente Lifeguard Headquarters - 1960s

I told the San Clemente guys I wanted to try out even though I was only 15 1/2. They encouraged me to show up and see what would happen. Inside I knew I wasn't as fast as many of college and other high school guys that were trying out but I thought I could maybe outsmart and out train them. Most would be just pool swimmers.

I started going down to San Clemente and running the beach and body surfing where the tests would be held. I got my mom to drive me down after school. She made me a deal: If I did my homework, she'd take Kenny Wollin and me surfing down there and at Doheny Beach after swim practice. That is the same Doheny Beach that is in the Beach Boys song "Surfin' USA." I did my homework.

I went down on low tide days as well as high tide days to see how the waves broke and to devise a game plan. I wanted to understand the south to north currents at high tide and low tide. The current usually ran into and away from the San Clemente pier. The bigger the waves the faster the current ran under the pier from south to the north. At high tide you couldn't run far into the water as it became waist deep quickly. At low tide you could run quite a ways in the water before you had to start swimming.

I prepared a lot and asked the lifeguards a lot of questions.

Finally, the Saturday morning tryouts came.

It was a cold winter foggy March Saturday morning. About 50 or 60 kids showed up for the tryouts.

There were three events that morning:

1.) A long swim out to the end of the pier and around an orange buoy and back.

2.) A "run-swim-run" up and down the beach with a shorter swim.

3.) A run-swim-rescue where you had to run down the beach and swim out around a lifeguard sitting on a Surf Rescue board and come back in and pick up a guy and run down the beach with him on your back. The second and third swims were about half as long as the first long swim.

There was about 10 minutes between each event. They started at 8 a.m. The water was about 55 degrees. The sky was gray. The air was damp and there was fog so thick at times we couldn't see the end of the pier. We wore our speedos. No goggles, no fins.

That day there were really good size waves. I was stoked. Some were pretty big. I could see on a lot of the swimmers faces, that they had never swam out through the surf before. There is a way to do it that is fast. Most didn't do it or know how to do it. The tide was pretty high. There was a pretty strong current with lots of churning white water. I was excited and prepared.

I knew where to start and it wasn't with the pack swimmers. It was off to the left closer to the pier. The current would be a big factor in getting to the orange buoy at the end of the pier. I needed it to carry me to the buoy and not past it. And it did.

If you lined up in front of the buoy, the current would take you off course. It would cause you to have to swim extra to get back to the orange buoy at the end of the pier and then around it. No one wanted to swim any harder than they had to in the cold water. There would be three events and I wanted to conserve my energy for all three and not waste it on the first longest swim.

It worked out that way. Almost all of the swimmers lined up directly in front of the orange buoy and ended up being carried way off to the right and off course. I felt awkward but also a little smart starting way off to the left of everybody else. Some of the swimmers just stared at me in bewilderment. "What's he doing?"

Thankfully, in the first swim, the current took me to the buoy. On the way back in, I was in about eighth place and there were really good size waves to ride as I had hoped for.

It was a pretty high tide day meaning you had to swim a longer distance. That was good for me as well.

After I rounded the orange buoy at the end of the pier, I swam as hard as I could to position myself to try to catch the first or second wave of a three-wave set. Then miraculously it happened. I waited for the second wave which was bigger than the first, and backstroked into it. Then I took a big breath and did an underwater take off rolling over on my stomach and caught it. As it turned out, I body surfed past all the faster swimmers into the shore.

I didn't know what had happened because I was holding my breath with my head was underwater. But when I stood up at the shore, I looked behind me. I was amazed to be the first to shore and out of the water.

The crowd was as shocked as I was. They were screaming and not all for me. I ran up the sand berm in front of the lifeguard headquarters and grabbed the popsicle stick being held by one of the lifeguards that had the #1 marked on it.

My high school lifeguard teammates ran over to me and hugged me as did my mom. I was breathless and speechless. They were going nuts. This was amazing.

All I knew was that I was really cold. I was shivering, a little blue and I had pulled an upset. Someone threw a towel around me and I watched in amazement the rest of the swimmers came in.

My mom gave me a cup of hot chocolate which was shaking in my hands and I could barely drink it. It was a life changing moment. Some of the better college swimmers were 22 and 23 years old. I was smaller than all of them, and I had won.

I tried to warm up before the second event but it never happened.

I ran OK and was probably fifteenth into the water. But I did not go in the water on a straight line to the guy sitting on his surfboard. I started again to the left of the others and let the current take me to my right.

When I got around the lifeguard sitting on the surfboard I was in about eighth position which was OK. I just kept switching from freestyle

Coming out of the ocean, running to grab a win.

to backstroke so I could see when the next set of waves was coming. Usually in a three-way set of waves the last wave is the biggest. But I didn't need the biggest. I just needed the first wave to be strong enough to take me all the way to the shore.

I noticed the set coming and nobody seemed to care about that first wave. I think they were waiting for the bigger second and third waves. But I cared. It was a strategic move to get in front of the faster swimmers. When it came, I just backstroked into it, took a deep breath, rolled over on my stomach again, and caught it all the way to the shore like the first one.

Again, when I stood up, no one was in front of me. I ran up the sandy berm and grabbed that #1 popsicle stick again. My teammates went nuts. I was the youngest guy out there and a sophomore, not even legal to work, with two first place wins to my name.

The third event, I bodysurfed again to the shore with a couple of other guys. But the guy that I picked up was pretty big and heavy. The sand was soft and I stumbled down the beach with him on my back. I finally carried him the approximately 50 yards for a third place finish.

By that time it didn't really matter because I had received the two first places and everyone knew I was in a good position going into the third event.

It was a huge win for me and the crowd went wild. I couldn't believe I had beaten the faster, older University of California-Irvine and the San Diego State swimmers.

All my beach lifeguard friends celebrated with me as well as my mom. The strategy had worked. Most of the other swimmers were mainly pool guys. They didn't know the ocean. Studying the beach and with the input of the older lifeguards, I'd found a way to compete.

Here was the big life lesson for me.

I knew I was average and had always been average. I now knew for sure this insight: If I would work harder and be more strategic than others, I would be more than average in my life. I learned I could beat more talented people just as Coach Urbanchek and Coach Terry had said. From that point on in my life it was only a matter of will and motivation. Today it is referred to as your "Why." How strong is your Why? If it was strong enough I would do whatever it took to compete. If my "Why"

Dragging a kid out of the water and down the beach was part of the test.

wasn't strong enough, I found excuses and reasons to not give it my 100%.

That Truth lives within me. That was 50 some years ago. It is the truth that was with me then, and was with me when I was going across Greece or doing Kokoro or the World Marathon Challenge.

When Jon Urbanchek and Howard Terry heard what had happened at the lifeguard tryouts, they hugged me and congratulated me that next Monday.

I mentioned to them that they had taught me how to work hard and work smart. And I thanked them for teaching me that the fastest swimmer doesn't always win, nor does the most talented water polo player. The winner can be the one who worked the hardest and used their head. Coach Terry would often yell at me in those three high school years, "Owens, use your head."

It was a life lesson for me. And I've never forgotten it. And I've never been the same.

The chief lifeguard and the lifeguard captain were to interview those who placed in the first 15 places in the tryouts immediately after the three events. They were probably going to hire the first 10 or 15 lifeguards pretty quickly. Training was going to start in two weeks during spring break. They knew I was only 15 1/2. But they chose to interview me anyway. I was the first interviewee. It was quite a moment. The others just watched as I was the first one called to go inside and

Jon Urbanchek, Me, Howard Terry in May 2019. Jon is 83 and still represents USA Swimming for the 2020 Olympic games in Tokyo. Howard is 81. Obviously, it is wise to stay in shape into your 80s. They exemplify the 20X Principle.

speak with the chief and the captain.

Maybe they were just intrigued or wanted to meet me. I don't know. They congratulated me and asked me about how I had trained for the event and how I did so well.

I told them that I knew I was too young by six months to be hired but that I wanted to see how I could do and compete. I told them my strategy and how I trained for that day. Then I told them that I'd be a great lifeguard.

I guess they were impressed because a few days later I got a phone call at home telling me they had gone to the city manager and asked for a waiver to be able to hire an underage 15 1/2 year old lifeguard. Amazingly, the City Manager checked with the city's insurance plan and granted them a waiver to hire me. I became the first and only underage lifeguard ever hired by the city of San Clemente to this day.

Interestingly, there was only one death that summer within our lifeguard department. It was with me at the pier. I had a kid die on me while he was surfing at the pier. He cut his aorta in half with his surfboard when the board "pearled" on him. He bled out on the beach in my arms. The ambulance came and took him to the hospital but they couldn't save him.

I had a lady die on me the second summer as well after being washed off the rocks in South Laguna Beach. When I finally found her, I couldn't resuscitate her. She had been under water, squeezed up and under a rock for over 10 minutes.

It was an unusual experience to go to some place and have someone say to me at 15 or 16, "How was your day or week?"

"Had a kid die on me this week."

It took some processing. I usually drank.

Back to the swim team. Coach Urbanchek and Howard Terry went nuts as did my high school teammates. It was a win for me but it was also a win for the mentality of our program. We worked hard and we were scrappy. And we won a lot. Four of our high school seniors were offered university scholarships.

That one experience radically changed me. I knew I wasn't the smartest kid, nor the fastest kid, nor the most gifted kid in the world. However I knew if I could be smart, and work hard, I could do more than I had thought and more than what other people thought for me.

After graduation, I enrolled at Orange Coast College to row Crew. Again, the program was outstanding and was known for our competitiveness nationally for a two year college. We were the only two year collegiate rowing program in the U.S., rowing against all four year universities JV teams. In rowing, the first eight guys were the varsity and the second eight guys were the junior varsity. Lots of universities were interested in our rowers and wanted them to consider transferring for their junior and senior years of college.

We worked hard as well. On the water by 6:30 a.m. after arriving for PT at 5:45 a.m. I have never done anything as hard as crew. Water polo was different and easier because of the technical demands of rowing.

In crew I learned to drive myself to the place of throwing up and nearly passing out.

Again, I found myself to be average. There were better and more technical oarsman than me, but I loved to work hard. It was my only hope of being on the team. I made the freshman and varsity team for those two years but not by much. I wasn't consistently able to make the eight man team and rowed a lot of "pairs" and "fours." But I enjoyed being with the guys and on the team. And I excelled at being in shape.

My challenge was, I was going nowhere as a young man. I had to make a change.

Me dragging a guy out of the water, down the beach, during the San Clemente lifeguard tryouts. I was 15 ½ years old.

BEYOND AVERAGE

The lifeguard tryouts where I came in first place, and became the youngest lifeguard in San Clemente history.

Note from John Urbanchek and Howard Terry

Preparation for life was the overall goal for the coaches at Anaheim High School who took on the task of leading the athletes in our aquatics program.

Robert was like many of our athletes who for varied reasons decided to swim and or play water polo while in High School. Some of them came with a great deal of experience while others had little to none. Bobby or Big O, which is what we called him, was one of those with little experience as a pool swimmer. However, he had spent a lot of time in the water at the beach. He was excited about being a part of the team and ready and willing to learn.

Through hard work his confidence level grew at an exceptional rate to the point when he left us we could see a major positive change. It was a joy to watch him grow as an athlete and as a person. Even more rewarding is to see him and others use those skills and attitudes as they continued through life.

Robert, we are very impressed and proud of your accomplishments and are thankful that we had the opportunity to be of some guidance to your years of success!

Remember Jon's slogans:

1. "The only way to swim fast is to swim fast".
2. "It is mind over matter but if you don't have a mind it does not matter".

Jon Urbanchek USA Hall of Fame Olympic Swim Coach and Michigan Swim Coach Jon Urbanchek

Coach **Howard Terry** from 1964-1998

Anaheim High School Swim and Water Polo Coaches.

LEADERSHIP LESSONS

1. Do you know your issues? There isn't a perfect person. Everyone has issues. Those who say they don't, have the most. Issues shape us. If you don't understand them and deal with them they can sabotage you. If you are going to focus and do great things you also need to figure out if your issues will sabotage your goals down the road.

> I hope you enjoy the next chapter
> where I take on some of my issues.

1968 Lifeguard Pic. I am in the back row, fourth from right.

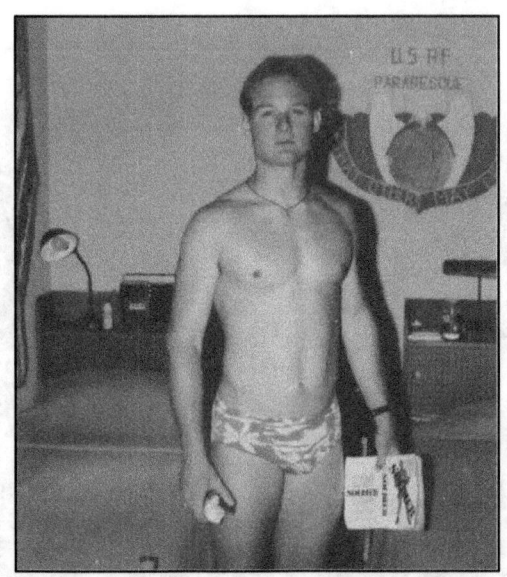

I'm 23 at INDOC, Pararescue training. Check out those camo speedos.

Me and my team at Dive School, I'm in the middle standing up.

If You Can Tolerate It, You Won't Change It

CHAPTER 2

Air Force Pararescue: Learning to Save Lives. Starting with my own.

During this time and during the Vietnam war, many of the beach lifeguards were being recruited by Navy SEALS to become Navy SEALS. They were looking for water guys who could go all day.

The Air Force was also recruiting beach lifeguards to be Combat Paramedics called "Pararescuemen." The Navy SEALS, Green Berets in the Army and the Force Recon guys in the Marines were the offensive units in the military. Pararescue guys were the defensive minded guys.

If a Navy SEAL or Army Ranger or Marine Force Recon guy gets shot or is in trouble then the Pararescue guys are called in as combat offensive or defensive minded paramedics to do the rescue work and escape with them.

If you liked rescuing people, like many lifeguards did, this was the big leagues.

At 23, my life was going nowhere. I had started and quit college three times. I had been in jail and crashed three cars screwing around. I was getting a master's degree in irresponsibility and knew I was going nowhere. Surfing, skiing, partying and working were getting old. All my friends seemed to be progressing in life. I wasn't. I was stuck. And I had excuses.

Consistently over the years, my lifeguard Pararescue friends had urged me to come join them and become a Pararescueman. But the last thing I wanted was to go into the military in the middle of the Vietnam

53

war.

But life has a way of getting your attention. Sometimes you have moments of clarity and perspective. I needed help and knew I needed to grow up. I realized I couldn't do it on my own. I needed help and to change my friends, environment and lifestyle. Structure would be good for me.

Pararescue seemed more fun than the regular military. I asked a lot of questions about going into the Air Force and weighed my options. I knew that I would get great training and have a lot of fun getting that training. Plus, the job skills that I would learn by being a Pararescueman would be of great value when I left the military.

I changed my mind. I would go into the military. It would help me.

It is interesting to me today to see how two or three Pararescuemen could change my world view about the military and going in.

I finally made the decision without talking to friends and family. Everyone I talked to about going into the military, including my parents, discouraged me against the advice of the Pararescuemen. But I respected them and knew they were the kind of guys I wanted to be like. This would be the best thing for me at this point in my life. I knew I wasn't going to find a lot of supporters. There was a controversial war going on.

My fear was that I was still an average athlete compared to the others who would be trying out. That fear was a real concern to me.

I went to training like my life depended on it. I asked a lot of questions. I began to run, swim and do body weight training. I knew I had to do 15 dead arm pulls if I made it in so I went to work on them. I started with being able to do four. I got stronger by the month. This went on for about five months. I think my parents were bewildered as I began to get really focused.

That wasn't like me.

I had gone down to the Air Force recruiter and told him I wanted to enlist. He gave me the basic test and I scored pretty well in two of the four categories.

That was all well and good, however I was going to be a Pararescueman and those scores didn't really matter much to me. I wasn't trying to qualify for any of those jobs.

He of course tried to discourage me about believing I could be a

Pararescueman. Almost all Air Force recruiters back then tried to discourage young men and women who believed that they could make it into the Special Ops community. I understood because they want us to be "realistic" about our future. But I thought I was realistic too. I had done my homework and learned about the Pararescue culture. I knew what to expect in training, and I trained hard. Really hard.

Finally, after about seven months, I told my mom and dad that I had decided to go in the Air Force. It was about a month before I was to leave for training to be an Air Force Special Ops Pararescueman. The Air Force didn't use the term Special Ops back then. When I said I was going to try out for the Air Force equivalent of the Navy SEALS, they got the idea. Then I told my girlfriend who lived about 90 minutes away. She couldn't believe it.

My parents understood my plan and were not happy. I can't think of many parents who want their son to join the military while watching a 10 year Southeast Asia saga on the nightly news. So many young men had been killed over the years. Vietnam was not a happy subject for anybody in America.

My girlfriend had come to the conclusion that I was a little strange. She had seen me go through a number of changes and this was just the latest. But to her, this was the biggest and stupidest change.

The night before I was to fly out to Lackland Air Force Base in San Antonio, Texas my parents had a going away dinner for me. It was more like a death dinner than a celebration or going away party. I was the only one who was happy. They all tried to be encouraging, but mostly there was silence and tears. My mom, the consistent encourager, thought that I would do well. She encouraged me to be the best I could be and I would surprise myself. My father, the Superior Court Judge, didn't know what to say. He was a Republican but he wasn't happy with the war. He kept silent.

My girlfriend Sandy just couldn't believe what I was going to do. She couldn't believe I would want to go in to the military. But she also knew that I was searching for purpose and direction.

That dinner didn't last long. Soon Sandy had left and my parents went to bed. Finally I was alone and so excited about the next day I barely slept.

The following day was a blur. Before I knew it, I was getting off the plane in San Antonio, Texas and stepping into a blue school bus that was taking me to the base.

In a flash they had shaved my head, taken away my civilian clothes and given me new, green clothes and assigned me to a dormitory. I spent the next eight weeks in Air Force basic training with all kinds of different types of guys. It was a trip.

As it turned out, I wasn't average this time.

The pull of a goal must be stronger than anything else in your life.

Have you ever been embarrassed in front of your peers? Have you ever entered an event that crushed you? Have you ever stood in front of a class paralyzed with fear? Have you ever been afraid that you're going to fail privately and publicly?

When I talked to my Pararescue friends, who are known in the military world as PJ's, about what I needed to do to get ready for Pararescue training, they repeatedly told me it would be the hardest thing physically and mentally that I would ever attempt.

I was 15 1/2 when I started hearing that. When I made my decision to go in the Air Force at 22, and try out for Pararescue, I was deeply insecure and afraid when making that decision. It was a four year commitment where if I failed, I'd be stuck in the Air Force as a cook or something. That had some fear built in for sure. But I had the knowledge that if I worked really hard before I got there I had a chance to make it. I was determined that I would not be a quitter or be eliminated.

For five months I trained like my life depended on it. I never wanted to be embarrassed and I didn't want to be a failure. I was going to college at that time and in all my spare time I trained. I ran stairs, thousands of stairs, did push-ups, did pull-ups, did air squats and swam.

I ran up and down the beach in the soft sand to work on my hamstrings and my glutes, I did bear crawls in the sand as well as forward and backward crabs in the soft sand. I did long runs, up to ten miles, often. And I did this all alone. I didn't have a cheering section encouraging me, except for a couple of Reserve Pararescuemen. They said I could do it.

When you train in fear none of your training is ever good enough. I had lots of fears. Fear of failure, fear of rejection, fear of being embarrassed and fear of being stuck in the Air Force being a cook if I flunked out of Pararescue school. Fear of my father shaking his head at another wild strange thing I'd done where I failed.

I knew about hard work from Coach Urbanchek as well as from rowing crew for two years at Orange Coast College. I wasn't afraid on either of those teams. This time I was afraid. I knew I had to step up my game and my intensity for this challenge.

My PJ friends shared stories of the things that happened in PJ Indoc School. Their stories, and my imagination, were in my brain every day as I trained.

In some classes the instructors would have the young man who quit stand up in front of the other trainees and be forced to yell out to his classmates, "Sir, I am quitting sir." The sergeant would say to class whatever number it was, "Everyone shut up and look here. This classmate of yours has something he wants to tell all of you." Then the instructor would say to the young man, "What did you say young man?" And the young man would have to say, "I am quitting sir!"

And the sergeant would say, "I want to hear you say that again louder son. Are you a quitter son?" And the young man would embarrassingly say, "Sir, I am a quitter, sir."

Then the sergeant would say to all the class, "Everyone look here. This is what a quitter looks like. Say it again son. We want to hear you say it again. This time shout it to your classmates." And the young man would have to shout out, "Sir, I am a quitter sir. You are looking at a quitter sergeant".

Then there would be silence. The sergeant would stare at the young man who was embarrassed and ashamed. Often the young man would begin to break down and cry and shake.

Finally, the sergeant would say to the young man "Go turn in your gear son, and get out of here. You are just another quitter."

Then the sergeant would turn to the class and say, "Any more quitters here?" And then the class would shout back "No Sir, there are no more quitters here." Then the training would continue.

The PJ guys told me over and over as I was getting ready to go in to be mentally prepared for a physical and mental beat down. They emphasized that the biggest and strongest, and best athletes often didn't make it. They quit. Guys who everyone looked up to and thought they were the biggest studs in the group would just one day quit.

The guys who would make it were the most resilient, the mentally strongest. They would never allow themselves to become mentally weak or emotionally drained. Or you could say, that when they were mentally weak and wanted to quit, they found a way to not give in to their emotions. They had an inner strength that others didn't have.

They told me to train with that in mind.

My question was where did those guys get that inner mental strength and how did they develop it?

It had to come from hard workouts and overcoming physical and mental pain and mental pressure.

With that in mind, I did pull-ups until my hands blistered and finally became calloused. The ends of my toes had continual little blisters that became wonderful calluses. Those calluses became my friends. I loved to feel them.

The guys from the beach and college thought I had lost my mind. They commented "Why in the world would you want to go into the military and to a war when you don't have to? That is so stupid." I finally stopped talking to almost all my friends because they just didn't see what I saw.

In a sense I went dark. I checked out. I just dropped out and focused. Why? I didn't need the mental distractions or the drama. I wanted to make it as a Pararescueman as much as anything I had ever wanted in my life. I wanted it more than my girlfriend, I wanted it more than acceptance from my friends. I wanted it more than getting drunk. I wanted it more than partying. I wanted it as much as life itself. I wanted to change and I wanted to be tested. And I did not want to be embarrassed or find myself being a quitter.

When I finally went into Pararescue training it was like I expected. All these trainees were in an old white wooden two-story barracks. The guys came in all sizes. There were tall ones and short ones. Some from the South where I could hardly understand what they were saying. Some from the Midwest. There were obvious studs, and short, skinny guys. There were beach guys from Florida that like to smoke weed like Jimmy Payton and there were super straight guys that didn't even know what weed looked like. There were all kinds. Garry Lewry was a runner from New Jersey. Bruce Hickson was a strong 18 year old athletic kid from New Hampshire who wasn't shaving yet. We had a 22-year-old African-American guy from Virginia by the name of Charles Harris. He came really buffed and with a huge afro. Problem was he couldn't swim. Most all talked a good game. All of them thought they had the stuff needed to make it through Indoc training for the next nine or ten weeks or so. Most were wrong

We were woken up at 4:30 in the morning and told to go in the basement and begin to do PT on old blood and sweat stained canvas wrestling mats. The basement had the smell and stains of years of trainee sweat, spit and tears. We did every kind of push up, leg lifts, mountain climbers and sit-ups that you could imagine from 4:30 a.m. until 6:30 a.m. five mornings a week.

We then went to breakfast and had our rooms inspected afterwards. Then it was outside for more pull-ups, more push-ups, more pull-ups, bear crawls and or runs until lunch. I remember having a brand new pair of white Tiger running shoes which was the new design that helped Nike get on the map in their early days. They were wonderful.

Then after lunch we went to one of two pools and we swam a lot, sprints, underwaters, more yards. It went on for days and weeks. For me that was the best part of the day because swimming was easy for me. But for others it was draining and discouraging. Many quit from the pool training alone.

Then often we would do another run of five to 10 miles or do sprints up the hill somewhere on the base. Finally, we would have dinner. Often there would be a meeting of some sort and then lights out at 8:30 p.m.

On Saturdays, we would be tested. We had a mile and a half run to do for time then more pull-ups and more push-ups and more sit-ups. We made the standards. However, the instructors kept raising the acceptable standards for us to attain. "You can do better", we heard often. We were never good enough. We could get better. And we did. As they expected more - we gave more. Life lesson is, people live up to, or down to expectations.

Our class did this every week for five and a half days a week for thirteen weeks. We were told that it would be eight weeks, but the war was winding down and we weren't needed as other classes were. Some guys had mentally prepared for 8 weeks of INDOC. When they heard that it would go on indefinitely, it rocked some. That meant we were not scheduled to go to our pipeline training until the Air Force knew what to do with us after our PJ graduation in nine months. And that meant that we had nothing to do but train more.

What I discovered for the first time in my life was that I wasn't average. I was doing well and excelling. I had the fastest swim times on record at PJ Indoc. That amazed me. I really wasn't that fast, I thought. Where were my high school friends? They would have smoked this place. I was told by Garry Lewry that my swim record stood for years.

My runs got faster. I became stronger. PT became no big deal. Just do it and get it over with. I wasn't being crushed. I was thriving in it. The hard work before coming in to the Air Force paid off. I had worked hard. I was mentally strong. I had an unshakable confidence that I tried to hide so I wouldn't be singled out and tested more. I encouraged others. I had new friends. I was so stoked.

Most of all I was gaining confidence.

What I learned was many guys may have been great athletes before they arrived for PJ training but many weren't mentally capable of handling the weekly day in and day out duress and stress. The workouts just went on and on and on. It was really mentally fatiguing. I had to break the workouts into weeks, days, and hours. It was hard to get up every day and know how long of a day it would be physically and mentally. But you just put your mind to it and reminded yourself that it wouldn't last forever. So ….. Just do it.

As I had been told before I went in by the Reserve Pararescue guys from the 303rd Unit in Riverside, many of the best athletes would just one day quit. They would say, "I'm done. This is bullshit. No more. To hell with this, I don't need this." And they would just eliminate themselves. The weeks took a mental toll on them. We all felt it. Or for a few, their bodies broke down. Knees, ankles, lower backs, hamstrings. All began to go. It was sad. We were all competing, but not so much against each other as against ourselves and the system. There were really good guys who quit or got Med dropped.

Every time, we would try to encourage them to not quit and tell them they were doing great and they had it in them to make it. But you could see in a guy's eyes when they were beaten mentally. One day they just didn't care to go on. They were done. They had lost their "Why" their dream just wasn't worth it anymore. As I said before, to me it was sad. We lost some great guys.

Also, lot of the guys grew tired of being yelled at. But it was the instructor's job to get in your head and get you out of your strength zone or comfort zone to see who you would really become under pressure. Could you keep a positive attitude when all hell was being thrown at you? Could you lead and contribute when you're exhausted? Could you be a team player when the pressure was on?

Actually, the intense hard brutal yelling ceased after a few weeks as we got down to a core group. The guys who quit were gone and we all had a pretty good idea who would make it except for guys who would unexpectedly be injured.

The instructors knew it as well and began to yell or give orders with a different attitude. They began to encourage us and do more talking than yelling.

I remember one day we were in the push-up position and Sergeant Bruce came up to me, got down on one knee and in my ear and said, "Owens, I am never going to touch you. I'm never going to hurt you physically. But I am going to crush you. Do you understand? I am going to make you really wonder if you really want to go through this. Do you understand?" I said, "Yes sergeant."

"Why am I doing this Owens? Because I like you. You have potential. And someday you're going to thank me for making you miserable. And the man's life who you're going to save is going to thank you for training like this. Do you understand me?" I said "Yes sergeant."

I was staring down at the brown, stiff, dry, grass with the sweat rolling off my nose. My arms were shaking in the push up position for some gawd-awful period of time in the afternoon Texas sun and saying to him "Yes sergeant. Thank you. I will appreciate this someday. Yes sergeant, I understand. Yes sergeant, I love this." And then he continued to make all of us miserable. But I found that I loved the challenge.

Sergeant Bruce explained it this way to our class of trainees:

"You want to be a Pararescueman? That means men and women are going to put their trust in your ability to get to them and help them and save their lives. They are putting their trust in you that no matter what happens in combat or not in combat, you will not quit on them. You would rather die trying to save them, than come back alive without them. You are willing to lay down your life for the person you've been called to rescue. That is why the Badge on the Pararescueman's maroon beret has this motto on it, "That Others May Live." You may not live, but they will live. You need to want to train so you will know you will never quit on anyone.

"We need to know at what point you will quit on your man. And YOU need to know when it isn't worth it anymore and quit on your man. That is why we need to discover what you're made of and if you are a quitter. There will be lots of reasons to want to quit now and in your career. Some of them will be good reasons. But we cannot allow quitters to be trained as Pararescuemen. It is OK if you decide this training is not for you. You may have come in with one idea of what it was like to be trained as a Pararescueman. Now you may see that it is different. That's OK. This job is not for everyone. There are other good jobs in the Air Force. We will help you find one. We need to discover what you're made of and you need to discover what you're made of. That is why we are doing what we are doing."

Then Sergeant Bruce said to all of us, "Class, do you understand why you are here and what you have signed up for?" And we all shouted back, "Yes sergeant. We understand."

And then we continued doing more PT.

This was a classic INDOC training ritual moment for me. One day, about four in the afternoon, Sergeant Bruce said "Class, get in the push-up position. I need to have four or five of you quit before dinner. We are going to stay out here and miss dinner and if we have to we will go to midnight until four or five of you help me out and your classmates out and quit.

"Would any of you help me out now and quit? It is not a bad thing for you to quit because I'm asking you to help your classmates out by quitting. So this will be an honorable quitting. You will not be embarrassed if you quit. We will understand. Would any of you help us out now?" No one said a word. He said "OK, let's keep going."

I don't remember exactly how long we continued but sure enough after an hour or so, a guy would quit. Then a little while later another guy would quit. Then the third guy would quit. Finally, Sergeant Bruce would say, "God, I miss my wife and I miss my dinner. This really pisses me off. I need one more of you to quit and this will be over. I need one more of you to quit now." And some guy quit!

I was amazed. How could they be so stupid and cave in. They had come too far to just quit.

It was dark. And Sergeant Bruce said "Great. I'm sorry to see you

INDOC training I'm on the far left.

go. You're a good man. Just go back and turn in your gear." And it was over.

Then he looked at us still there and said "OK."

We all went back to our barracks and that guy quit. Sergeant Bruce went home and we went to dinner. Those guys were gone in the morning.

And so it went during the early weeks of training.

Why do I share these stories with you? It is because, I was fortunate as a young man to be tested and broken and reshaped. I have never forgotten those experiences. Quitting isn't an option.

Ralph Waldo Emerson said it this way:

"When a man is pushed, tormented and defeated he has a chance to learn something."

I believe that.

I am fortunate to have been pushed, tormented and defeated in my 20s.

I was mentored by some great men like Sergeant Bruce. I share this with you here on purpose: I have learned to look for mentors and people I could learn from since then. I have asked for a mentor to teach me and train me. In some ways, I needed them to break me and test me. I knew that there was more in me than I had ever allowed to be shaped and developed. I knew I was lazy and an undisciplined punk.

And today at 67 years old I know there is still more in me to be tapped into.

The things I learned in Pararescue laid a foundation for the rest of my life. They shaped me for everything I thought about, or attempted to accomplish in the years to come. When I planted a church in a non-church environment, or started a live call in radio program, or TV program that lasted 22 years, or ran for a state legislator seat in the early 80's where I won a four way primary, I had learned to focus, train and learn from others.

The culmination of my transformation from an irresponsible young punk, into a leader in Pararescue Indoc Training came when Sergeant Bruce summoned me into his office.

I knocked on his door. "Come" he bellowed. Seated behind his desk with a big wad of chew in his right cheek and a Styrofoam cup for his spit – he was still imposing. I stood at attention in front of his desk and announced my presence, "Owens here, Sir."

He looked at me for a little while and then scooted his chair back away from the desk and stood up. He picked up his cup and came around the left side of his old wooden brown beat up desk and stood in front of me. He spit in his cup and said, "Owens you know I've been watching you. You always seem to hide. You don't say much and you try to stand in the back of the line. You just try to stay invisible. Do you know that Owens?"

I said, "Yes Sergeant Bruce. Just doing my job and staying out of trouble, Sir." He said "No. To me you are hiding. You know you are a leader amongst these men. They watch you swim and do the other events and you are hiding from being a leader. Why is this Owens?"

I said, "I'm just trying to do my job Sergeant."

Then he spit in his cup again and took a step forward and slowly without him blinking he put his nose on my nose. Talk about invading your space. I could smell that tobacco breath and he had little pieces in his teeth. He rocked my emotional world and said, "Owens, do I own you yet?"

He had been trying to break me the whole time I was there. But I wouldn't show weakness or vulnerability. I just kept my head down and did whatever he said. I didn't complain. I didn't whine. I wouldn't give him eye contact unless I had to. But I knew he wanted more. He wanted me to cry "Uncle" in some way. He wanted to know that he had won and I should show brokenness before him. But I hadn't done it. And I was proud of it.

Instantly, the tears began to roll down my cheeks and I said, "Yes sir, you own me sir. What do you want of me?"

And he slowly backed away and spit in his cup again and said to me, "Good Owens. I own you and you will do what I say. Right?"

"Yes Sergeant, you own me. What do you want of me?"

"Owens, we're getting ready to graduate this Indoc Class and go into the Pipeline and I want you to be the Team Leader. I want you to lead this team of men and be responsible for them. Do you understand me?" I said "Yes Sergeant, I understand what you want."

Then he said, "I'm going to give you responsibility for these men for the next nine months. If one of these men under your leadership gets in trouble in one of the schools, I'm going to fly there and have your ass. Is that clear Owens?"

That made me really nervous because we had some wild guys in my class. Getting in trouble wasn't hard for the guys. I think I was picked because I was a little older and it was known that I didn't drink anymore.

Master Sergeant Bruce knew these guys were young stallions too. He was proud of us. They were ready to get away from Lackland and into Pipeline training. He was glad to get us out of there. I was too.

"Yes Sergeant. That is very clear." And then he slowly walked back around his desk and sat down and spit in his cup again. Then he said "Good, I'm glad you understand. Tomorrow you will be the Team Leader." Then he said "You're dismissed." And I turned around and opened the door and left his office.

That moment I grew up. It was a life impacting moment. I became a leader instantly. More of one than I wanted. I just changed. Responsibility has a way of doing that. All thirteen weeks' worth of experiences changed me.

I mentally grew up.

I learned how to dig deep and overcome pain.

I learned how to develop endurance and mental toughness.

I learned about the difference between physical pain and mental pain.

I learned that I could handle a lot more adversity than I had ever imagined.

I learned that I could do far more than I ever thought I could do.

I developed confidence.

And the greatest gift a young person can have is the gift of confidence.

Lastly, I watched as other guys developed, changed and grew up too. That was an invaluable experience.

Mark Divine, who founded SEALFIT, calls this the 20X Principle. That we all can do 20 times more than we think we are able to do. But that most of us have never allowed the 20X Principle to be worked inside of us.

Therefore we have all limited our potential because we don't like pain and adversity. But without pain, pressure, adversity and suffering, we never have the chance to grow and develop into the person we can be. Everyone wants to live victoriously but no one wants to have a battle. But you can't have victory in your life without a battle and overcoming adversity. Confidence comes with hanging in there and persevering.

Therefore you need to wrestle with your inner person and win over him or her in different areas in your life.

You can't understand my five events until you understand the struggle. And everyone has struggles. More importantly everyone needs to struggle in lots of areas. You need to stop running from them and run to them. The 20X Principle only works in the struggles. You must learn to be an overcomer. You must choose to end accepting yourself as you are, and quit just existing. The chicken has to struggle to get out of the egg to gain the strength to live. The butterfly has to struggle to force its wings to expand.

Life is what you make of it. There are no perfect families. No perfect relationships. No lasting great situations. Life happens. We are not victims. You are where you are now by the choices you've made. We make good ones and bad ones. I would say get over your stuff and grow up.

Here's my last thought:

Change your diaper,

get over your stuff and grow up.

LEADERSHIP LESSONS

1. Will you allow yourself to be coached in the battles in your life?

2. Are you willing to REALLY focus on something?

3. Do you know that there are seasons in your life when you will not be able to live a balanced life?

4. Have your significant relationships signed off on your unbalanced seasons of life, or will your focus ruin close relationships?

5. Are you willing or able to "go dark" relationally for a period of time? Can your relationships withstand long periods of relational or emotional absence?

6. Do you love "The Test" and being tested?

7. Do you love, and are you willing to go through, the mental, relational and emotional pain to achieve your win?

8. Are you willing to be changed in how you think? Do you have a mental coach? Are you willing to hire a mental coach?

9. Is your "Why" strong enough? Would you rather die than not accomplish your goal?

10. Do you have a bulletproof strategic plan that is guaranteed to get you to the win?

THOUGHTS YOU SHOULD TAKE AWAY FROM THESE FIRST TWO CHAPTERS:

1. Dreams and Goals have huge costs attached to them.

2. "Why" you are doing something is so important. To all of us, our "Why" has to be unshakeable. You must be willing to forsake everything to attain your Why. Otherwise you will find a way to quit.

3. There are costs to pursuing your dreams and goals.

There is a Mental Cost.

- Mediocre and average men and women don't understand Champions and Overcomers.

- Champions and Overcomers don't train with average mediocre men and women. They eliminate them mentally from their daily lives.

There is an Emotional Cost.

- Paying the price required will be hard and challenge your inner person. You will hear your excuses scream at you to find reasons to quit.

There is a Physical Cost.

- Growth and change may take a while.

There is a Financial Cost.

- You reprioritize your short term and long term spending to go and do whatever it takes to be around winners.

There is a Relational Cost.

- You must change your friends and eliminate losers and excuse minded people from your friendships.

There is a Relearning Cost.

- You must be teachable and willing to change everything in your life. EVERYTHING!

4. You cannot live a balanced normal life if you are pursuing extraordinary goals.

- People will not understand you. You will be doubted and criticized. You will go dark. You can't confide to excuse minded people who want you to be normal and more balanced. For a season of your life or forever, you must do what you need to do to reach that dream and goal. Balanced people don't accomplish much. They watch from the stands. They read about you!

5. You must find and train with Winners. Only Winners.

- These are people that have done what you want to do and have excelled at it. You share with them what you are going to accomplish and ask for accountability from them. They may encourage you or scoff at you. It doesn't matter. You just do what they do and get good at it. You may do this for six months or six years. But you must train with winners. Not occasional winners.

6. You must relish going through mental, emotional and physical barriers.

- Mental toughness is a learned skill. It comes slowly. But it comes. It comes as you do what you haven't done before. You will have subtle but significant breakthroughs.

7. You must rewire your mind with positive self-talk.

- Every day you must strategically set time aside to watch videos, listen to speakers. Read books every day. You have to feed yourself mentally.

- You MUST read the book "Relentless" by Tim Grover. It is a MUST. You must also read Mark Divine's three books, "The Way of the SEAL", "Unbeatable Mind" and "8 Weeks to SEALFIT". You must watch Mark Divine's SEALFIT (SEALFIT.com) YouTube Videos. Learn to "Box Breathe."

8. You must set new positive mental and physical habits.

- It starts the moment your eyes open in the morning. It changes your eating habits and sleeping habits. It changes the first words that come out of your mouth as you wake up. It changes your first 30 minutes of every day.

9. You must not let your feelings derail your goals.

- Feelings lie and steal dreams and goals. You don't care how you feel. You do what you need to every day no matter what the voices in your head scream or whisper to you.

- The voice of your WILL and your WHY will take on the voices of your feelings and overcome the other bothersome and distracting weak voices. Then you daily do your work harder than you thought you would. Mental and physical tiredness is a fact in your life. But you learn to become mentally stronger.

10. You learn when to schedule mental, emotional and physical recovery time.

- You have a plan and you work your plan. You recharge with the same focus as if you were working out.

> The next chapter is another confidence building block.
>
> You must continue to get "wins" in your life.
>
> You can't get wins without risk of failure and enduring mental pain and suffering.

Robert doing a "Scuba Jump" out of a C-130 in the Arctic. The parachute is on the top with the scuba tanks underneath. The knife is strapped to the left leg. The crew chief's helmut is in the upper right corner of the door.

My PJ graduating class.

Getting ready for IRONMAN 1980. In Honolulu the day before the race.

On the road in Honolulu, 1980 IRONMAN.

CHAPTER 3

After Pararescue:
1980 IRONMAN: Year 3

The IRONMAN in Honolulu was definitely one of the most memorable and transforming experiences of my life. In order for you to really understand this experience you need to please go back and read the Sports illustrated article from May 13, 1979 before you read my experience. If you don't read the article, you'll not understand the context of the event. It was a crazy sports event. Much of the sports nation was captured by it. (Google: Sports Illustrated VAULT May 13, 1979 IRONMAN). When you read the article, you'll understand why I read it over and over during my training. For me to read the article and then immediately the next day choose to start training for it has led many to question my sanity. My experience in 1980 in many ways mirrored the Sports Illustrated account. After finishing IRONMAN 1980 I knew that the 20X Principle was working inside of me again. I also knew that impossible challenges seem to bring something special out of me. The next year, Iron Man was moved from Honolulu to the Big Island and Kailua-Kona where the World Championships have been held ever since.

Somewhere in there the original name Iron Man was changed in Kona to Ironman.

The 1980 IRONMAN is one of the most asked about experiences I've done. Most people do not know its history. I had just turned 29 years old.

BEYOND AVERAGE

I had been out of Pararescue for two years in January of 1980. Back then we rode our bikes with toe clips, no aero bars and no helmets. I just rode with a baseball cap and shorts.

In year three, 100 people read the article from May 13, 1979 and showed up with their "A-game." It was a life experience that fortified what I learned in Pararescue and shaped how I would think thereafter. This was one of those experiences that live within your mind and spirit forever. I pushed myself so hard during the IRONMAN that I passed out from dehydration in the marathon in some guy's yard. I flopped around for a while on his driveway until I could get it together and continue. (Please go to 1982 Wide World of Sports video of Julie Moss on YouTube and you'll see exactly what I went through.) Overcoming that was an experience that built another layer of confidence in me. I learned that "hitting the wall" either challenges you or crushes you. I had never hit a wall like that before. It was another building block. I learned again about developing mental resiliency and confidence.

After that experience, I made a choice that I could, and I would, overcome the challenges in my life! I didn't really have any more excuses. You don't really know someone until you watch them under mental, relational and physical pressure. That is when the real person leaks out and shows through the façade. I was finding out what was in me. And I was surprised.

I have always enjoyed watching great players play during the most intense moments. Great players like Kobe Bryant, Michael Jordan, LeBron James, Roger Federer and Tom Brady seem to always rise to the moment. They always want to ball. Others, on the other hand, shrink back from those big moments. The potential for failure is too much for them. I think those moments expose the real you.

The Ironman Triathlon was known at the time as the toughest and most insane endurance race in the world. Only crazy people attempted it. And some were crazy. They dressed up in Superman costumes or like Cow Man who ran his races with cow horns on. Some just drank beer at the beginning or during the race. That is why ABC's Wide World of Sports weekly TV program showed up in the IRONMAN's third year to film it. Its national reputation was huge after only its second year. It was something the Sports Illustrated writer had to see. It is fun now to think that there are less than a handful of IRONMAN triathletes competing today that have finished both IRONMAN Honolulu and The Ironman World Championships in Kona. Most of the Honolulu finishers of years one, two and three, have retired or died. Fortunately I am one of those who has finished both of them and is still in the game at 67.

When I read the long article in Sports Illustrated it instantly captivated me because it sounded so wild and so impossible. Except for a US Air Force Pararescueman, it didn't seem that impossible. Just wild!

I thought to myself "What a challenge... What if....."

A small voice in my head said, "I bet I could do that. I think I Gotta do it! That rough water swim is cut out for me. I AM GOING TO DO IT!"

The race was a dare event where you were to do Honolulu's three toughest races in one day. First, would be the Honolulu rough water swim. It would be two and a half miles starting at Waikiki Beach. You would swim out through the surf and down the coast and back. Second would be the Honolulu around the island bike race. The road around the island was 112 miles. Third would be doing the Honolulu Marathon at 26.3 miles. The debate at the time was who was the fittest athlete: the swimmer, the bicyclist or the runner. It was thought up by John Collins and others who dared each other to do all three in one day. The most obvious challenge was not just being a swimmer but being an ocean rough water swimmer. You almost had to be a beach local to be able to do that. That's where I got excited being an ex-beach lifeguard.

Immediately, I made a plan to be a part of that next January 1980 IRONMAN. I first purchased some two and a half pound wrist weights and began to run with them on my ankles. Then I borrowed a friend's bicycle and went to a bicycle shop and borrowed some stationary rollers. Rollers are like conveyor belt rollers where you put your bicycle on top of the spinning rollers and you ride your bike while still being stationary. It took some balance and focus or you could ride off the rollers and crash. You can work out with people standing next to you and talking to you. The reason I put my bike on rollers was because back in Tulsa the roads were too narrow and without shoulders for people to ride their bicycle safely. So I rode every day on rollers because I had to find a way to ride my borrowed bike and find a way to win.

For the next semester starting in late August, I would go to the pool and swim at lunch between classes. After the swim I would put my bicycle on the rollers by the side of the pool and I would ride for at least an hour five days a week. I usually put 20 pounds in my backpack as well, so as to strengthen my lower back. I was trying to prepare for everything that might zap me of my strength and endurance in this thing.

Then I asked to join the University Cross-country Team. The Coach said I could join as long as I could keep up. I was 26 and the guys on scholarship were 18 to 22. They were real runners, like the small skinny type. I was a straining six foot "want to be" runner. But it wasn't long before I was running 16 miles a day with the Cross-country Team and keeping up.

We averaged between 80 and occasionally 100 miles a week that semester. We would have our first run at 6:30 a.m. and run until 7:30 a.m. Then I would be in class by 8:00 a.m. I would go to my 8:00, 9:00, and 10:00, classes. After that I would go to the pool and swim and bike until my 1:00 p.m. and 2:00 p.m. classes. Following them I would go meet the Cross-country team at 3:30 p.m. and finish off our miles for the day. The university asked me to move into the athletic student dorm because they thought I would be a good older role model to the scholarship athletes. Plus they needed a Resident Advisor. That was great because I could eat at the athletes training table three times a day. And the school also paid half my tuition for being an RA. I knew I needed to develop sustained intensity and learn how to fight mental and physical fatigue. I needed to feel like I was back in Pararescue training. So running that mileage was needed for my mental conditioning, as well my physical conditioning.

On Saturdays I'd be running by 6:30 a.m. I had increased my physical stress by putting the wrist weights back on my ankles just to make my runs more taxing. Then I'd run 14 to 16 miles by myself.

By November this training had worn me out. I had diarrhea every day and ran with a big wad of toilet paper in my shorts every time I went out. I got to know more places to hide in the bushes than you could ever imagine. My biggest hope was that my large meal at night would stay in my body and I could absorb its nutrients by morning. Sleeping with food in my stomach was my salvation. I could absorb enough nutrients to handle the next day. If I ate lunch, I was sure to see it again on the run. Even then I got to see breakfast often. I lost about ten pounds that semester but I felt great. People said I looked gaunt but I was feeling lighter and stronger as the semester progressed. People stopped encouraging me because they thought I was obsessed and a little crazy. Diarrhea every day? The Cross-country coach thought I was too extreme and asked me to rethink this thing. But I pressed on! He didn't understand the power in a "What if I could pull this off when everyone doubts your reasoning and ability?"

Just before the end of the fall semester I advertised that I was raising money for the trip by running a marathon indoors around the indoor track. It took eight laps around the track to make a mile if I remember right. It was one of the stupidest experiences of my life. I started at 6:00 a.m. and ran till about noon. I got dizzy after a while and so started running the other direction around the track to unwind my brain. It was a long morning but I made it. I think people donated about $50 to my disappointment. It was a lot of work for $50.

Two weeks before the race, (Christmas break 1980) I still did not own a bike. But I had an entrepreneurial idea. The most famous American bicycle manufacturer at that time was Schwinn. They had a bicycle called The Paramount. It was the hottest thing on the road, except for a few European bikes. Schwinn had a distribution warehouse in Diamond Bar, California which was about 40 minutes from my parent's house. I searched for Schwinn's number and the name of the manager, and I called him. I asked him if I could come out and meet him and introduce myself. He probably thought I was nuts, but he said, "Sure come out anytime. I am always here."

So I borrowed my mom's 1968 two door Mercury Cougar and drove to see him one afternoon. I took my Sports Illustrated magazine article with me and introduced myself to him. When I met him I shook his hand with my right hand, and in my left hand I had the article about this crazy endurance race in Honolulu. I thought I'd get him to read it and then maybe he would want to help me out. What was great was that he recognized the article because he had read it!

Back then almost everybody in sports read Sports Illustrated. It was the Bible of weekly sports. Then he said to me, "Are you going to try to do that thing?" I replied, "Yes... I've been training for five months in Oklahoma even though I'm from California. I don't have a bicycle and I need to find a bike to ride. Do you think you could help me out by renting me or loaning me a bike to take to the IRONMAN?"

I was really hoping he would say, "You should ride a Paramount!" Sure enough he said, "If you are going to do that crazy thing you need to be riding the Paramount. I'll loan you one and box it up for you, if you will just bring it back when you're done using it." I was amazed! This guy had become my friend instantly when he knew I was going to attempt that crazy race he had also read about in Sports Illustrated. He actually became excited for me!

I was also excited because in junior high school my father had purchased me a gold Schwinn Continental bicycle, which was a level below the Paramount. All through junior high school and high school I wanted to have a Paramount but they were too expensive. Only the rich kids had Paramounts.

He called some guy in the back of the distribution warehouse and he rolled out a new Blue Schwinn Paramount. They proceeded to take it apart and put it in a box for me. Then he gave me two t-shirts to wear... a red one and a green one that both had in big letters "Schwinn" on the chest. He said, "Wear this shirt and tell people where you got your bike, OK?"

I said "Sure, be happy to! Thank you so much for your help!"

They carried the box out and put it in the trunk of my mom's car and off I went with a brand new Schwinn Paramount bicycle to ride. I was going to ride this bike around the island of Hawaii having never ridden it before. It was going to be fun and crazy. By today's standards, it was a heavy bicycle with nice toe clips. It was also pretty stiff and rigid. But back then it was "the bomb". He also gave me two water bottles and clips for the water bottles, a couple of wrenches and everything I needed to prepare my bike once there. I was living the dream!

I also had shared my dream of doing the IRONMAN with friends in a couple of different states and sure enough they all contributed financially. I had worked for a guy name Tom Lingo before I had gone into the Air Force. He was a very athletic and successful realtor in Laguna Beach and he said he'd cover whatever I couldn't raise. True to his word, he did. I've never forgotten his generosity and kindness. He was a wild, athletic adventurer too.

My friends and family thought I was crazy as usual but they gave money. I'm sure a few expected that I wouldn't make it but that's what made it fun. In my mind, I was attempting the impossible and something amazing. All I had to do was get through the IRONMAN and then relax for a few days in Honolulu. I felt like a genius.

I checked the bike box on the plane to Honolulu and off I went to the IRONMAN. When I landed in Honolulu there had been a severe storm. When we landed there were gale force winds on the ground. It was typhoon weather. The next day the storm slowed down but there was still sporadic rain. Two days before the race the word on the street was that it was going to be nearly impossible to do the "Honolulu Rough Water Swim" in these conditions. The waves were huge and the water was whitecapped.

I rented a white Plymouth station wagon, and drove part of the course around the island to see what the road was going to be like. In those days everyone had to have their own support team and support vehicle. All your supplies and change of clothing was supposed to be in your chase vehicle. That meant that there were 100 competitors and 100 vehicles following the competitors. The chase vehicle was supposed to stay near their bicyclist or behind their runner during the bike and run phases. The IRONMAN people didn't provide anything for the competitors, as I remember it.

Can you imagine how fun it was to have a chase vehicle behind each bicyclist? There were 100 vehicles on the race course that the bicyclist had to maneuver through and around. The way you were to get the food and drinks to your bicyclist was to have the driver pull up alongside them and have someone hand them the food or drinks through the car window. Those support experiences provided for some safety issues as well as some fun moments. It meant that I had to find someone local who I didn't know and ask them to be in this adventure. One person was to drive and one person was to hand me my food and my liquids whenever I signaled for them. I can't remember who they were but they were great guys and really nice.

When it came time to have the race, the people in charge said it was still too rough of an ocean for the two and a half mile swim. What complicated things, was that Wide World of Sports had sent Jim Lampley and Donna De Varona to cover this race that had been written about the year before in Sports Illustrated.

We ocean beach guys said, "Let us swim. If you can't swim in these conditions don't swim. These are supposed to be the three toughest races in Honolulu. The first is the Honolulu Rough Water Swim. These people who came knew this was not a pool swim or a smooth water swim but a rough water ocean swim out through the breakers. What the hell! If they can't do it they should not have come and should go home. They knew what they had to prepare for rough ocean water. They are screwing this thing up."

Others said, "No these guys are going to drown. It's too rough for anyone to go out and attempt the swim." It was just like year one and year two. Again, in the big picture the ocean swimmers only advantage over these fast pool swimmers, great bicyclists, and great runners, was a rough ocean. They did not know how to swim in the rough choppy waters.

The arguing went on for a while about the race that morning until those in charge canceled the race. They said "Come back tomorrow morning at 7 a.m. and we will see what the weather is like then."

A few of us were really bummed. Others were relieved. We felt like we were losing our ocean advantage to all these people from Wisconsin, Boston and North Dakota. It sucked. The next day we showed up again with Wide World of Sports already set up to film. Again the water was really choppy and the waves were still booming. It was a beach lifeguard's dream. Of course the arguing started again. Many said it's still too rough to let people out in the ocean. People were going to drown. We shouted, "They should drown! They don't belong here. This race isn't for them. They shouldn't be here. Either we do the race and they stop complaining or they should go home."

The race organizers debated and they canceled the swim and the race for a second day. They said come back tomorrow. It was unbelievable. Sure enough we came back the next day and the Honolulu Rough Water Swim was gone. The Wide World of Sports film crew and Jim Lampley and U.S. Swimming Olympian Donna de Varona said they were going back to the mainland if they didn't start the race.

The next day they had moved the swim into the harbor area where the water was smooth, as a safety issue. We ocean swimmers were angry and bummed. The whole point of the IRONMAN triathlon was to see who could rise to the challenge of doing the three toughest races in Honolulu on the same day. Now the 2 ½ mile Honolulu Rough Water Swim was dumbed down to pool type swim in the harbor. And that's IRONMAN history.

The good news is that no one drowned that day. The terrible news is they dumbed down a crucible event for people who should never have showed up in the first place. IRONMAN was never designed for pool swimmers.

My concluding thought: the IRONMAN has never again been as tough as it was supposed to be. They messed it up to make way for pool swimmers. But that is just my commentary. I am sure very few IRONMAN triathletes agree with me today. But I don't care.

The next day the race started with a beautiful peaceful swim in the harbor. Out of 100 participants, I came out of the water in 11th place with a swim of 1:11. I was sort of amazed at being number 11. I said to myself "Who me? That's great. Who would've thought?"

Then on the bike it was an interesting, fun ride with all the different vehicles weaving in and out on the highway. Imagine being on a two lane road for probably 80 miles with no shoulder and a faster bicyclist passing another bicyclist. That meant the chase vehicle had to pass the other chase vehicles to stay up with their cyclist. There were some pretty interesting moments with enthusiastic drivers trying to keep up with their bicyclist while dealing with oncoming traffic. It almost wasn't a race at times for me. There were so many things happening on the road that it was great fun. There was honking and swerving cars and people yelling at different vehicles. Vehicles were trying to stay with their bicyclist while passing out food. It was crazy. It was an event in and of itself. Oncoming drivers had no clue that 100 vehicles were weaving in and out before them. It was sort of captivating to have all this going on while trying to ride your fastest. I don't believe we ever saw a policeman the whole day.

I did pretty well for a while but then the day became really hot.

Especially on the backside of Oahu in those sugarcane fields. Those stretches of highway were seemingly airless and suffocatingly hot.

I remember US Olympian John Howard blowing by me about two or three hours into the ride as if I was standing still. I was amazed as well as demoralized. He was just so fast. Have you ever heard the "whoosh" as a bike comes up on you really fast and screams by you? It is a unique sound and moment.

I guess John was the last one out of the water on the swim but by the end of the bike he had caught up to Dave Scott and was now in second place. I was thinking, he shouldn't even be here! If it was a rough water swim he wouldn't have made it. He probably would've drowned. It wasn't fair. But since it was a pool swim type morning, he was able to make it. How am I supposed to compete against an Olympic medal winner? How are any of us supposed to compete with an Olympian?

Looking back on IRONMAN history, this was the year that IRONMAN really took a giant leap forward. Real athletes showed up like Dave Scott and John Howard. And the guys who were still wearing costumes and drinking beers before the race, quickly became fun guys of the past. This IRONMAN turned into a real race with amazing athletes in 1980. I was just a "want to be athlete" compared to them. When you saw Dave Scott and John Howard blow the place up, everyone knew the "Nautilus Triathlon" was going to another level really quick.

It is fun to have these memories.

On the backside of Oahu in the sugarcane fields I began to fade. It was so hot that I began to get dizzy. I was thinking I may not make it back to Honolulu on my bike. I kept motioning for my support van to pull up alongside so I could pour water on my baseball cap and shirt and drink some Gatorade. I did that many times thinking if I could keep my shirt wet and my hat soaked with cold water I may make it. Finally I limped into Honolulu and looked for my support car. I have a picture of me sitting in the back trunk of a Plymouth station wagon changing clothes. But I don't really remember that part clearly.

There was a big public fountain in Honolulu on one of the streets with a lot of water and ivy in it. It was brown, mucky water but I didn't care. I got down to my Speedos and thought I would submerge myself in this big fountain to refresh myself. It felt so good but it was full of dead and alive bugs. The water was slimy, and brown from all the rotting ivy and vegetation in it. The stench was horrible. It felt great to cool down though, even if I was covered with slime. But I really didn't like the smell on me when I got out. Neither did anyone else. Someone took a picture of me in that water, probably because they were amazed that I actually got in it. Mercifully when I got out someone started pouring clean water on my head and shoulders to wash the bugs and smell off. It worked.

I remember that it was oppressively hot. I decided to walk in between the high-rise buildings because it was too hot to run. When I got to the shade of the tall buildings I would run. I did that all through downtown. Run in the shadows and walk in the sun all the while drinking as much as I could. Finally, I got out of the downtown area and onto the main road of the Honolulu Marathon course. In time I got into the suburbs towards Diamond Head. I was weak but doing OK. I was hoping to survive by going easy until the sun set and it would cool off.

I found myself in the pack of runners who seemed to know that they were in places 15 to about 20. They were all laboring in the heat like I was. I remember being encouraged thinking that I was doing pretty good just to be with them. I remember at about the 12 to 14 mile point in the marathon course coming to a highway overpass by a shopping center. At the bottom of the highway overpass one or two people, who I guess were volunteer officials, were seated at a brown, school type, portable table. They were sitting in folding chairs. At the table they had a clipboard with a list of runner's names and their bib numbers and were checking them off as the runners came through. They also had, next to the table, one of those white metal height and weight scales that you see in doctor's offices.

All the runners started walking and came over to the table as they were asked their names. Then a lady asked me to stand on the scale. I did as I was told and the lady moved a little black thing on top and said, "Oh my, Robert, you've lost 11 pounds since you started this race. You need to drink more." I was feeling pretty weak at the time and a bit dizzy but I couldn't show them any weakness or else they might pull me from the race. I said, "OK. No problem I'll do that." Then one of the people at the table said "I think Robert, we need to take you off the course." It was just what I figured. They said "You've lost too much weight to go on. This isn't a safe situation for you anymore."

I said "No no, everything's gonna be fine. I'll just drink a lot of fluids right now and everything will be good." Of course I remember the concerned looks on their faces but just walked away. I had to act like everything was good. I pointed to my chase vehicle and said "I'll go over there right now and start drinking. Thank you very much." I think they probably became distracted by the other runners that they were checking in and I escaped.

Then I went down the cyclone fence a little ways away from them under the off-ramp and tried to pee. It was dark brown like sludge. How do I remember the cyclone fence? Because I remember my fingers grabbing the fence tightly as I was dizzy. I was happy to just hold on to it in the shade for a few moments. By now I was really wobbly. Having stopped running got to me. I was in a zone while I was running. When I stopped everything hit me. Stopping for five minutes in the hot sun to talk to those officials hadn't helped me either. I hadn't felt this bad before in all my training times.

The other runners had taken off and I was alone trying to cross the main highway. Fortunately I was now out of sight of the officials. I wobbled across the highway and aimed for a corner house that had some green grass in the front yard. I remember stepping up on the curb and then falling over on the driveway. I started do the involuntary "flopping fish on the boat deck" movements. It was like having involuntary convulsions. My head told my body to stop but it wouldn't. It was a unique situation to say the least. I've never had one of these before. I was slurring my words and having trouble talking. I felt like I was peeing in my pants but I didn't have any pee. My body had a mind of its own and I did not have control over it. When I saw Julie Moss have her moment on Wide World of Sports in 1982, it made me smile in a sick way. It is a strange experience. I related in a weird way like a fond memory.

Out of nowhere came two guys who said they were in the Army. They tried to talk to me. I could see them and hear them pretty well but was having a hard time getting my words out. The next thing I knew, the one guy was putting his arm under my neck. He lifted my neck up and help me drink a big bottle of orange Gatorade. His friend took off for a 7-

Eleven that was close by and came back with four more big orange Gatorades. The first Army guy gave me the second bottle and then the third bottle, all the time talking to me. Finally, after the fifth bottle of Gatorade went in me I remember thinking "Where did all that fluid go inside me?"

Little by little I regained mental and physical stability. After about an hour, the first Army guy got me to sit up. Strangely my body began to become normal again. My legs stopped flopping around and my head was feeling better. It was a pretty amazing experience. Finally the Army guy encouraged me to stand up which I did with both of their help. They had me just stand and try to get my balance. After a minute or so they helped me walk a little with my arms over their shoulders. It was a weird thing to be like that. Never been that out of it before.

After a few minutes, I was able to let go of them and begin to walk around the neighborhood. Finally, the one Army guy said to me "You can do this. You can get back in the race." I agreed. I could see the runners on the highway and I just walked back over to where they were running and started to jog again. The Army guys had given me another bottle of Gatorade to carry with me which was great. I'd run a little then walk and drink some more fluids and then put the cap back on and run some more.

By this time the sun was setting and it was cooling off. A nice breeze came up which was wonderful. I began to feel much better like I was getting a second wind. I had survived the worst part of the day. As crazy as it may seem, I began to pass more and more runners. The longer I ran the better I felt.

I passed 15 runners to my amazement. It was now dark and I was feeling good. Then all of a sudden some people began to direct the runners to run into a park that was filled with big trees. I thought, "This is the first time we have been off the street the whole day. I wonder why they're having us run through this park." Then all of a sudden I came upon a bunch of tables with a lot of people and some guy yells "Congratulations. You've finished!"

I said to him, "No, the race can't be over. I'm just getting going. I can do better! It can't be over!" But it was over. Somehow I had started running and ended up finishing 39th place. My time in was 13:11.

Triathlete Magazine December 2009 article calling me the
"MOST INTERESTING TRIATHLETE IN THE WORLD."
The picture is me after the Honolulu IRONMAN.

Thinking back on it today, I must've been in pretty good shape for a 29-year-old. I rode that old heavy Schwinn Paramount bike with toe clips and without aero bars. I hadn't ridden a bike a day before on the streets. I spent some time on my back and still got a 13:11. I was so bummed. I knew I could've done better if I had just drank more. But I learned a lesson: Equipment and hydration were essential in these events. It was a bittersweet victory for me. I knew I could've done better. The race was not too big for me. The 20X Principle was alive and well. When under pressure I was able to do more than I thought I was capable of doing. I had more than survived, I had won. I wasn't just average. I had finished the greatest endurance race in the world at that time. I had put another mental "Win" in the bank. When I took the bike back to the Schwinn guy, he asked me all about it had high fived me. He was really stoked.

**My plaque and official times.
They don't give these out anymore.**

Winning that "What if I could do this... when everyone said I shouldn't even try" was worth everything. They were all wrong. Now they admired me for trying and more for accomplishing what they wouldn't dare to do, and said I couldn't do. Honestly, I was amazed too. That "What if" was so rewarding.

Know this: If you are not careful, you will allow others to shrink your world down to their size. You will be average and mediocre like them. You have more potential in you than you know.

Bring it out!

BEYOND AVERAGE

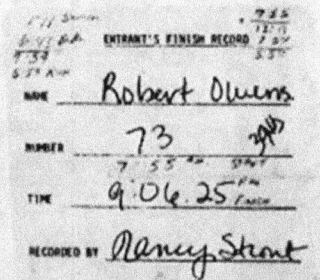

Far left: Robert cruises through the bike leg of the 1980 Hawaii Ironman on a borrowed bike. Center: Did you know the 1980 Hawaii Ironman was actually officially called the Nautica Triathlon? Below: Owens' official finish record from the event. Note that "9:06.25" refers to the time of day when he finished, not his race time.

Finishing time 13:11. Not bad for a heavy metal bike, no aero bars, never riding a bike in the street before the race, and passing out in a guy's yard in the marathon.

My winning t-shirt.

LEADERSHIP LESSONS

1) Ask for audacious things – I had a corporate sponsor for my first race only because I asked and was willing to put myself out there.

2) There are always those who will try to "protect" you, and keep you small – ignore them.

3) Try to achieve amazing things, and you will find support in the most unlikely of places – like two Army guys coming along to get me back in the race.

4) Discover the 20X Principle in you. It comes when you embrace suffering and "The Moment". You must believe that you can get through "The Walls" and "The Moment" isn't too big for you.

The next chapter will encourage you that it is never too late to dream and grow. Enjoy!

IRONMAN FLORIDA

CHAPTER 4

My IRONMAN Comeback at 50.

I took the next twenty years off from IRONMAN competition, and raised five children. I worked out regularly and did some local endurance events, but no like IRONMAN training.

When I was about to turn 50 my oldest son Matt made the comment, "You're getting really old dad, I mean like really old." I didn't like that. Something inside me was offended. How dare he tell me what I was thinking, which was, "I'm turning 50. This sucks. You know what, I'm gonna make a comeback. I'm going to do an IRONMAN again because I'm not old." And so I did.

My strategy again in 2000 was as it had been in 1980. To get in overall great shape. Plus I thought it would be fun to see if I could do this race like I'd done in 1980. This time instead of a borrowed bike on rollers, I would train indoor at my gym in spin classes. I decided to again not ride a bike outside one day before the IRONMAN. Why? Just to see if I could do it again. Remember I'm not a real triathlete. I am just a guy that can do them. I wondered if I could still show up on race day fit enough to ride a bike 112 miles after swimming two and a half miles. I knew I could swim and probably ride the bike. Now I wondered if I could still run a marathon afterwards. With those thoughts, I began to train for my comeback. I would train using an outdoor pool, take spin classes and run on treadmills. And just for fun, I purchased those two and a half pound wrist weights for some of my runs and my swims. When I did my swims, I did not swim for time, but for distance. About a month before the IRONMAN, I started by swimming 10 laps, and then 20 laps, and then to 36 laps which was a mile. Within eight days I was back swimming 50 laps with my wrist weights and feeling strong. Two weeks before the IRONMAN, I was swimming two miles or 72 laps in a little over an hour with wrist weights on.

On the bike, I got up every morning at 4:30 a.m. and was in a spin class by 5:30 a.m. five days a week. On Saturdays, I would spin at a 7:00 a.m. and an 8:00 a.m. class back to back just to practice being more fatigued. Oftentimes after the bike, I'd run ten to fifteen miles outside. It all seemed to come back as I focused.

The big question was, could my 50-year-old back and butt survive again on any bike seat for 112 miles.

I took my wife and kids to IRONMAN Florida in 2000 and made the kids sit at the finish line to observe all the different types of finishers. It was a wise move. They saw a little bit of everything. They saw tall people as well as many wide body people finish. They saw some people crawling over the finish line and some people not even being fazed at the end of the race. And they saw young people as well as middle-aged and older people all finish. As I had hoped, they had much to talk about after I finished the race.

I was especially pleased to finish again on a borrowed bicycle that I had never ridden before. My butt was raw but I made it. Back then, you could run through the finish line with your kids or loved ones and I ran through the finish line holding hands with three of my children who had jumped out of the stands to greet me. It was a very special moment for all of us.

We were walking back to the hotel when we saw a bicycle lying on its side near a building with bushes at the base of it. As we got closer to the bicycle and the bushes, we could see someone lying behind the bushes. As it turned out, there was a doctor, who had passed out and fallen over into waist high bushes walking back to his hotel room.

Ever the Pararescueman, I helped him and fortunately he regained consciousness and stood up. We were quite concerned for him since he was alone, but he assured us he was fine after a few minutes. So we walked with him for a few minutes and then let him go by himself to his room. I think of it as a little karmic payback for the Army guys who helped me in Hawaii.

When we got up to our room, I took my shower and lay down on one of our double beds when probably the same thing hit me. I thought to myself, "Oh my God, something is happening to me too. I am fading."

As I lay on the bed I broke into clammy chills and began to shake. And pretty soon I said to my wife, "I feel like I'm slipping away and dying. I'm not trying to be melodramatic but I feel like I'm gonna pass out and die."

I asked her to call an ambulance. It was the weirdest feeling, like the world was closing in on me and I was sliding into a dark tube. My vision began to close in to the point where I felt like I was going blind. And I just lay there as my wife freaked out. Within minutes the ambulance guys were in my room and they were talking to me but I really couldn't say much. One came to my left side and said, "I'll get his blood pressure" when the other one went to the right side and said, "I'll get his pulse." I remember listening and the one guy say, "I can't find his pulse" and the other one said, "He's dropping, I'm having difficulty getting his blood pressure."

I remember asking the guy on my left "Does that mean that I'm dead?" He said no and quickly stuck in IV in my arm. Then they got me on to a gurney and rolled me out of the hotel room and then to the ambulance. My wife was trying to figure out what to do, as my kids were saying to her "What's going to happen to Daddy?"

They hopped in the car and followed the ambulance to the first hospital but it was full of IRONMAN competitors. So they got on the radio and called the second closest hospital but it was full too! So they called a third hospital and that's where they took me.

When they rolled me into the hospital there wasn't any room for me in the emergency room as there were so many other IRONMAN participants on stretchers. So they rolled me into the entry hallway and said this is where you can stay. And that's where I spent the night receiving my second and my third IV bags. They told my wife she could go home because I was safe. But they wanted to keep me for the night for observation. They released me at about 6:00 a.m.

It was a hot day in Florida for the IRONMAN and many others had difficulty with dehydration, but it was the second IRONMAN where I became dehydrated. I took consolation in not being alone, but that wasn't good. The challenge was that I trained in the mountains and I'm never around humidity. So for the second time I didn't drink enough. I had to get better.

The good part was that I had persevered even though I had become dehydrated. I made it to the end even in my condition. That gave me another dose of confidence especially at 50 years old. Plus I beat my time of 1980 by about 20 minutes. I did it in 12:48. That wasn't bad after a 20 year break on a borrowed bike.

In 2001, I went back and did IRONMAN Florida again. I had about the same results. I used the same borrowed bike and trained about the same and did a 13:20. This time I went right to the hospital tent and told them I needed some IV bags because I didn't want to go back to the hospital. They believed me and took me into the hospital tent and gave me two IV bags. It was great. I was in there probably an hour and a half and walked out feeling much better.

It had been another really hot day for the non-humidity training guys like me. Again I became dehydrated but I was getting used to it now.

Each IRONMAN was a personal win for me because I wasn't trying to be a big time triathlete. I was just enjoying competing against myself. I was disappointed having a slower time than the year before, but in the big picture I was good with it.

It was so much fun to be on the bicycle and passing guys with these $3,000 to $5,000 bicycles with all the gear, and me on my borrowed bicycle. I can't tell you how much satisfaction that brought me. I remember giggling with joy more than once about six hours into the race passing these guys. And they were younger than me too! Those again were tremendous moments that put something in my mental tank. It is called confidence. It makes it all worthwhile. I was still in the game.

A big challenge that year was that I became hungry when I started the marathon. At the aid stations they had different types of food. I grabbed a banana and ate it but found that the second half of the banana got stuck in my throat. I think from the dehydration, my throat had closed. But all I knew is that I had this banana that I couldn't swallow that was somewhere down my throat which caused me major mental concern. I wanted to drink it down but as I drank the Gatorade, it stayed stuck.

Then I thought I would go in to a Porta-Potty on the side of the course and try to throw it up, which seemed like the next best idea. However when I came up upon the row of Porta-Pottys there were all these people throwing up inside them or there was diarrhea all over the insides of the Porta-Potty. The heat was again affecting all kinds of people. I remember feeling so bad for this one lady who had her butt sticking out of the Porta-Potty while she was throwing up and had a diarrhea covered toilet seat. She was desperate and she was paying the price. So I just moved on.

I drank sips of Gatorade and kept running. It was the strangest and most awkward kind of situation as I couldn't get the banana to drop into my stomach which made me want to feel like throwing up. I remember thinking "Wow this is a bizarre experience. I wonder if this banana will ever get out of my throat. But I'm going to have to find a way to win, to just keep going."

About halfway through the marathon the banana just went down my throat. It was like I swallowed, but I didn't swallow. It just went down. And a moment of euphoria went over me because I had powered through that situation. I had run for probably 12 miles with my gag reflex going on. It just made for mental gymnastics. It was uncomfortable, difficult and weird but I hadn't let it get to me. That was a win in and of itself.

By the time the race was over it was not even an issue. That was like 13 miles ago. It was just another bump in the road on a long hot day.

To this day I've never eaten that much banana on a marathon again. It was a great lesson on small bites, when you're running.

When reflecting, what I really liked was being back in shape. It didn't take that much effort to go from general conditioning to IRONMAN conditioning. It just took more time. I had to spend extra time in the spin classes and get used to longer runs on asphalt and not just on the treadmill. But I was figuring it out.

My family again had a fun time being a part of it, and I even had some friends come with us for the IRONMAN experience. They were amazed and quite moved as they watched all the different types of athletes compete, and especially cross the finish line.

LEADERSHIP LESSONS

1. The Unexpected Happens. Have you developed the confidence to handle the unexpected things like a stuck banana in your throat?

2. You must enjoy the unexpected challenges that is where the 20X Principle is discovered.

3. You've got to keep going through the unexpected to develop your mental resiliency. There is no other way.

Next up – Success is in the planning.

Robert H. Owens

Training gear for Kokoro. Weight vest runs in combat boots.

CHAPTER 5

Making A Plan To Get Stronger.

Each year that I do an IRONMAN, I look at the older age group athletes to see what kind of shape they are in. And every time I looked at the 65 to 70 and the 70 to 75 and 75 to 80 old age group I could tell that their muscles were losing their size and strength. They were getting flabbier.

Oftentimes I would go up and introduce myself and say "Hi, my name is Robert Owens from Southern California and I admire you. It's great to see you here. How's it going?"

And then they would happily tell me their story. But in each case they would say to me "You know Robert I can go all day but I can't pull the water like I used to and I can't push the pedal on the bicycle the way I used to. I'm just not as strong and fast as I used to be and it is discouraging." I understood.

I had a coffee one day with a nice lady named Mickey Schapiro who is a multiple IRONMAN finisher who was now in her 70s. In the course of our conversation she mentioned "The Iron Nun" Sister Madonna Buder who has been the world record holder for the oldest IRONMAN Finisher in the world at 83.

She mentioned how Sister Madonna had finished a number of IRONMANs in her early 70s but could not finish in her late 70's. But she chose to hire a strength coach in her early 80's. In doing so, she said that she became stronger in every way and went on to finish IRONMANs in her 80's.

When Mickey mentioned that to me, the light turned on in my head. I knew I was getting weaker and my muscles were shrinking. And my runs were slowing. The only way for me to stay physically fit and able to continue to compete for the next 20 years, was to get into strength training.

Jack LaLanne was a guy on TV in the 1950s, '60s, '70s, and '80s who talked about weights and weight training well into his 90s. I immediately thought of him. Many people remember he was an early weight training advocate pioneer and role model for seniors and younger people urging the usage of weights to stay fit.

But I also knew that I was a lazy IRONMAN. I've only just done enough to get by all these years. Submitting myself to a coach and a regimen would be a whole different experience. I honestly didn't want to do it but I knew this: I needed to change. I knew this Truth: If you always do what you've always done, you will always get, what you've always got.

I knew a little bit about CrossFit. I had begun occasionally to watch the CrossFit Games on TV a few years earlier and admired the level of physical strength and fitness they had. Those athletes were unbelievably aerobic and anaerobically fit.

I begin to look for a CrossFit gym close to where I had been working out. A man by the name of Roy Heine mentioned to me that he was also working out at a CrossFit called Eternity Crossfit in San Juan Capistrano.

He said they called their gyms "boxes" not gyms which I thought was unusual, but fine with me.

So after a few days of contemplation I finally agreed to meet him at Eternity Crossfit which is owned by Gary Villegas.

When I met Gary I instantly liked him. He is a tall, handsome, long-haired Venezuelan. He has a great smile and you would never know by looking at him, but he is super strong. I came to learn he was one of CrossFit International's instructor trainers.

He welcomed me with his infectious smile and asked me what I was looking for. I told him that I had hoped to grow older and stronger at the same time. He just broke into a big smile.

He then said he had two categories of Athletes #1) Competitors and #2) Health and Wellness Athletes. Which would I like to be? I mentioned that I wanted to be a Health and Wellness guy. I didn't see myself as a CrossFit games competitor like the guys on TV.

I mentioned that I did IRONMANs and I wanted to get stronger in

Gary and I. I'm 6'0" so you can see how big a guy he is!

my 60s. I said, "I hope to continue to do them into my late 70's if possible. I want to be a guy who ages gracefully but could still compete if I wanted to. I wanted to see if strength work would help me in everything over the next 20 years." He just smiled and said, "Of course it would."

Then Gary introduced me to three other over 60-year-old guys in the box who were doing the same thing. They were nice guys doing CrossFit for the sports that they were in. Tom was six months older than me and was a golfer, Roy was a 60 year old mountain biker and Frank was 70

Developing my pull-ups with a rubber band assist at the Eternity Crossfit Box.

year old mountain climber. I was impressed. I decided to try it and started working out four to five days a week.

The CrossFit workouts radically affected me. I liked the way my body and my strength levels were changing. I lost body fat but grew in muscle size. I didn't get "big" but just filled out. Everything in my body began to change. I was amazed and encouraged. My weight stayed about the same but my body reapportioned itself.

I'd been a regular for probably four months when someone mentioned SEALFIT.

What in the world was SEALFIT?

I went online and read everything I could about SEALFIT. I read about the SEALFIT Academies, and Mark Divine's book "The Way of the SEAL." In it he expounds on The 5 Mountains and about the 20X Principle. I read everything I could about SEALFIT and watched all of his YouTube videos.

Mark was a 22 year retired Navy SEAL Commander who had taken a CrossFit Box and designed it to train young men who wanted to become Navy SEALS. Then somewhere along the way, more and more non-military people would also come in and train at the SEALFIT facility in Encinitas, California. Encinitas is about 10-30 minutes north of San Diego and Coronado. Fortunately for me it was about 45-50 minutes south of Laguna Beach. What made SEALFIT unique was that had a military and Special Ops/Spartan like atmosphere or "culture."

Over 10 years, Mark has been very successful in preparing young men before they enlisted, to get them ready for Navy SEAL training. He has a 95% success rate. If you make it through his training you could make it through Navy SEAL Hell Week and BUDS. That is saying a lot. Mark has strong views on training and is specialized on how to develop mental toughness and emotional control.

So one Saturday morning I found the courage to drive down to see if I could do one of their Saturday morning workouts. I paid my $20 drop in fee and met about thirty other 20-60 year olds. Most of the regulars had non-military backgrounds.

Each gym or box has their own culture. SEALFIT was different than anything I had experienced since the military. Mark teaches that you are to get self-centered and focus on your work out. He teaches and models that real Warriors suffer in silence. Meaning that in the workouts people were to be quiet. Not much talking, not much noise. You never hear anyone cussing, and there is not much interaction with others. You could encourage others but that is about it.

BEYOND AVERAGE

At SEALFIT you focus on your workout and not becoming a distraction to others. You don't find loudmouths, attention seekers and super-egos and whiners. If they were like that, they knew they didn't fit

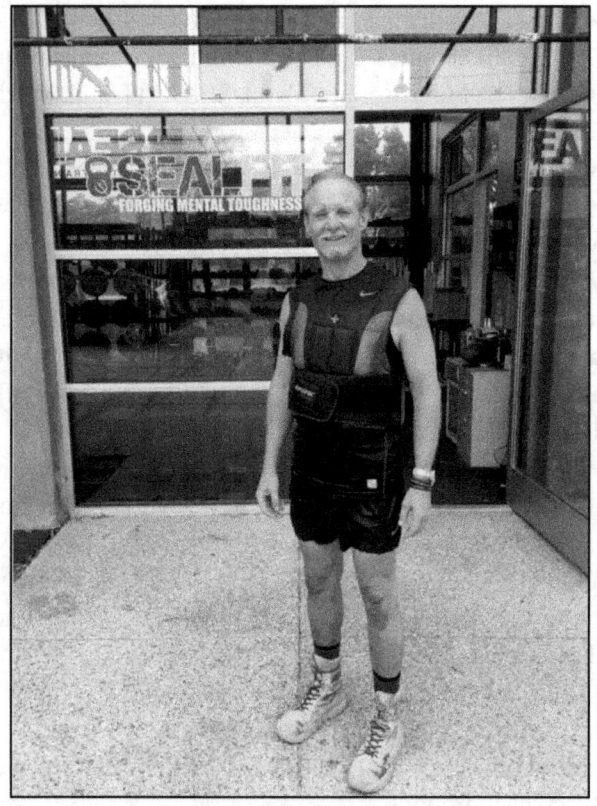

Working out at SEALFIT with weight
vest and military boots on.

and they never came back.

That was so refreshing. Just shut up and do the work.

In a sense, I found a second home. From that time on I looked forward every Saturday to seeing that group, and doing their 8 a.m. or 9 a.m. workout.

While working out at SEALFIT some of the guys told me about the different challenges and academies that SEALFIT offered.

1.) A 12 hour nonstop CrossFit/Navy SEAL type challenge.

2.) A 24 hour nonstop challenge.

3.) A 50 hour nonstop Navy SEAL Hell Week formatted challenge called Kokoro. It was their most difficult challenge with less than a third of each starting class finishing.

4.) A three day two night Leadership Academy which taught mental and physical fundamentals in "The Way of A SEAL."

When I heard about Kokoro it was like when I read about the IRONMAN in Sports Illustrated in 1979 or The World Marathon Challenge in 2015. I knew I had to attempt it. It was audacious. It was super difficult. It could be impossible for me. It would be epic. It scared and intimidated me. And it would give me a great set of goals to inspire me. Plus, there had never been a PJ or Pararescue guy to ever attempt it. I thought maybe I wasn't a good representative at 65, but it had bragging rights.

Then I figured out that I would be the oldest guy to ever try Kokoro. That did it. I knew I had to have that record. Especially as an Air Force guy.

In a passing conversation one Saturday morning, it was mentioned that every IRONMAN man or woman who had tried a Kokoro had quit during their first attempt. That really got my attention. I just wondered if that was true? Really?

Shortly thereafter one of the SEALFIT Coaches heard that I had done IRONMANs and that I was asking about Kokoro. He mentioned how the Kokoro instructors love to crush IRONMAN finishers. "They were never as tough, or in as good of shape, as they thought they were" said one of the Kokoro instructors. IRONMANs were almost an embarrassment to this group. It was like a junior achievement. No one cared if you had finished one or not. The SEALFIT staff or Kokoro instructors just asked, "Have you done the 12 hour Challenge? Have you done the 24 hour Challenge? Have you finished Kokoro?" I learned that many of the SEALFIT coaches had finished IRONMANs. However, Kokoro was the standard by which all physical tests or competitions in the world would be evaluated. On the SEALFIT website, Kokoro was advertised "as the toughest civilian training in the world."

I never brought up anything about IRONMANs again.

A few months later, I heard there was a Kokoro coming up and thought I'd be a good guy. I said to Mark, "I'd be happy to volunteer at Kokoro if you need some help." Mark quietly just smiled back and said "Thank you but you can't. You can't volunteer to help at a Kokoro unless you have finished one."

He smiled and walked away. I walked away sheepishly. I felt stupid and naive. I didn't know enough about Kokoro. It was a closed event. No visitors. No guests. No one allowed to observe. And no one would tell me much about what happened there. Finding that out drove me more.

That day everything changed for me mentally. I was not going to be told "no" again.

The coaches loved to mention how NFL guys had quit their training. Army Rangers had quit. FBI, Homeland Security and ICE Agents had

Sandbag, weight vest, and a backpack for Kokoro training.

quit. And lots of young men who thought they wanted to be Navy SEALS had quit and never came back again.

The game was on. Now I just needed to shut up, do the work and watch and learn from others. I had been training to get older and stronger. But now I had a real goals. I knew I wanted to attempt the World Marathon Challenge and my next IRONMAN but they weren't strength events. They would be easier than Kokoro. Kokoro was way out of my league. You had to be strong to meet the strength standards along with tremendous endurance to try to compete in Kokoro.

Over time, I had come to discover that there would be a basic strength and endurance test after about the first six hours of PT in the 50 hour challenge. It is called "A Murph." It consists of a mile run up a dirt and sand road in the dark, soaking wet, then 100 pull-ups, 200 push-ups, 300 air squats and then another mile run all with a 20 pound weighted pack on. It had to be done in 70 minutes in the dark.

I knew about Murphs because we did them often at SEALFIT workouts. In Kokoro you had to do it wet, and with a 20 pound pack on.

Pass it or go home.

All the testing activity in the 50 hours would be in wet t-shirts, wet fatigue pants and wet boots. Expect blisters from 50 hours of wet feet in wet socks in wet boots. You better have broken in your boots before you got there. Much of the PT would be on sandy, rutted dirt roads. There would be wind sprints up hills repeatedly with burpees and push-ups at the bottom. There would be a four to five hour pool PT of swimming in those same clothes. There would be two all night tests. One eight hour night would be doing PT in and out of the ocean, summer or winter. Expect to become hypothermic and colder than you have ever been while doing the beach all night PT. The other night would be climbing up a mountain and running down the same mountain in the middle of the night. Expect broken ankles, broken legs and lots of falling. Many participants became delusional and a bit out of their minds during the mountain 'evolution' or event.

Most PT was done in mud. The instructors kept you hosed down in the dirt. Their goals were to keep you uncomfortable and mentally and physically stressed the whole time. In Special Ops combat, you never know what is coming or the changes that can unexpectedly happen. The instructors wanted to simulate combat like conditions. The Taliban wasn't going to stop chasing you and ask you how you are feeling or how tired you are. They were going to pursue you and kill you.

Remember the movie Lone Survivor about Marcus Luttrell? Many of these instructors knew Michael Murphy, Marcus Luttrell and the other men who died. How will you handle being that mentally fatigued and physically tired? Many combat fights lasted 10 to 24 hours in Afghanistan. Could you do that?

The Navy SEAL instructors wanted to test your mental strength while you were mentally and physically fatigued. Could you be a leader in those conditions? They wanted to know. You didn't know.

One of the mental tests that would rock a number of people was submerging yourself in water filled horse troughs that were also filled with ice. And do it often. I knew going into this that they would probably do this repeatedly during the day as well as in the middle of the night. It was meant to wear you out mentally, especially if you were already cold and shivering.

In that test was also another test. You would be told to go under the ice water and hold your breath until the instructors allowed you to come up. No one ever knew how long they would be told to hold their breath to mess with their minds. Or they would tell you to go under the ice water and give you a plastic bottle to put in your mouth that had the bottom of the bottle cut off. It was a makeshift snorkel. They would just say, "Go under and breathe" until they allowed you to come up. If it bothered you or freaked you out, they'd keep you underwater longer to get in your head. If it didn't bug you they would let you out and not bother you with it again. It was mind games.

I'd seen it at SEALFIT when working out down there, when groups came through and wanted training. I had watched how many people reacted. So fortunately, I prepared. But the first time you do it, it can get your attention or rock your world.

For me, being a water guy helped a lot. I was a scuba certified guy from Pararescue. I've spent lots of time with something in my mouth underwater. I did scuba jumps in the winter out of a C-130 in Alaska. The water was 33 degrees and like thick soup or a 7-11 slushy on our dives.

At SEALFIT, I'd seen some men and women quit on the spot by refusing to go under the ice and water in the horse trough. It can be a phobia issue for some.

Remember: Navy SEALS scuba dive from the ice filled ocean or inlets up onto the snow, often in the Arctic.

When I was a Pararescueman in Alaska in the 70s, during 24 hours of darkness and winter war games, I'd watch as Navy SEALS simulated the Russians assaulting the Army from the sea. Often it was minus 20 degrees during the war games called "Jack Frost". Pararescue guys were there in support of the Navy and Army personal who had physical issues or injuries during the training exercises.

Our job as paramedics was to helicopter in and rescue the cold and injured, and get them to a hospital. I was always amazed as the SEALS, in that 24 hour darkness, crawled from the Arctic Ocean or seawater inlet, up onto the snow and sniper attacked the surprised US Army. Often it was -20 below outside. Then they would disappear again back into the ocean and to their submarine or recovery boat offshore.

Here's a fun story of what war games can be like. I was doing a

US Air Force PJ Student Airman Robert Owens, PJ Pipeline, after a training scuba dive @ US Navy Dive School, Diver 2nd Class, San Diego, CA, May-June 1975. PJ Class 76-03.

"remote duty" in Fairbanks Alaska during Jack Frost. We received a distress call concerning an Army guy. They just said he was in trouble and needed immediate medical assistance and or evacuation. So the helicopter crew and I flew out in the dark to the middle of nowhere where the annual Russian Invasion war games were being held.

Our HH53 helicopter finally located the location. I was requested to give medical assistance. It was probably around -20. As we open the side door that blast of cold air game in along with the rotor wash wind. It was shocking to say the least. It took my breath away and made my face sting. I grabbed the "penetrator" that was attached to the outside cable line that is used to lower PJ's down as the helicopter hovered overhead. I

Me on the tarmac in Alaska. Those big boots are super warm and called "Bunny Boots".

also attached a recovery basket to the cable as well. The rotor wash was causing the snow on the ground to become a white out.

I had no idea halfway down where the ground was going to be and I could barely see the helicopter above me. Plus, I didn't want to look. The snow felt like needles hitting my face. Finally I hit the ground and got my bearings. I detached the basket as the helicopter lifted off.

In a couple moments two army guys ran out to me and thanked me for coming. Then they carried the basket as I followed them to a large tent about 30 yards away. Inside there was a kid on an army cot shaking and looking ash white. It was warmer in the tent because of some big heaters but not by much.

I thought to myself, "How can you have war games out here in this dark cold weather?! Nobody wants to leave the tent! This is crazy!" That's how the Navy SEALS attack the Army without being detected.

The kid was probably 23-24. I was 26. I tried to get his pulse and couldn't find it and also couldn't find his blood pressure. I looked at him and asked him what his name was, and he couldn't talk to me because his speech was slurred. The officer in charge told me his name and rank as I couldn't understand him. He was in bad shape. I knew somehow I had to get him warm as it wasn't warm there in the tent and it would not be warm in the helicopter.

So I thought how in the world do I get this guy warm and only one thought came to mind. I had to get my body against his. I thought about it for about 10 seconds as this wasn't in any medical manual. But Pararescuemen are taught to think on their feet and solve problems because many of the situations they face are challenging, and may be unusual.

I told the Army guys to get their 2 biggest sleeping bags and get this guy undressed and in a bag. Then in the cold I also took off all my clothes except my socks. In those days I always wore speedo's because I could daily always wash them in the shower. It was one less thing to wash that was dirty at the end of the week. I thought to myself, this is going to be weird but it's the only hope for this guy. So as they stuck this guy in the biggest sleeping bag that could fit two of us I had them turn him on his side and I got in and bear hug him skin to skin, chest to chest, and had them zip us up in the bag. Then I had them get another sleeping bag and put us in that second bag as well. This guy stunk from being out in the field big time. But I told him to hug me as my left side of my face touched his right side. Then I told the guys to put us in the basket and radio the helicopter to come back and get us.

I held this guy for probably five minutes in the tent. The Army guys just stared at us in sort of disbelief. I told him to soak up my heat. He didn't say much but just hugged me tightly. We waited for the helicopter to return, and then they carried us out back into the snow and rotor wash of the helicopter. I told them how to hook us up to the Penetrators line that had been lowered again. The crew chief in the helicopter turned on the winch and pulled us back up.

Once secured in the helicopter, it took off for Eielson Air Force Base in Fairbanks and the hospital. I talked to this guy for an hour or so and gradually he warmed up. By the time we got there he was better. We landed and some medical personnel came and unzipped us and put him on a stretcher. The helicopter Captain and Co-Captain just stared at us, as did everybody else in the hangar. We both didn't have any clothes on except his underwear and my speedos. I wish they had taken a picture. It was classic. Thankfully he lived. He was all plugged up with stomach issues.

The Captain and crew asked me "How did you think of that? Was it in your medical training?" I said "No. I just had to get him warm and I was the warm. So I did what I had to do." They said "Wow!" I said "Wow" too, because the guy stunk really bad. We all had a good laugh about it for a few days.

The lessons here are valuable life lessons: 1) Be Creative in problem solving, 2) Do what it takes to win – I only won if he was alive, 3) Don't let others opinions of you stop you from your mission. These are some of the things that make Special Ops special.

Handling mentally tough, physically challenging events is what the Navy SEALS do, that's why the Murph, and the water trough test had real world Navy SEAL applications. It was just a small civilian taste of SEAL Training and Pararescue training.

Lastly, after "The Murph" you had to have the physical strength and endurance strength to go non-stop for 42 more hours. It was daunting. The unspoken expectation with the Navy SEAL instructors was that usually half the Kokoro class would have quit by the end of "The Murph." Something inside me loved it.

Thinking about it, I knew it would take at least two to three years to try to get strong enough to prepare to attempt it. I don't mean strong in muscle size. I meant strong in body weight strength, and endurance. Most of the men and women in the Crossfit world or Special Ops world don't stand out in a crowd for their big muscles. Honestly, most just look fit, and in really good shape.

I was not strong, nor had I worked on real strength since my 20s in Pararescue. I could do three dead arm pull-ups when I started my Kokoro training. I had to get to 10 for my "standards test" then 20 pull-ups with my 20 pound vest on to be confident.

I was just a lean, swim, bike, run type guy. I asked Gary at Eternity Crossfit and some guys at SEALFIT to give me advice on making a plan for my goals and they gave me good suggestions. I set a plan for The Murph standards and started on the strength and endurance goals. I believed that if I focused I could become stronger even if I was older. This whole vision was doable. I just kept doing my research and developed an evolving strategy. Then weekly I'd recount the "cost" of the preparation.

My big picture thoughts were: This would be a whole new challenge for me but would fit in with my long-term goals. I'd be in good shape to transition to the next IRONMAN three weeks after Kokoro and then the 777 seven weeks later. It could all line up.

The big encouragement I had inside me was that I had finished Honolulu 1980, and I'd finished Kona in 2003. Both had physical and mental difficulties that I had overcome. I'd finished 11 IRONMANs with their different challenges and I had done well in Pararescue when I thought I was just an average athlete.

I had a bank account of deposits of confidence from my previous training experiences. I had picked myself up after passing out more than once. I had willed myself to get off my back and get up and press through difficult situations often. I had resolve and determination. I had overcome different types of physical and mental pain. Wonderfully, buried deep within me were the thoughts that said, "Train hard. Train smart. Stay focused. Give yourself time. Work out harder than the event might be. Practice mental and physical pain. Practice doing it while exhausted. You can do this." And behind all of that was the same thing David Goggins says, "What if..." I fed off the thought "What if I could pull this off? It would be epic and legendary."

My main thought was, "You can accomplish this if you focus and train right."

I was all alone. I tried to tell a few people what I wanted to accomplish but it was stupid talk to them. They just laughed or stared at me weirdly. After a few times of saying "This is what I'd really like to do in the next year", I stopped talking. No one understood. No one thought it was a good idea. No one said, "Tremendous, you'll do great and accomplish great things." No one said, "Those are tremendous goals Robert." Just mentioning seven marathons on seven continents in seven days brought all kinds of reactions, much less mentioning Kokoro. No one knew what to say, but a few said with raised eyebrows "Wow..... OK."

I was alone, except for my wife Sandy. She said, "OK, go for it!"

With that in mind, I begin to train at Gary's Monday through Friday and then go test myself at SEALFIT on Saturday mornings. The great part was that I had a real strong "Why." I knew my Goal. I knew how to focus. I knew I wanted the bragging rights to being the oldest man to ever survive Kokoro. I wanted to do it on my 66th birthday. And I wanted to do it as a PJ in a Navy dominated environment. Most importantly, the big picture was that I was going to grow older and get stronger.

Soberly, I also knew this truth: You cannot do great things and live a balanced life. You must focus. You must say No to things that are normal and OK for others, to be able to say Yes to your goals. Average people do average. I am not average. I knew I had to focus intensely.

Quickly, I became a sort of hermit. I started to say No to lots of things that would detract from my psychological focus. I am best mentally and physically in the early mornings. I had to prioritize my early morning trainings.

When I work with athletes or business people, I know their commitment to the things they say they want to achieve by the things they are willing to give up or change, to achieve their goals. The Why has to be your everything. There is a cost to meaningful accomplishments. Most don't want to pay the price. Most quit after they understand the real cost of their goals. To do epic and legendary things has epic and legendary mental, emotional, psychological, relational and often physical costs. They don't come easy.

I explained this to Sandy, and wonderfully she shook her head in bewilderment and supported me. Again. She has known me long enough, since I was 16, to know I have always been a little bit over the edge.

Monthly, my workouts matured and I continued to do more of everything: pull-ups, push-ups, sit-ups, core work, running of stairs, air squats, thrusters, 20 pound wall balls, box jumps, run repeats and long runs after long morning Crossfit workouts, etc. Then I upped the stress by doing all of that with a 20 pounds weight vest on.

After about five months of training I found myself in a fun box jump competition with the other over 60 year old guys at Gary's Eternity Crossfit. It was a Friday morning social thing that seemed harmless. The goal was to see how high we could jump. Simple.

We had wooden boxes and we continued jumping higher by putting flat barbell plates on top of each other on the boxes for increased height. I had been keeping up with Roy Heine and the others when at the 38 inches height, I caught my left toe on the front of the box and fell over the box and the plates. Somehow, as I was falling forward, I broke my fall with both my elbows. I couldn't get my hands out in front of me fast enough. When my right elbow hit the tumbling barbell plate and box, I jammed my shoulder upward and blew out my right rotator cuff. I heard something go "tear" if there is such a thing. It was a bad sound that I heard deep within my right shoulder. It wasn't fun or pretty.

After it happened, I just sat down and looked at my bleeding shins which I had scraped on the upper corner of the box during my fall. There was blood all down my right and left shin but it didn't hurt like my shoulder. Guys looked at me and laughed and pointed to my shins and said, "Shark bite, shark bite." I said "Yep.... shark bite. But the shark bit my shoulder too!"

There is a reason why gyms are getting away from wooden boxes to softer boxes for box jumps.

I didn't know what I'd done to my shoulder but I knew it was bad. I was bummed because I knew immediately I was going to have to have surgery to fix it and lose all my strength gains I had been working on for six months.

And that's exactly what happened. The injury could have become a very discouraging time, but I fought those feelings and refocused. I moved my goals back. Athletes get injured. They make comebacks. Get over it and don't whine.

I found a shoulder doctor and lined up the surgery. It was a severe rotator cuff tear. I had surgery in June of 2016. As I imagined, I couldn't do a push-up or pull-ups until January 2017. To try to stay a little in shape, I ran on the treadmill often with my shoulder in a sling or I did spin classes not leaning on my right arm much. The good part is I could focus on my core work. Not planks, but other exercises. My core became really strong.

Those were really challenging days. I had worked so hard and made great progress, only to watch it dissipate. I had to keep saying to myself over and over: Many athletes in the past had become hurt. If they had found ways to come back and survive, so would I.

I recovered and got well. The challenge was staying positive in my six months of recovery. Thank goodness, I focused on the positive and what I could do vs. what I couldn't.

Why do I say this more than once? Because it is easy to become discouraged at any goal you attempt. Life happens.

There was a bumper sticker that used to make me laugh. It is crude but true. It said in big white letters on a dark red background: "Shit happens." When I think of it and share it I usually say "Stuff happens." But it isn't quite the same. Making lemonade out of lemons is easier said than done.

I remembered this truth: Setbacks can rob you of vision, if you let them. It is your choice.

I had hurt my arm in May 2016, had surgery in June and missed my yearly November IRONMAN Mexico for the year. By January 2017 I was able to do my first push up again and was ready to start over. I went back to Gary's and said, "I'm back." Then I went back to the SEALFIT Saturday morning workout and said, "I'm making a comeback." They welcomed me back with smiles and encouragement.

What I didn't say to any of them was that my goal was to do Kokoro in October 2017. I had 10 months. Some things are better off left unsaid. Talk is cheap. I knew I should be smart, shut up and just be glad to be back. Then work really hard. 10 months isn't a long time.

Then the new challenges arrived.

One of the guys working out at SEALFIT was Dave Crandall. He is an attorney who had finished Kokoro after two attempts. In his first

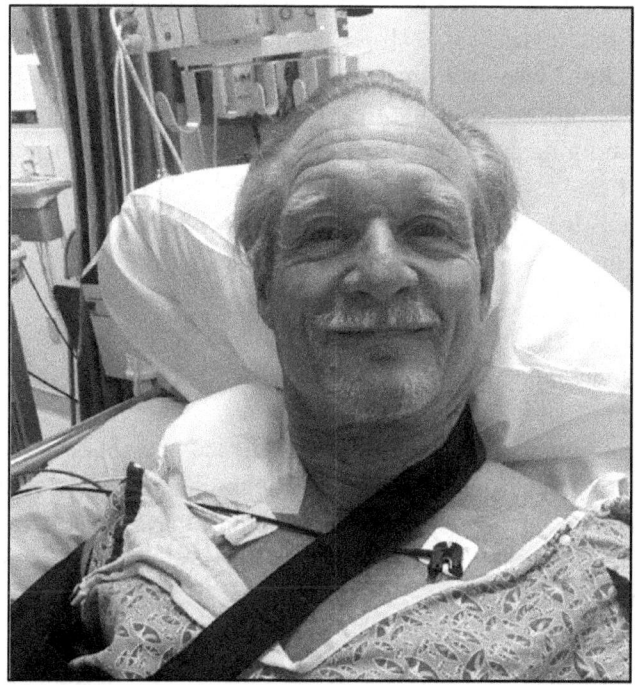

Post shoulder surgery. Many thanks to my wonderful surgeon and the kind nurses who took great care of me.

attempt his back went out on him at the 40 hour point. Can you imagine doing non-stop 40 hours when your back goes out doing beach PT? How frustrating.

On his second attempt he made it through and finished. I couldn't imagine having to do the 40 hours again, but he wasn't defeated by his injury. He got well and attacked it again.

Before and after my shoulder injury, on Saturday mornings when I would go down to SEALFIT, he was my role model. I watched everything he did and tried to keep up with him. I never could, but trying made me better in every way. I was not as strong as Dave as he was a bigger boned and heavier guy, than me, but I tried to follow his example. He wasn't fat at all. He probably weighed 195 and I was 180.

He'd been at SEALFIT for a while and knew every evolution or exercise we did. Dave was kind enough to be nice to me even though he was really quiet. He'd say, "Hi Rob" when I showed up and sometimes, "Good job Rob" when we finished. That was it. Dave was also the oldest guy to have ever finished Kokoro at 62 I believe.

One morning Dave said to me "Hey Rob, have you heard about Greece?" I said "No, what's going on in Greece?" He told me that there was going to be a Navy SEAL fundraiser for the families of those who died with the US Ambassador in Benghazi Libya. He asked me if I had seen the movie "300"? I said I had.

"The guys going to Greece are going to do a warriors march like King Leonidas and his "300" warriors had. They are going to march from Sparta to Thermopylae."

It was going to be 238 miles across Greece in eight days. He said he was going to go and be a part of it. I thought it sounded great and asked "Were there any openings?" He said he didn't know but I could contact Retired SEAL Master Chief Lance Cummings who was going to be setting up the event.

I didn't think much about it before I went online and found the details. I emailed the Greek travel company that was hosting the event and asked if they had any room. They wrote back that yes, and there were people coming from all over the world to participate. Some would be running the 238 miles and some would be marching and/or run-walking the distance.

I came home and mentioned it to Sandy who is Greek and said "I'd like to do this fundraiser in Greece with the Navy SEAL guys and others." I mentioned that I thought it was a great cause. She said, "You want to do what? That's crazy! 30 miles a day for 8 days?" But after letting it sit for a while and not bugging her about it she relented and said "OK if that's what you wanna do, do it. All these things you've lined up besides IRONMAN seem crazy."

About the same time, an old lifeguard friend of mine, Steve Bro mentioned to me at the 24 Hour Fitness in Dana Point that there was an Annual Beach Lifeguard Memorial Run the second weekend of August from the San Clemente pier to the Newport Beach pier. It was a 25 mile run swim run swim run that lasted about nine hours. You had to have been, or presently be, a beach lifeguard to participate.

It was a memorial run to honor the beach lifeguards who had died while trying to rescue swimmers at the beaches in Orange County, California.

He asked me if I wanted to do it with them, since he and others thought that I was getting in to pretty good shape. He said, "You'd be the oldest guy to attempt or finish it. It was mainly 16 to 30-year-olds who did this thing."

When he said that, I knew I was doing it.

So now they all lined up:

May 2017: 238 miles across Greece in 8 days.

August 2017: 25 miles, 9 hour Beach Lifeguard Memorial Run, Ocean Swim, Run etc.

October 2017: SEALFIT's Kokoro.

November 2017: IRONMAN Mexico.

January 2018: The World Marathon Challenge: 7 Marathons in 7 Continents in 7 Days.

I'd be the oldest guy in Greece, the oldest guy ever in Kokoro and the oldest guy ever in the lifeguard memorial run.

Wow.... they all just worked together. I'd be in great shape to attempt them. Plus, the eight day Greece event would give me an idea of the mental and physical stamina needed to do the 777.

Again, I need to say here that when I shared what I was thinking of doing with a few guys they just stared at me with that look that said "You're crazy". Actually, some looked at me like "Who are trying to impress?"

I remember thinking, "These guys think I have inferiority issues and that I need affirmation; that I need to impress others for my own self-worth."

I didn't like their responses, or those thoughts of mine, so I shut up about it. No one got it.

Two thoughts:

First, I mention this because you can't expect affirmation all the time. People won't understand. They can't. Don't expect them to, or else they'd be doing it.

You have to decide to go it alone and go dark.

Michael Jordan, LeBron James and Kobe Bryant all could care less what others thought. They lived and trained at a different level.

You can read about it in "Relentless" by Tim Grover. He coached all three. It is a tremendous book.

It doesn't matter what people think. Don't care about it. It is your insecurities that want their affirmation. Stop being needy. Focus.

Secondly, in my different way of thinking this stuff just seemed to make so much sense to me. The draw was that I was so out of the box to attempt this. Again: No one I was training with or around, believed in me. You have to embrace that. I knew that all I could do was talk to myself. I would do it or fail. Then I eliminated the fail thinking and said to myself: "I will do it or die trying. I thought...Life is supposed to be an adventure."

All the slogans I'd heard in the past came to life:

1. Some people just dream empty dreams and envy others. Winners risk and dare.
2. Go big or go home.
3. Nothing ventured, nothing gained.
4. Live safe and be like everybody else or risk and maybe become legendary.
5. Anyone can be average and mediocre. Live Legendary.
6. Safe is for the insecure.
7. Adventurers get questioned all the time as to why they need to be the first to do something.

My mantras were: This moment is not too big for me. Breathe...Easy day, good day, fun day, Looking good like Hollywood.

Smile.... Breathe.....

I also knew that once you get in to shape, you should use it as much as possible. You don't get in that kind of shape very often, especially at 65 and 66. I know from experience that it can and will fade quickly when you stop. I was going to make the most of every opportunity. I also knew that I may never ever have these opportunities again. I am getting old!

I started adding long rucks up hills wearing my 20 pound weight vest to my weekly workouts.

From January 2017 until May 2017 I worked out five days a week about two and a half hours a day. I got up at 4:00 a.m. and made it to the 5:30 a.m. work out at Gary's. Then I got my runs in. I could be done by 8:00-8:30 a.m. and then have a life.

By May 15th, I felt like I was ready to go with Dave and tackle this Greece 238 mile experience. We would meet a whole new group of active and retiring Navy SEALS, Marines and other guys when we got there. I would be the oldest. I didn't feel challenged by that at all.

The hard part was mental because we didn't know what conditions to expect. We rucked in military combat desert boots but also purchased some cross training stiffer trail running shoes. I hoped that I had the right equipment. Wrong equipment can ruin great training.

Sandy finally put me on my flight to Greece to meet the others. I was really anxious and excited. Dave took his wife and booked a weeklong vacation in the Greek Islands afterwards. I booked three days afterwards by the sea near Athens to recover before I was to come home. Boy, was I glad I did that....

LEADERSHIP LESSONS

1. Saying NO is crucial – and extremely difficult. You must learn to say "No" if you are going to "Yes."

2. Having a Personal Vision is a MUST.

3. Keep your counsel wisely – only share with the bare minimum of people who will support you. Remove the nay-sayers from your life.

4. Mentally prepare for Unknown Unknowns. The 20X Principle means you prepare for the Unknown Unknowns. They are the game of the 20X Principle, and going through the challenge is how you find your 20X Potential.

**This next chapter is a story of surviving improper research and the price you pay.
It is what you don't know that bites you. Knowledge is positive power.
Wisdom is applying it.**

Robert H. Owens

Me at the statue of King Leonidas, in Sparta, Greece.
He's the Greek George Washington.
Before we begin on the first morning.

CHAPTER 6
Greece Part 1

I arrived in Greece a couple days early to get acclimated; I was just outside Athens by the ocean and got some rest. The area was great and the Greek water was wonderful. Finally the day came where I went to the Athens hotel to meet the rest of the guys. We all met in the lobby with Chief Master Sergeant Lance Cummings to be updated on everything. Guys came in from five nations. There was also an Air Force Reserve Triathlete lady named Jodie from Idaho with us. Lance welcomed and thanked us for coming, and for our commitment to raise funds for the different foundations. I had previously asked if I could raise funds for needy Pararescue guys from Afghanistan and Iraq. He said that would be fine. At that point I was disappointed that I had only been able to raise a little over $5000.

He laid out the game plan for our travel to Sparta, and the trek starting the next morning. He reminded us that we would be doing approximately 30 miles a day for eight days. Lance encouraged us to get a good night's sleep to be ready to catch the bus the next morning.

Sure enough, the next morning we loaded onto the busses and made the two hour ride to Sparta, Greece. What I noticed on the bus ride was the beauty of the hills and mountains of the Greek countryside. It didn't cross my mind how challenging that beautiful countryside was going to become.

We arrived in Sparta in the afternoon and got settled into our hotel rooms. I was glad that I had two small rolling suitcases and a backpack. Some of the guys had large duffel bags and large suitcases. I came to appreciate my packing decisions as many of the countryside hotels we would stay in didn't have elevators.

We were greeted by the Greek travel company that had arranged for all of our hotels and provisions for the next eight days. They were great people who were really excited to be hosting us on this special challenge. They mentioned to us that in their research, no group has ever tried to duplicate what King Leonidas and his 300 warriors had accomplished. The legend said that they had marched from Sparta to Thermopylae, covering 238 miles in eight days.

This travel company felt it was such a special undertaking that they

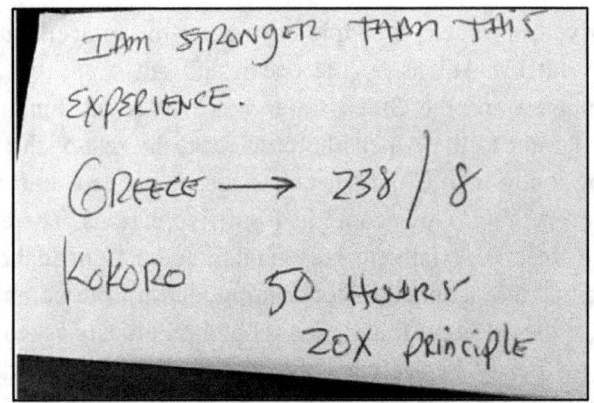

Another motivational card I carried with me daily.

had notified the media that this adventure was about to take place. The Greek national media covered our event. They also hoped that this would turn into a yearly national event. As it turned out, after our ordeal they didn't think it should ever be done again.

Some of the guys were friendlier than others and it was easy to get to know them. Others were quiet and a bit standoffish which is normal. I knew by the time we got out walking and running we would get to know each other. Thirty miles a day is a lot of time for interaction.

I especially wanted to know who the Navy SEAL guys were as well as the other ex-military guys. I wanted to hear their stories and understand their reasoning for being on this adventure. Many of these men knew the four fallen Navy SEAL contractors who had died in Benghazi. Of special interest was having Kyle Maynard with us. He was about 30 and born with a condition where his arms stopped growing at his elbows and he only had part of his right thigh. To many, he was a well-known adventurer. He had been a high school wrestler and avid athlete who had mastered many amazing mountain climbs. He enjoyed being told that he couldn't do things.

Kyle Maynard is such an inspirational young man. He has a total "can do" attitude that infects those around him. He's climbed mountains, literally Mt Kilimanjaro and others.

Kyle would be using an electric tricycle which he would pedal with his arms. We often see on TV athletes without legs using special wheelchairs in races. This tricycle was somewhat like that except he had special attachments for his arms. When he would come to the steep climbs, then he would use an electric motor to get him up the mountainside roads or trails. It was really quite amazing to watch him set up his low to the ground tricycle. It brought tears to my eyes just thinking of what he was going to attempt over the next eight days.

The next morning we met early for breakfast and then gave all of our gear to the travel people to load into support vehicles that would follow us for the eight days. Then we walked down to the street and the tall statue of King Leonidas, where an official from Sparta welcomed us and read to us about the legend of King Leonidas and his 300 brave men. He congratulated us on coming and attempting this unique feat.

You can read about King Leonidas and this nation changing story by reading "Gates of Fire" by Steven Pressfield. It is a book about Spartan culture and this suicidal mission to save Greece from the Persian invasion. It was a mandatory read for us before we came to Greece for this adventure. And I am glad I read it.

The Spartans were a unique, warlike clan who were known for their severe culture. They were the most feared City State in Greece.

At the statue, were a number of civic leaders and townspeople milling around and clapping for us as we had our pictures taken.

We also had a guide to lead us across Greece. His name was Pavel and was about 50 years old. He was an experienced ultra-marathon runner who had run races in and around this area and around Europe for years. He had mentioned that one of the races he enjoyed doing was a 50 hour non-stop running race around the base of the Alps which went through three countries. Those ultra-marathon types are unique endurance athletes. As I came to find out, he was really tough to keep up with, even when he was walking.

At the end of these festivities, Pavel said "It is about 8:30 and time to get going. We have a long day ahead of us. We have 30 miles to get down before 6:00 p.m." We waved at all the locals and off we went. It wasn't long until we came into the next village or town, where we had a police escort along with the community band, accompanying us. I think there was even a helicopter overhead covering our event. The media was there and it seemed like a pretty big deal to these folks. I was a little awed.

It helps for you to know that King Leonidas is the George Washington of Greece. He's the biggest national historical figure in Greek history. It is because of him and his band of 300 warriors that the Greeks today are not speaking Farsi. The Persians were coming to invade Greece and King Leonidas and his men marched out on a suicidal mission to confront and hopefully slow down the Persian army.

King Leonidas and his 300 men hoped that the way they would fight and die would motivate the rest of the Greek city states to rise up and fight the Persians. He wanted to shame the other Greek city states for their refusal to take on the Persians. And that's what happened. The Spartan wives kissed their husbands and sons goodbye and told them to fight and stop the Persians or else they would become Persian slaves. And so they did. King Leonidas and his men fought the Persians heroically and died in such a way that the other Greek city states were ashamed of their lack of courage and rose up and thwarted the Persians. So reenacting King Leonidas's suicidal march to Thermopylae was a really big deal to the Greeks.

Finally we got through the towns and villages and started our first 30 mile day. I started in my solid leather walking boots which I had trained in. We were told by Chief Master Sergeant Lance Cummings that there would be a lot of trail rucking and hiking. I guess that's what he had heard from the Greek travel company. Or at least that's what he thought he heard. But it soon became evident that we were going to be on asphalt roads for a long time. At the end of the first or second day I remember asking Pavel, "Where are all the trails?" He smiled and said, "They got paved over!" I laughed while shaking my head. Of course they had. That was 2,000 years ago. Somehow, we had the wrong information.

That day we left Sparta at 8:30 a.m. and climbed up and out of the Sparta valley until about 1:00 p.m. All of it was done on a warm, cloudless morning, on hot asphalt. It wasn't long until my feet begin to swell in my boots. I was hot and sweaty in my boots, and outside them as well. I remember thinking, "Oh my God we just keep climbing up and up." Continuously, the top of one mountain revealed another. "Will it never end?" On top of that, Pavel said "Listen, this is the pace we have to keep if we're going to make 30 miles by six o'clock. Don't fall back. You've got to keep up."

On the climb up and out of Sparta, by the third and fourth hour many of us were getting blisters because we had the wrong shoes on.

Equipment can make or break you. A person can train all they want, but if they have the wrong equipment all the hard work can quickly be negated. All the work we had all put in preparing for this thing was evaporating. Most of the guy's feet were blowing up.

When we finally got to the top of the mountains Pavel said, "Things will be easier now. We just have to get down the mountain."

By this time, I had multiple blisters on top of blisters. I didn't complain because none of us were complainers. This was a Navy SEAL led adventure and no one complains. But I heard other guys say that they had multiple blisters as well. The challenge was now getting down into the next valley. I had no clue that there was now going to be a fast four hour descent.

I didn't know if it would be better to speed walk down to make our time deadline or jog. Everyone was silent and trying to figure out how to cope. Both options were really painful. I found myself splitting my time speed walking and jogging. But what I did know was that on the descent I could feel my big toes pushing against the front of my boots. As you might imagine, the four hour descent became a new challenge. I stopped a few times trying to loosen up my boots to get some extra room for my feet but that didn't work. It became a long afternoon. The good news was that after a while my feet hurt, but sort of numbed out if I kept moving. If I stopped too long, the pain from the blisters and big toes would awaken and scream at me.

Mercifully, we finally made the 30 miles about 6:00 p.m. We had left at 8:30 that morning. But just prior to the finish I came upon 28 year old Mitch Aguiar who was an active-duty Navy SEAL from Norfolk, Virginia. He was sitting in the middle of our one lane rural road under a large shady tree. We hadn't seen a car all day so it wasn't shocking. He had been in the group ahead of me. He had had enough and just quit by stopping and sitting down in the street. He said it was his feet.

I said, "Hey Mitch, what are you doing?" He probably was surprised to hear me say anything to him. And I enjoyed saying it. It was fun and satisfying to see him sitting there.

"I'm done. This is the fuckingous, stupidest thing I've ever done in my life. I am done. I'll take Navy SEAL training any day over this. Deployments were easy compared to this. This speed walking and jogging bullshit in these shoes is miserable."

A Navy SEAL buddy of his and mine just laughed and encouraged him to get up because it was almost over. Mitch was supposed to be the

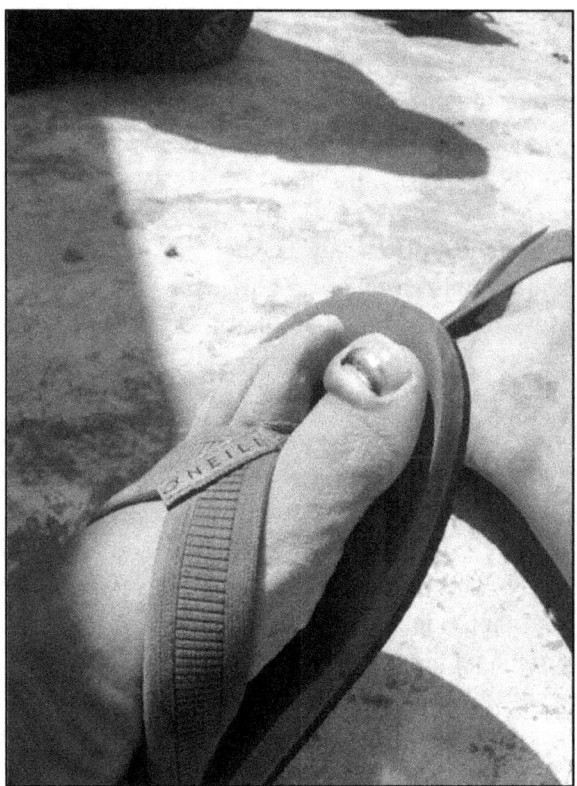

**300 of Sparta - Day 1. Thank God for flip-flops.
That nail is about to come off.**

biggest badass of the group. He was also a MMA coach and fighter. In the beginning I had tried to stay away from him because he wasn't friendly and seemed to leak a lot of contempt for others. Matter of fact, at the Sparta Hotel he looked at me when he first saw me and said, "What the fuck you doing here? You're old!" I just kept walking. But this was now a different Mitch.

It took some time but he got up and shook his head and said "What am I doing here? This is fucking crazy." Fortunately, our first day was about over. We gingerly walked the last part together just laughing and commiserating together. Mitch was my new friend.

When we arrived at the gathering point, there were mostly guys lying on the ground under some trees, being silent with their eyes closed. A few were laughing and moaning. Then there were other guys behind us who came in later, trashed.

The Greek event organizers were a little worried. We were supposed to be the badass Navy SEAL group. We weren't badass guys anymore. The hot day and hot asphalt had won. Everyone except a couple of guys had blown up their feet. As guys took off their boots or shoes there were bloody feet and deep blisters everywhere. Fortunately, the Greek organizers had hired a physio medical guy named Theo to come on this trek with us. He worked his butt off the next seven days keeping us together.

Master Sergeant Lance Cummings saw all this and told us to suck it up. I think he had a few blisters as well but wouldn't show any concession to them. We slowly walked to our bus and were driven to our hotel. It was a beautiful four or five star place. I was amazed. I thought how I'd love to come back with Sandy sometime and enjoy this hunting lodge type of hotel. The challenge now was that most guys had a real difficulty carrying their suitcases up the stairs to their rooms. It was our first day of experiencing hotels without elevators.

Theo went right to work lancing blisters, repairing feet and taping them up. He was busy for probably four hours that first night. Plus, a number of the guys made appointments starting at 6:00 a.m. to get their feet bandaged in the morning. I was one of them.

I hobbled to my room with my two bags, and sat on the edge of my bed. I couldn't care less about dinner. I didn't want to go back down and back up those stairs again. After I got my hiking boots and bloody socks off I found that I had blisters on top of blisters. But I also had black and deep blue big toes under both the nails. I had popped them both off. The right big toe nail had lifted off and was held by the skin in the back of the nail. The other was held on by a little more skin. I just stared. This was day 1 and I had 208 miles to go. Wow.... this was going to be a challenge. It would be a unique adventure beyond my expectations. My feet were oozing and throbbing.

Taking a shower was an experience. The water stung. The shower had

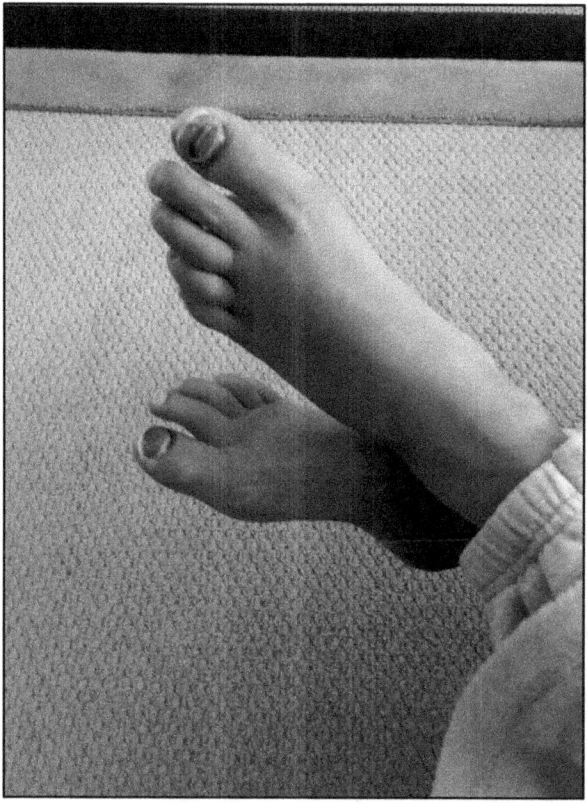

Big toe agony. The "Sufferfest" was just beginning.

a place to sit so I used the flexible water head to clean up with the least amount of water getting in my blisters. Then the challenge was to dry them off and get downstairs for dinner. It was a slow shuffle for sure. Thank God for the railing on the wooden stairs. I leaned on it with each step down. And thank goodness for flexible flip flops. They became life-savers all week.

I had brought some Moleskin pads as well as some supplies to dry out my skin. I applied the drying-out lotion and saved the Moleskin hoping that my feet would dry out a little by morning. Fortunately, I had paid extra to have a single room for every night. I knew I'd want some alone time on this thing. Everybody else was doubled up in rooms. It was a smart decision.

The next morning was painful. Putting my feet on the floor for the first time was excruciating. My feet were stiff and swollen. I remember just putting them on the floor and easing my weight on to them. It was like stepping on broken glass. Then the slow shuffle to the bathroom. My blisters had dried out a little. There was hardened ooze in between my toes, and on my heels. I slowly hobbled again downstairs and I waited in line to have my feet taped before breakfast. My blisters were a little drier but not much. I had three blisters bigger than quarters with blisters beneath them on the balls of my feet. My heels were raw as were the pads under all my toes. And there were oozing blisters between many of the toes. All had to be lanced and drained. With all the blisters being taped by all the guys, we were late getting out of the hotel which displeased Lance. He let us know we had schedules that we had to keep to make this thing work. We got it.

Somehow we got our stuff downstairs and hobbled to the bus and got to our drop off point. There wasn't a lot of conversation in the bus. We were hurting but there wasn't any complaining. We got off and stretched, received our briefing on the day and started.

The surroundings were beautiful. We had another 30 miles or so to do. We immediately walked by an old monastery that we all wanted to photograph. Then we headed out again. What I found out was that if I could get my feet in my boots, and start walking, the pain would subside after 15 to 20 minutes. I just had to push through the pain until they deadened. It was just like what David Goggins talked about in taping up his feet in "BUDS". You just had to push through the pain and it could be done. And so the day went. My goal was to not be the last guy every day. It was easy to just fall to the back of the group but my ego demanded that I not be in the back. I didn't want Lance thinking that I was old and a liability to the group. Honestly, it was hard to keep up with Pavel. That first day I didn't try.

Day two turned out to be OK. I survived. I got into a rhythm, kept my head down and powered through it. The uphill stuff I walked as fast as I could, and most of the downhill stuff I jogged. The key was to find my pace, which meant I had to go it alone most of the day.

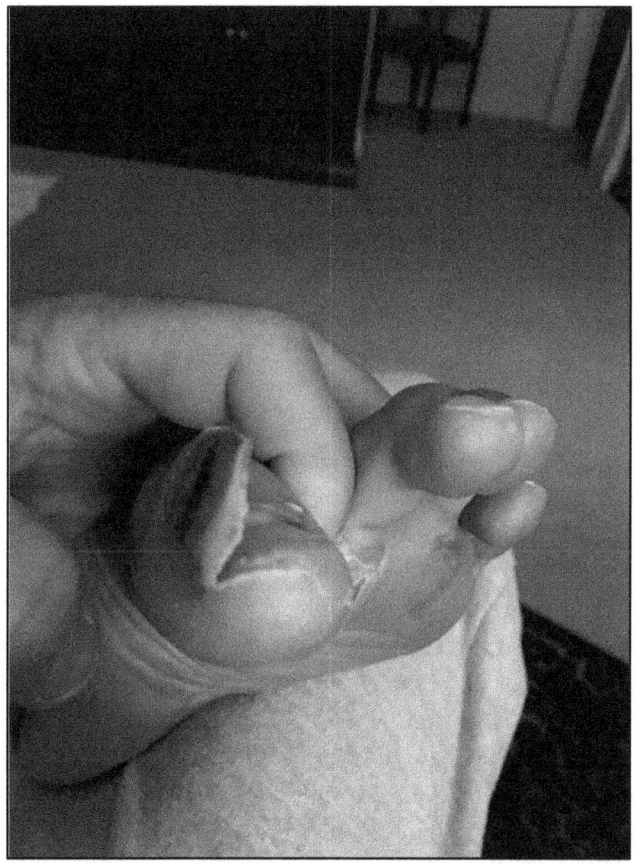

Day one Sparta - big toe nail about to come off.

The guys broke into groups according to speed. Then they would gather together again at the morning break or at lunch. Lance wanted us to stay all together but it just wasn't possible. Different guys were hurting, which meant the real hurt guys lagged behind. The big thing I learned quickly was to not stop for long on the morning or afternoon breaks, or at lunch. As long as I didn't stop too long, my feet stayed dead. But if I stopped for more than five minutes all the walking on broken glass pain would come back. So I would just grab something to eat or drink, and down it while walking. I kept going non-stop the whole day. Occasionally I would think on this and say to myself, "I guess I am in pretty good shape at 65 to go all day without stopping." But what I feared, was also happening. My feet seemed to be getting tighter in my boots. What did that mean with six days to go?

There was quite a bit of elevation again on day two. By non-stop walking or jogging I developed a time cushion ahead of the group. Once ahead, I could walk and run at my pace without the pressure of the group. I had a feeling that most of the group would catch up to me by mid or late afternoon, which they did.

My macro goal was to get such a lead in the morning that when I began to peter out in the late afternoon, I'd built up such a lead that I would finish near them. My micro-goals were to break my day into one hour segments and set goals for myself. I had mini races against myself all day. I didn't know what the other guys were doing to get through the day but I was competing. Sure enough I didn't see anyone from probably 10:30 a.m. until 4:00 p.m. because they took the first morning 10-15 break. I just kept motoring along, but I looked behind me at 4 and there was a group gaining on me. And now it was all uphill. Again we went past a Greek monastery that was way up on the side of a mountain cliff. I walked and ran to it for probably an hour. I just wondered how they got their food up there. It was out in the middle of nowhere.

Wonderfully, as they caught up, and then passed me, we were near the end. It was 5:30. We'd done 30 miles. A really nice guy named Levi Hensel, who was an Olympic caliber cross-country skier, congratulated me on doing so well as the oldest guy. When we all finished in some small village we had a beer and shared stories. Levi then encouraged me to get up against a wall and put my feet up against it for as long as I could to get the blood and fluids drained out. It was fun to get my boots off and my feet up on some building while drinking a beer and commiserating together. It worked. My feet stopped throbbing. I had brought my flip flops in my backpack for this moment and slipped them on. What a relief. My socks were bloody in the heels and I had new blisters. My big toe nails were detached and bloody. I'd gone non-stop since 8:30 a.m.

Finally we were told to get on the bus that had pulled in to get us. We all slowly shuffled up its steps and found a place to sit. Mitch became the funniest guy talking about his day and feet. He struggled again like the rest of us. But he had changed. He wasn't badass Mitch anymore. He was just another sufferer on the trek. He could make anything funny. Then he said to the group, "Even my Dad did well today" as he pointed to me. Somehow, I had become Mitch's Dad. I was accepted. I had finished before him.

He labeled our adventure "The Suffer Fest." It resonated with all of us. Day two was in the books. It was 6:00 p.m., only five more days, and 170 or so miles to go. Get me to the hotel.

One of the motivational cards I carried
with me throughout this journey.

Day 6 - On the way to Thermopylae.

CHAPTER 7

Greece Part 2

By the end of the second day two things became very clear: One, speed walking isn't walking. It is really hard to sustain that speed because it uses a completely different set of muscle groups than regular walking. Maybe that is why it is an Olympic sport. There was a reason that the Bataan Death March in WWII was seen as torture. It is hard to walk faster than at a comfortable speed. Plus we had to make 3000 foot vertical climbs over and over at an uncomfortable pace. None of us had trained for this.

Two, it became obvious as well that I couldn't wear my stiff brown hiking boots any longer. My feet were too swollen and the boots were now too small. I had brought with me a pair of rock running trail shoes that were about the same size but had a softer feel. Neither pair helped but I knew I couldn't continue to wear the stiffer hiking boots. And so I made the switch.

Each morning when I woke up I started the same ordeal. I would wiggle my toes to see if my toes were crusted with dried ooze. Then I'd swing my feet out of bed over the floor and stare at them. Gently I would lower myself onto my feet to see how bad they were going to feel, to start the walk to the bathroom on them. Every morning it was like walking on broken glass. With that process, it took me about five minutes to get from the bed to the bathroom. But I'd make it.

I'd get dressed and painstakingly slide my flip-flops on and hobble downstairs to breakfast.

Breakfast was usually oatmeal or eggs and bacon and orange juice. There was always a great European spread with wonderful rolls and cheese if I wanted them as well. Then I'd get in line with the other guys and have my feet bandaged by Theo and slowly hobble back upstairs. Getting my feet in my trail shoes was work. They didn't fit either, because now they were also too small. Plus they were a really stiff shoe. But I'd stuff them in. It was just part of the process. Then the challenge was getting my stuff together and carrying it down the stairs. That was the worst. Even today as I rethink about those mornings it causes me to break out in a sweat. It was really painful. However, I had to get that deadening process going so that by the time we got walking or running my feet could handle it. The group was pretty silent in the mornings. We were just dealing with our pain the best we could. Actually, about three or four guys out of the 17 were not having severe blister issues. I should say... not yet.

We'd get our bags to the bus and get our briefing from Lance and Pavel. After the briefing on how much elevation we would climb that day or what kind of roads or trails we would be on Pavel would always say, "Make sure your bottles are filled and you have an extra pair of socks and Band-Aids. Theo is here if you need him." And off we'd go.

Those first 10-15 minutes were crucial. Usually the group started slowly which was helpful to most of us. Pavel wanted us to start faster but we just couldn't do it. We would be talking about how we felt and how we were doing. The key was to share your woes with a laugh and lightheartedness. Whining or complaining wasn't manly or viewed as being a good teammate. This was a Navy SEAL led group. Suck it up and get it done was the tone over the group. On this third morning I remembered yesterday morning. After a few minutes my feet would numb up and stop screaming at me. I just had to power through. That was good news for me because I was finding a way to cope. However, for many of the guys, their feet were getting worse.

By the end of the third day I believe Jimmy from Miami and someone else, had found a taxi driver near the hotel and asked him to drive ahead to some town that had a place that sold running shoes and buy some. They had to have bigger shoes. I did too but I didn't think quick enough to say, "Me too!" They asked him to find running shoes with thick soft soles in their sizes and buy them and bring them back to them. The thick soft soles had two intended purposes: For comfort, but also separation from the hot asphalt. The asphalt was hotter than anyone anticipated. Our feet felt cooked in our shoes after the early mornings, turned into hot afternoons. And the taxi guy did it. Off he went with a bunch of U.S. dollars to find some shoes.

Amazingly, later that morning he returned with boxes of shoes. But he had to find us which wasn't always easy. We were always out in the middle of nowhere and rarely saw traffic or cities. Usually we were in villages or in small towns. They were all beautiful with monasteries and old buildings surrounded by lush fields or valleys.

The guys were elated and picked out the ones that fit best. Their bandaged feet slid into the new shoes wonderfully. For them it was like a new lease on life. Then the taxi driver took the other unpurchased new shoes back to the store.

Jimmy said to me, "Robert, get some new shoes. You've got to do it. They work!" So on the fourth day I said to the race director, who was so kind and concerned about all of us, "Can you find someone to go get some bigger shoes for me as well?" He said "Yes," and talked to the hotel manager who sent someone to find me new running shoes.

That day was a tough day. I got my feet numb but we went off road and walked on dirt and gravel through a forest area for part of the morning. It was up and down. My feet were always being pressed onto new pressure points from the uneven surfaces. That day other guys began to fall apart. By early afternoon we were back on asphalt which I became grateful for.

That afternoon Jimmy tore his Achilles tendon. You could see him hobbling until he could barely walk. He said it was an old injury that he seemingly had re-torn. Lance told him to get in one of the support vehicles and go ahead to that night's hotel. Lance encouraged him to get a room, and get into a bath of cold water. Jimmy thought that was a good idea, along with having a beer while soaking. We were envious because he got the go ahead to the hotel. We dreamed of being done and off the road. We were only on day four and we all just wanted to finish and have this "adventure" over.

Levi's feet were infected and oozing green pus from multiple spots. Actually his feet were turning purple. Everyone was concerned. But of course Levi would not stop.

Jolene had shin splints and was struggling. She was limping and falling behind. Soon the race director found a bicycle for her and she began to ride it for the rest of the days.

Lance had developed new blisters as well but never showed any weakness. He was Lance. Dave Crandall my SEALFIT lawyer friend had really bad blisters and was struggling. Ferris, a retired Marine with one prosthetic leg was struggling. His one foot was blistered up. But he refused to slow down and just limped. Ferris had lost his leg in combat but was also a Kokoro finisher as well as a Kokoro instructor. He was tough as nails and had blisters on his one foot. Levi and another guy from San Diego named Graham Dessert were Kokoro finishers. Others had issues as well.

That evening, the small mountain village hotel lobby had cold beers waiting for us in a refrigerator case. It was like the greatest thing in the world. I am not a beer guy and maybe have one beer a year. But when they are cold and you've just done 30 miles on the road on a hot day, that European beer tasted tremendous. I powered the first beer like I was on a TV commercial and then grabbed the second. I got my bags, hobbled up to my room and gently slipped off my shoes. It was a ritual to welcome my new blisters on top of my old ones. I pulled my socks off, then the bandages off ever so gently and surveyed the day's damage. Then I laid on the floor and forced my feet up in the air on the hotel room wall to enjoy the feeling again of the blood draining out of my ankles and feet. I then took out my iPhone and made a video of me talking to myself. I knew my kids would love to see me in this position later. I was so cooked. This experience needed to be chronicled. I play it now sometimes on my phone to just enjoy.

Let me expound a little here: Chronicling pain and damage for me is sort of necessary in its own sick sort of way. I want to have a clear remembrance of the moments. Pictures and videos remind me how crazy this thing was. Also, there is a point where you know you are over the edge mentally and physically. Maybe even close to being delirious. Speed walking up mountains for hours at a time and running down mountains was taking a toll.

I kept my feet up in the air on the wall for probably 30 minutes. But I knew I had to get back downstairs for a team meeting before dinner.

I quickly took a painful shower, got my flip-flops on and hobbled back downstairs. As I was sitting in the little dining area, the race director and his sweet wife came in with four boxes of running shoes that the driver had found for me that day. He came walking in carrying two boxes with his wife carrying two boxes. Both of them looked like they had brought me my Christmas presents.

I just looked at him incredulously and said with my second beer in my hand, "Hey what's this? You guys are tremendous!"

He and his wife smiled at me like loving parents and said "Robert here are some shoes. Try them on." There was a man behind them that must've been the driver who just smiled as well. You could tell he was quite interested in seeing who was going to get the fruit of his labor. He didn't speak English. He was captivated by the situation.

I slipped on each pair and none really felt really good. But one pair had a real nice thin cloth top and a wide toe box. They were made by a company I'd never heard of.

I said to the race director "I'll take these. These will work fine. My usual size is an 11 and these were 12 1/2. Thank you so very, very much for having this nice man find them for me." He looked at the price on the box in euros and told me they would be 150 US. I said "Great!" Those were the most expensive shoes I have ever purchased in my life. But they were going to be worth it. They took the other three boxes away and I asked the hotel manager if he had a pair of scissors which he went and got.

I then proceeded to cut up the tops of the shoes in the areas that were the tightest on my feet. Pretty soon my shoes looked like a bad convertible top on an old car. They were all cut up and missing certain areas. And they felt so much better. Now my feet could swell into those loose areas. It was so much fun customizing my shoes with a number of the guys in the race director and hotel manager watching. They smiled and shook their heads. Ruining a perfectly good pair of shoes.

Our Greek hosts were so kind and thoughtful every day. Actually the whole support team did whatever possible to make our 238 mile experience as nice as possible.

This 238 mile trek was the most boring, difficult, stupid thing any of us had ever done in our lives. As James Lawrence who is known as the Iron Cowboy, because he did 50 IRONMANs in 50 days in 50 states, said to a group of us out the middle of nowhere on the third day, "Everyone needs a stupid one on their resume. This is my stupid one." We all laughed. None of us had ever speed walked up mountains, and jogged down the other side over and over and over again. Speed walking and running for eight days in silence now seemed really stupid. The adventure of it, and the fun had worn off. It was a "suffer-fest." The goal was to just get through each day. For some reason I had thought that the trip was going to be more flat but every day there were more mountains.

On the good side, when we were in the beautiful valleys we saw lots of picturesque farms and vineyards. Often we'd come across shepherds with their herds of goats. We saw the lakes and streams as well as the sea. Occasionally we'd come into old villages where the men and women looked like the black and white photos I'd seen of Europe in World War II. It made me want to come back for a vacation with my wife who is Greek, and enjoy this beautiful place. But for the moment it was just a lot of hard work at 30 miles a day.

When I mention doing this thing in silence it is because most of the time we all trekked on in silence. Occasionally there would be conversations but after while there wasn't much to talk about. We had talked about everything to talk about already. And for me, I was always trying to get out in front of the group in the mornings so I did almost every day in silence.

Here is an interesting side note about walking in silence and being alone a lot:

In the first two days, when walking in a group I would hear and see all the guys. Some had long strides and some short strides. I kept my head up and would pick a guy to stay with him. I focused on his back and just worked on keeping a certain distance.

If I looked down I'd try to find a guy who had the same length of stride as him and walk in rhythm with him. But both were hard for me for some reason. The sound of the guys walking and talking kept helping me lose my best pace. Inevitably, I'd fall to the back of the group. It was frustrating to be in the back. Often I'd run around the guys to the middle of the group and try again to stay in that place. But inevitably I'd be passed by the guys behind me. Once Lance said to me, "Come on Owens.... pick it up." That was humiliating. I wasn't going to ever hear that again.

The third day, I made a crazy decision to go to the very front of the

Me and James "Iron Cowboy" Lawrence on Day 4.

whole group with Pavel who was the fastest guy out there. He was always in front, urging us to keep up. Sometimes if he wasn't too far ahead of us, he'd turn around and walk backwards urging us to keep up the pace. He made everything look effortless.

That morning I said to him, "I need to be away from everybody else and concentrate and focus on doing this. I want to see if I can stay up with you. Which is crazy." He just smiled and said "OK. Stay with me!" Here was the oldest guy there, trying to speed walk, or jog with the fastest.

He smiled and then said with his thick Greek accent, "Stay real close to me, and stay with me." So as he took off, I attempted to take the his exact steps going up the hills or mountain sides that he took. I drafted behind him, being as close as I could. If he didn't tell me and slowed down, within one stride, I'd walk into his back. It was like we were attached. I continually looked down at his feet and took the stride he took. That meant I broke a sweat within four minutes in the morning and was using my breathing techniques to stay with him. It was a real workout.

That third morning, he took off and within 30 minutes we couldn't see the rest of the group behind us. I guess we just sort of got into it. We really motored up the mountain that had continual switchbacks. By 10:30-11:00 a.m. we had a 20-30 minute lead on the group.

We finally got to the top and looked back down on the road and could see the guys way behind us. We were elated, or at least I was. I went to the side of the road overlooking everything and yelled at the top of my lungs, "I am a Spartan!" Pavel just laughed and said "Good job Robert." I felt like Rocky on the steps in Philadelphia. Some of the guys looked up, seeing how far ahead we were on the mountain. It was a moment.

I was amazed that if I focused on doing exactly what he was doing and kept everything else out of my mind, I could do more than I thought, and probably the group thought, I could do.

More than once someone who saw me later on in the morning said something like, "Way to go Owens, you crushed that last section." And amazingly I had, and we did. The interesting part was that he and I never talked. We just worked, or at least I did. Occasionally after an hour of being in silence he'd say something like "You doing good? You OK?" And I'd say something.

By our first break, he'd be there before the others. Since I couldn't stop because the pain would come back into my feet quickly, I'd grab a bar or juice or something and keep going. Pavel then waited for the group. He didn't like to walk as slowly as the group or groups. That meant from that point on I was in silence in my world by myself the rest of the morning and into the afternoon. Usually, I'd start to get tired and slow down by mid to late afternoon.

The game was on. I was now mentally racing every day. How far ahead could I get before being reeled in? Like in cycling.

You might ask, "What did you think about out there on the road?" My answer would be foot placement, foot angles, my speed and the length of my stride. I learned to walk differently for different types of terrains. Different hills and different roads require different lengths in my stride. I needed efficiency and I needed to conserve energy. I was trying to go all day non-stop. And that was a trip. You try going seven to nine hours as fast as you can, without stopping on bad feet.

It was a mental game to see how I could be the fastest and most efficient each hour. I'd practice the Big Four: #1) Breathe correctly. #2) Visualize what I was doing. #3) Break everything into micro-goals or mini races against myself. #4) Use positive self-talk to keep the negative voices out of my head. Whenever the negative voices tried to talk to me, I'd counter with speaking out loud to myself positive affirmations. They really worked.

Let me emphasize, we could never just walk and be relaxed. Every day was a physical and mental test. You would never make the mileage if you walked and enjoyed yourself each day. You had to speed walk with intent and purpose up the mountains and then figure out how you wanted to descend them. Interestingly, I found that running downhill pigeon-toed was the least painful. It was much better than speed walking or walking.

I also refined my arm swing and hand placement on my "weapon" for swinging balance. Lance had everyone carry a four foot long large PVC pipe filled with about three or four pounds of sand to simulate a rifle or weapon the whole time. Some did and some discarded it by the end. I learned to hold it differently going uphill than downhill. And I learned to use it to pull me up hills with my arm swing. It actually became my friend and helper even though it was a stupid thing to carry for eight days. I began to think fondly of it after a while. I often would say, "Come on Baby, take us up this hill! And it would.

My main focus was to get to the next checkpoint or lunch spot within a certain amount of time. They were spaced at about every 90 minutes. There was a break around 10:30 a.m. then the lunch break around 12 and then the last one around 2:30 p.m. I would set 90 minute speed goals or micro-goals that kept me racing against myself continuously because it made the time go by faster. I wanted to have a mental win at the lunch spot then take on Part II in the afternoon. However, if a group of two or three, or four or five, caught me sometime in the afternoon, then I'd walk at their pace the rest of the afternoon knowing that all the others were behind us. Dave Crandall and I were together once or twice suffering together in the late afternoons. His feet were miserable with blisters.

By the third or fourth day, Lance didn't like my strategy because he thought we should be doing this as a team thing especially in the afternoons. However, it became obvious quickly that there were faster guys and slower guys. It was hard and impossible to be all together over nine hours. So I took advantage of the situation and found a way to survive my feet. I just didn't stop.

Once Lance had a guy go out on a bike and find me and told me to stop and wait for the group. That really pissed me off. It made no sense. That day, Pavel and I had broken out in the early morning and set the pace. I'd left Pavel after the first break and was motoring along. He stopped for the break and I didn't. I was about 45 minutes ahead of everyone. I stood still with the bike guy doing what Lance wanted, waiting on the side of a road with my feet screaming at me waiting for them to catch up.

Lance wanted us to be closer together and encouraging each other. But it was obvious to me by now that the guys were just wanting to make it, and survive each day. There wasn't any "team" happening. The group fun part had worn off. There were groups but we were not a group or a team. We were survivors. Everyone was finding their way to cope. The attitude of the group was way more, "Figure out a way to finish each day. You are on your own." There wasn't much "Be a Team" attitude left.

When Lance and other guys finally caught up to me, Lance didn't say a word. Finally, he said to me, "What the hell are you doing?" with a disgustful voice. I told Lance my situation with my feet which he understood I guess because almost everyone had bad feet to some degree.

I said if I stop at the breaks my feet scream at me after one minute of standing around or sitting. I mentioned how the group usually caught up with me in the afternoons so it was my way of not being a slow guy at the end of the day. I guess he understood.

So he made me ask for permission to leave the group on my own for the last three days, which I did. He could be a real Navy Chief Master Sergeant sometimes. I'd say "Lance, I'd like to take off now to keep my feet dead. Is that OK with you?" With irritation he'd say "Yes." And I'd smile and say "Thank you" and leave all of them. We didn't talk much after a few days.

Again, my goal was to be the fastest and to be in first place at the end of each day. It never worked. I never was the fastest and I never was in first place but that goal helped me finish in the top third almost every day. I was not going to viewed as old or slow. That second day when Lance said to me "Pick it up" when I was the last guy was the turning point. He was never going to tell me to "Pick it up" again. It is a guy thing. He never said it or saw much of me again.

After 3:00 p.m. I began to sometimes walk normally and maybe cruise to the finish. Of course we never knew where the daily mileage would end until we came upon the race organizers around some bend in the road or when we entered a village who said "Good job. You're finished. It could be at 5:00 or 6:30 p.m. We never knew how long the days would, or could be.

Back to the new shoes. The next day was better as the new customized shoes were like marshmallows. The friction points were gone. However my feet moved around now too much on the downhill walks and runs. But it was better than before. My toes would slide to the front of my shoes on my dislodged toenails but that didn't really matter anymore. As long as the toenails stayed somewhat attached there'd be some protection on the top of my toes.

On day three or four, we made it to Corinth, which is a beautiful coastal city. We stopped for a little bit of time at a mile long, deep canal that was dug by slaves between two cities. Prior to the canal, the slaves used to put ships on rolling logs and pull the ships with stabilizing ropes from one sea to the other. It was an amazing historical place and is still used today.

When in Corinth, we were directed to walk by the restaurants on the right and the sea on the left. It was beautiful and so European except the beaches were pebbles instead of sand. I don't like lying out on gravel, yet people had their towels laid out on the pebbles. I was thinking, "You guys are so hard up to be lying on pebbles by the sea. Not good. There has to be places that have sand." But I never saw any.

What we didn't know was that afternoon, we had to climb up from the sea on a winding road up a 2,000 foot mountain and go until 6:00 p.m. It was a really long day.

The next day, we went back down to the sea and climbed up that afternoon to over 3,000 feet. I couldn't believe that we ended up in the cool fresh air of a ski resort. That was a lot of climbing. The resort we stayed at was beautiful and had expansive views of the mountains and a long valley. It even had a swimming pool where some of us, after showering and getting our bandages off our feet, went and jumped in the pool. Maybe not a sanitary thing to do for us, or the pool, but it was so worth it.

Dinner that night was in a small Greek village where all the locals sat outside and ate at big, long tables. The travel company had ordered a special buffet for us and all the food was gone. The dessert was Greek yogurt with honey on top with pieces of lemon skin sprinkled on top. Tremendous. It was so Greek and memorable. I ate with Dave Crandall and his wife who was following us daily in a chase vehicle.

I enjoyed having such nice moments in the middle of such difficult and painful days.

Looking back and writing this is a little difficult as the exact days are a bit blurry. But there are fun stories I should mention.

One morning we started our day where the very first marathon was finished. I was really taken by the setting. You could visualize the spectators yelling and screaming from the dirt embankment, trees surrounded the open space that had become our first "stadium" in the world.

It was really something to understand the origins of the marathon. Another morning we started in a beautiful, lush, green valley. Later in the march, we started on top of a mountain in a really small village. We speed walked up from our small hotel to the top of the mountain, then spent four hours going down the other side. Every day was different.

All the hotels were unique and special. The whole time I just kept wondering, "How did King Leonidas make it with his 300 men, their servants and animals to Thermopylae in eight days?" They couldn't have done this. It must be a legend and not reality. All the guys made comments about the legend. It was a stupid legend. There was no way they did it.

All I knew was that every day was one day closer to the end. And I couldn't be happier.

On the last day, Levi, who lives in London, wanted to make a statement. The doctor had taken him off the course on day five or six. His feet were just too infected and swollen to go on and he was now on antibiotics. His feet were all bandaged in white stripes of gauze and wraps with green ooze coming through. They had told him to let his feet dry out and heal. Actually I had never seen feet as ugly as his. Those feet belonged in the hospital but he wanted to finish.

So on the last day, with his feet in those bandages, he put on his flip-flops and got out two walking sticks and began the last 30 miles. But he also brought with him a large U.S. flag on a stick which he stuck in his backpack.

The last day was a really hot, and windy day. It was like having your face in front of an oven with the fan blowing heat on you. I wanted to have my best day and go out strong. There were much better athletes doing this than me. There were war vets, active and retired Navy SEALS, Olympic hopefuls, Kokoro finishers and 2 Kokoro instructors. And there were some great guys who wanted to raise money for the foundations and participate. I was an old guy. I wanted to make this a statement day too. I wanted to finish really strong.

Pavel and I took off early. Again, my goal was to be in first place at the end of the day. I was going to go out with a statement performance. I was with Pavel in the early morning and alone by 10:30. I was leading at lunch and just motored through the lunch that was set up on the side of the road. I grabbed a cookie and a couple of waters and kept going.

Somewhere about two or three in the afternoon two young guys motored past me. It was OK. I was in the game. Then coming up behind me on a long open stretch of road was Levi and his rubber flip-flops. Even though he was encouraged to not get back on his infected feet, he wanted to go out his way. He was going to finish strong. He is a natural runner type, and a U.S. Olympic qualified marathon distance cross-country skier. He was in his groove. He had all this blood and ooze coming out of his discolored white bandages which didn't bother him at all. His feet were purple and swollen. And he was smiling. He was using walking sticks and had this large American flag flying on a stick from his backpack like you'd see flying from the back of a pickup truck somewhere.

He smiled at me and said, "Hi. Good job Robert!" I turned and smiled at him and got tears in my eyes which he couldn't see. I had sunglasses on. I replied "You're tremendous Levi. Go for it." And he just motored by me like a real marathon guy. It was a display of raw courage. He had a strong "Why" within him.

Everyone wanted to finish strong. It was so inspirational, as Levi speed walked past me, he gave me his unique smile and then began to jog away from me. It was a classic moment.

I worked the last day the hardest probably of any of the eight days and ended up coming to the end of that road in fourth place. I was so happy and so proud.

There were some people from a local running club welcoming us outside of Thermopylae with cold drinks. They tasted so good. The young guys who finished in front of me were sitting down off the road in the shade of some trees. Levi was talking to someone off to the side.

One spoke loudly, "There is Owens. Amazing job Robert. Hey Robert...you killed it today!" Another said, "Great job Rob. You really powered today." I had.

It was so satisfying to be in the first four guys of the 17. It was the last 30 miles, after pushing my way through the first 208. I had survived and made it.

To my surprise the last of the guys came in over an hour behind us. I'd finished 238 miles. Never once after the first day did I find myself in the back of the pack where most expected me to be. It was a personal win for me.

Finally everyone arrived. Lance gathered us together and

congratulated us. We had done 237 miles and now we would do the last mile together. We did it with the Thermopylae running club cheerleader 40-50 year old ladies with us. We marched to the national statue of King Leonidas and the memorial park built in his memory. This was the believed location of where the battle was to have taken place.

There, we met the mayor of Thermopylae and a few dignitaries. They had a celebration ceremony for us. We were given nice plaques, had our pictures taken and people said nice things. But I was dying. The longer I stood on that hot dirt in the sun, the more feeling came back in my feet. No one knew that I was almost in tears.

Finally, I was called forward to receive my plaque and had my picture taken with the mayor, the race director and the dignitaries. I smiled, said a few words and went back to my place. Soon it was over and I went and found somewhere to sit down. I grabbed my flip-flops out of my backpack and took my bandages off. Then I gently slipped my flip-flops back on and let my feet begin to dry out. My socks were filled with yellow pus ooze.

We then hobbled to a big Spartan national museum where there were exhibits about the Spartans retelling the story of the battle with the Persians. There was also a food court. The city government treated us all to food and a few beers. Again, I found that this Greek beer tasted pretty good. We sat and interacted for about an hour and then wonderfully were ushered to our awaiting buses.

Lance being Lance, wanted to commemorate this moment in a special way. He had us all get in the circle on some dead stiff dry grass near the flagpoles. He felt it would be a good thing for us to do 50 Burpees. I couldn't believe it. I was tired my feet were screaming, I was in my flip flops and Lance wanted to do 50 Burpees in the hot sun. I did most of them but they weren't the best Burpees in the world.

A new situation arose because instead of getting on the buses some of the guys crossed the street and went in search of the spring of water that tradition had said had given the Spartans their water. I just wanted to get back to Athens and the hotel, but now we were searching for our missing explorers.

We searched and searched for probably 60 minutes until finally we went down a road off the highway and came across a re-settlement camp of Muslim refugees. It was so sad. Out here in the middle of nowhere and outside of Thermopylae city limits were about 30 Muslim refugee families living in some abandoned buildings. I guess they heard about the freshwater spring as well and decided to make the area around the springs their new home. These people had nothing. Little kids were running around everywhere, while the men were in groups talking and smoking. The women were huddled in and around the abandoned buildings.

I couldn't help but think about their escape from their country. Somehow they had made it to Greece but it seemed that the Greeks were doing nothing for them. As I later learned there already were over 30,000 Muslim refugees and in around the Athens area. I also learned that there was a great controversy going on about what to do with them. It seemed so sad to me.

We finally found our guys in their underwear in the fountain. When they saw us, they quickly got dressed and got on the bus. Maybe they drank too many beers. Then we left for our hotel. Hardly anyone spoke. We were exhausted; most just slept. After two hours, we made it to our hotel where in silence everyone just got off and gathered their belongings. We were assigned rooms and I just went up to my room. I immediately took out my dirty clothes and took my $150 shoes and put them in the trash can. There was a little bit of an emotional attachment to them and I thought about taking them home to show Sandy but then I thought "No way" they're going in the trash.

I took a shower, ordered room service and went to sleep. When I woke up in the morning and went downstairs for breakfast, the lobby was quiet in the breakfast area. There weren't any of the guys. I never saw any of them again. They had left earlier than me I guess. That was sort of weird.

After breakfast, I went upstairs and gathered my belongings, came back downstairs, checked out and got a taxi to the hotel in Glyfada. It was the little beach town where I had rested when I arrived in Greece. I took a 20 minute taxi ride to a wonderful friendly little hotel I'd found online. It was about 40 yards from the water, and cost $60 a day, breakfast included. Across the street from the hotel was a restaurant and bar beach resort. I found a beach chair under an umbrella and settled in. I had brought a couple of special books to read from home for this occasion. It was wonderful. The key was to keep my feet in the sun to dry out. Also I went in and out of the sea to get my feet in the salt water; in the sea then in the sun, and I recovered.

To keep my new found tradition going, I ordered a beer and took out a cigar that I had brought from the US for this occasion. Actually, I brought four cigars. I thought maybe on one day I might want two. The beach, the umbrella, the lounge, the beer, the book and the cigar made for an ideal situation.

It wasn't too long after the beer and cigar that I fell off to sleep. I must've slept for an hour or two. When I awoke, it was late afternoon. It was peaceful, warm and beautiful. The tide had come in, and the clear warm water was lapping softly about 15 yards from my feet. I got up and again walked in the warm sand and into the warm Aegean sea and had a tremendous time.

I repeated this routine for three days. I read my books and took my naps. I didn't speak to a person except when eating. It was bliss. I hardly moved it all. I made sure to be in the shade under the umbrella but kept my feet in the sun. The blisters, as I hoped, dried up pretty quickly.

By the time it was time to leave my feet almost felt normal, even though they didn't look normal. All the blisters had dried up and become dark brown, thick, stiff calluses. Everything was much better.

On the fourth day, I took a cab to the Athens airport and flew home to Sandy. It was time to go home and go back to training for Kokoro in October.

When I got home in June, I resumed my Crossfit and SEALFIT training. I was finally getting stronger in my shoulders and arms and my anaerobic stamina was coming back. My ability to do repeat stairs, box jumps, burpees and sprints was encouraging.

I enjoyed Saturdays at SEALFIT workouts more than ever. And it was fun to see Dave again. He was still quiet but so was I.

One day I ran into an old lifeguard friend and we struck up a conversation about the lifeguards at San Clemente. He mentioned that "The Quest" was coming up for the guards who wanted to do it. And I said to him, "Is that the run to Newport Beach?"

He said, "Yes."

"Tell me again about it? It has been years since I've heard of it."

He reminded me that the second Sunday of August, there is a lifeguard memorial run from the San Clemente Pier in South Orange County to Newport Beach. It is only for beach lifeguards and is a memorial to the lifeguards who have died while trying to rescue swimmers in the cities the run goes through. These are San Clemente, Capistrano Beach, Dana Point, Laguna Beach, Corona Del Mar and Newport Beach.

It starts at 6 a.m. from the San Clemente Pier and finishes late in the afternoon, in Newport. He told me Larry Moore, a legendary San Clemente guard, set it up years ago. And he still does it each year. That means Larry has done it probably over 20 times. It is 23-25 miles long and when you aren't running on sand, you are swimming or on the rocks. He reminded me that "Larry is Legendary!"

I asked, "Is he in his 60s now?" and was told "Yes." I thought "Wow.... he is a real stud! That is a tough marathon beach run, with swimming."

I called the Lifeguard department or as it is now known, The Marine Safety Department and asked the guy on the phone about The Quest. He said it was on this year as far as he knew. He mentioned that Larry Moore wasn't going to participate this year.

I thought to myself, "If ever I could do this thing, it would be this year. I've never been in as good of shape as I am now. And I'll bet I'll be the oldest guy to try to do it as Larry has been the oldest so far."

So the week before The Quest, I went to my gym in Dana Point where I swim before the IRONMAN and got into the pool. I swam some laps and figured that I didn't need a lot of practice because the swims along the coast are relatively short. "The Quest" should be mainly a soft sand, endurance run with some climbing over rocky points occasionally, and some swimming around other points. And the thought of doing the rocks again lit me up.

Let me tell you about doing the rocks.

As a three year San Clemente lifeguard in high school, I loved the rock training and the pier jumping the most. Unless you are a Southern California beach guard you probably will never get this but I love washing up on the rocks and being washed off the rocks. It takes skill to not get cut up. I loved the waves booming and breaking on the rocks and the timing it took to navigate on and around them. If you missed the timing between waves, you could get pounded and hurt.

There is a place called the Blow Hole in South Laguna where there is an underwater narrow channel that comes under the rocks and blows a big splash of water into the air like Old Faithful in Yosemite. The waves would break on the rocks and then this blow hole would explode upward when the underwater wave went up an channel and hit a dead end. Then the water would go out again and in less than a minute the next wave would come and this geyser would shoot up and explode again.

The Blow Hole really happens to best on big wave days. Big days were the key. When it was big, people would come from all around, if they weren't afraid of the surf and rocks, to see the geyser or blow hole explode at low tide to medium tide. It was too dangerous to be out there at high tide.

As a 15 ½ year old kid, I came with all the lifeguard trainees and had to learn about the rocks for potential rock rescues. My second lifeguard death happened after my Junior year in high school. It occurred down the beach a mile north of the Blow Hole when I was 16 and in my second lifeguard summer. A lady got swept off those rocks at Aliso Beach by a rogue wave as the tide was coming in. She was swept off those rocks in a second and disappeared. When I finally found her, she had drowned and had head injuries, but that is another story. The rocks were no joke on big days or even on medium sized days. I loved the rocks.

As trainees we would train on the rocks, and each of us had to take his turn jumping in the Blow Hole as the water rushed out and back into the ocean.

It was scary and intimidating. You had to hold your breath and go under the rocks for about 5-10 seconds, while bouncing off the sides of the rocks in the dark, churning, rough water. It was a test of how kids handled the rocks. Some kids wouldn't do it occasionally but most did. I missed those days. If you didn't do it you were eliminated from lifeguard training. But after a while and figuring it out and gaining your confidence, you'd ask to be able to do it over and over. It was a huge rush to say the least!

I knew that in The Quest we would go by the Blow Hole again.

Maybe it would be booming again!

As I would drive to SEALFIT, I'd think to myself, "This is wild. If I could do The Quest, that would be five major endurance races or events in seven months which would be unbelievable." They would be:

> Greece
> The Quest
> Kokoro
> IRONMAN Mexico and
> The World Marathon Challenge

> At 65-66 years old!

Four of the events would be aerobic endurance events where I just have to have the stamina to finish. Kokoro would be the anaerobic spike your heart, Crossfit and Spartan Games strength test, and ball buster.

Ok, let's do this "Quest" with these young kids!

LEADERSHIP LESSONS

1. Equipment is Everything. Don't sabotage your training with poor, incorrect, misinformed equipment research.
2. You can press through pain. Where the mind goes, the body will follow. Practice pain and pain management before the test.
3. 20X Principles: Breathe, Mini-Goals, Self Talk and Visualization.
4. Train with winners and experienced athletes. Learn from them.
5. Believe that there is more ability and potential in you, even when you feel maxed. "Breathe" and ask for advice.
6. Embrace "The Suck". It is where you grow.

The next chapter reminds me that I didn't do what I knew to do. Poor equipment means suffering needlessly. Plus I suck up my fear and jump...

I carried my Los Angeles Adventurers Club Flag the whole way !

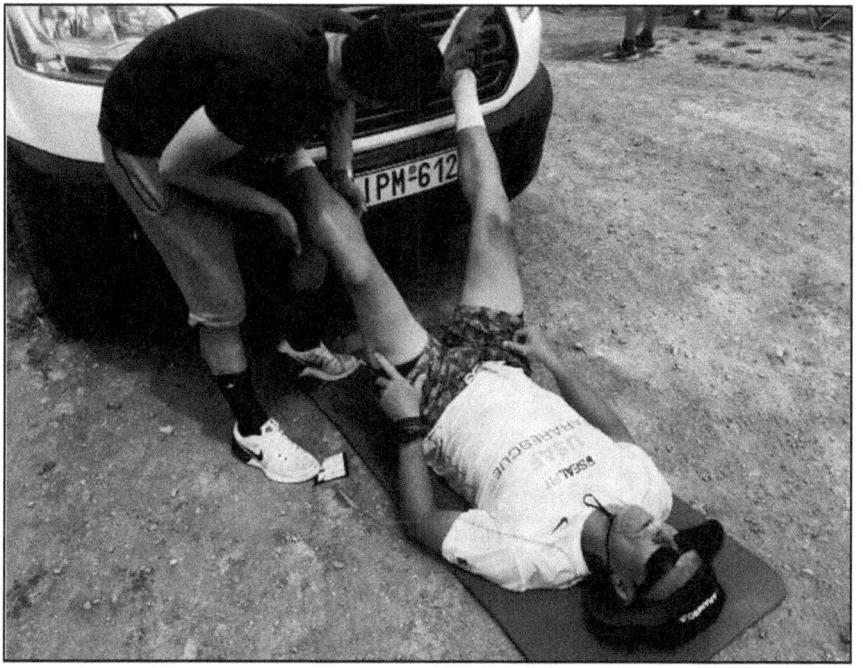

Legs locked up on me on day 6. Theo the medic rubbed out my thighs.

BEYOND AVERAGE

The Pre-Race photo op. I'm on the far right, totally unprepared for what is coming...

Chapter 8

The Quest Run

I called and reconfirmed on Friday morning that The Quest was on for Sunday and showed up at 5:45 a.m. unannounced. Sandy and I had gotten out of bed around 4:00 a.m., had our coffees and made the 40 minute drive from Newport to San Clemente. We walked to the end of the pier on a cool foggy morning in the 60s at 5:45 a.m. I could see that there were about 20 kids and some girlfriends and parents milling around by the rail at the end of the pier talking and laughing. The parents had jackets on and the participating lifeguards had t-shirts, shorts and running shoes on. Sandy and I walked up and just looked around. I had a light jacket on. They all thought we were parents so no one said anything to us. We didn't know anybody.

After a couple of minutes, this older beach lifeguard guy named Steve said, "OK, let's get together for a picture and let's get going. They all lined up and I walked over and got on the end of the line. The kid next to me just looked at me like, "what are you doing here. This isn't for parents!" but didn't say anything. We finished and the older guy said, "OK. Let's go!"

And the game was on!

They started running down the pier fast!

I had my jacket on, my regular cargo shorts on and water shoes. Why the water shoes? I assumed when we started, we would run down pier and get in the sand on the beach. But I thought wrong.

They were running away from me on the pier and I was there with

165

Sandy taking off my clothes and stunned that they were running. I got down to my speedo, t-shirt with my rubber water shoes like you buy in CVS or Rite-Aid in beach cities and sprinted to catch up with them. By the end of the pier, I'd caught up to the back of the pack and some 16 year old looked in amazement and said "Hi. You doing this?" I panted "Yes" and he just smiled, turned away from me and ran.

When we were at the end of the pier we turned left and north. I thought they would veer left onto the sand but stayed up on a dirt path that was 20 yards above the beach sand. This path went below the cliffs and parallel to the railroad tracks for a mile. I couldn't believe that they didn't get down to the sand and water. This was a sand run event I thought. But it had changed a few years ago. No one told me, because I never asked. This was now a regular dirt to asphalt running event in the beginning. Unbelievable!

I was running without socks in stupid rubber water shoes. I didn't say anything but I was working really hard on getting my breathing down and my heart rate lowered. These mainly 16 to 25 year olds were talking and laughing like they were on a school lunch break and running fast. It was just like being back in high school on the Cross-country Team my junior year. Back then every afternoon the runners would stay in a pack and talk and tell jokes until it was time to go to really go to work. It was fun and effortless.

That was this group. One guy even ran backward, occasionally talking. Another guy was barefoot. And there were two guys over 25 and they were fit.

These kids were having such a good time talking and laughing and I was trying to just get it together and stay up with them. I was out of breath and just trying desperately to get my heart rate down from the adrenaline rush. I couldn't talk. I was maxed. I knew that on this route we'd hit the Pacific Coast Highway and be on asphalt soon. It was four miles to the end of Dana Harbor. I'd run this area in training for my IRONMANs since 1980. I knew there was no way back to the beach until Capo Beach. And I was perplexed: "Why weren't they choosing to get over on the beach and on the sand! Later on, I was glad they weren't on sand. How would I have kept up with them there?

We finally left the dirt path and transitioned to the Pacific Coast highway and I was starting to get blisters on my toes in these hard rubber shoes. But it was a price I had to pay. By now I had my wind and I could keep up if they didn't ask me to talk. A couple of times a kid did try to talk with me but I couldn't answer his question. I said I couldn't talk with a smile. It was all I could do to stay up with them. I was sweating and breathing deep. But as usual, the longer I ran the more comfortable I became and more relaxed I could be. The panic finally subsided. The pack ran to Dana Harbor in 25-30 minutes from where the dirt ended and the asphalt began. I stayed at the back of the pack all the way. To my relief, they had scheduled a pit stop to drink and refuel at the very end of Dana Harbor parking lot past Baby Beach.

When we stopped to drink fluids by the day tables, this kid David Coy said, "Hi, I am David. Who are you?" I said, "I am an old guard that wanted to try to do this thing." He said "OK" with a big smile on his face. "It is break time." I replied, "Great!"

"Hey David, I thought this was a beach run?" He replied, "Oh yeah, a few years ago they changed it. This first leg was changed to the highway run. Sorry for any misunderstanding." "No problem" I replied. But now I had these blisters on some of my toes from those rubber shoes.

Then I made the mistake of changing out of my hard bottomed water shoes to a slipper type surf bootie with a softer sole. I didn't want to swim with the heavier water shoes if I didn't have to. I thought the lighter sole water shoes would work better on the rocks and when swimming. Sandy had followed the parents and friends in our car and was there at the harbor when I arrived. She just stared at me in my speedo and rubber shoes and said, "You OK?" I must have looked pretty out of it and stupid running three miles down the highway in a red speedo and black rubber rock shoes while all the kids were in running shorts and running shoes. Sandy tried not show concern or laugh. However I really was an oddity.

It is what you don't know, and what everybody else does know, that will kill you.

Within five minutes, the refueling was over. We said goodbye to Sandy and the parents, and made our way to the rocks. This would be our first rock work. We had to traverse north towards Dana Strand which was around the corner from the harbor. I had put a blue Pararescue shirt on for the rest of the day. It was a different t-shirt than I wore to the start. I hadn't time to put it on at the start.

Once on the rocks, I knew I had made a mistake. My softer sole shoes were too soft for the rocks. The rocks were sharper than I remembered and cutting through my rubber soled booties.

We kept going and I kept going. Unbelievably, one kid didn't wear any shoes all day. He was the kid that ran the highway barefoot. When I asked someone, "What's the deal with that kid?" I learned he never wears shoes doing this, and he does it every year. He just motored across the rocks barefoot talking to his friends. I was amazed. I was watching every foot placement I made and was slow.

We finally made it around the corner to Dana Strand but we had to jump off the rocks and swim over to the sand. I was the last one out of the water as I expected. They were all waiting for me.

By this time, I was embarrassed. I was in the rear, I was slow. The rocks had begun to shred my rubber booties. I noticed it on the sand run.

David Coy came back to check on me as we ran the sand together and I shared a little with him. He was about 22 and a real natural leader. He said, "You're doing great Mr. Owens. I am so glad you are here. By the way, how old are you and when and where did you guard?"

I was smiling and looking him in his bright unfazed eyes, "I am 65 and I guarded San Clemente City from 66 to 69. Like way before you were born." He said, "Wow, that's amazing. You are doing great."

I knew he was trying to encourage me. Even though I didn't want it, I liked it. I needed the encouragement. The first two phases of the day's marathon experience was harder than I anticipated.

When we jumped off the rocks into the ocean for our swim to the beach at Dana Strand, there was a good size swell coming in and breaking. It was fun to swim in those sets. We were going to have some fun waves after all.

Then David said "OK let's go." And the group ran for the next 20 minutes down the sand to where the beach ended again. We ran through Dana Strand and Salt Creek and finished at Monarch Beach. At Monarch, we got back on the rocks and made our way again towards the point.

My feet were really tender and David could see it. He stopped and waited for me and said, "Mr. Owens, you've got the wrong booties for this. Here, take mine. Give me yours. I'll be fine with yours. I've done this before and your booties won't be any problem for me." I was now really embarrassed. He was having no problems at all on the rocks. My feet felt like they were walking on the tops of screw drivers. Plus they were getting cut and my blisters were really talking to me. I said "No thanks" but he was relentless. After about another 20 minutes on the rocks he watched me struggle and he appealed again. I gratefully caved in. He had the kind of rubber shoes I had run the highway in. Why hadn't I kept mine on? Why did I exchange them for these softer ones? I was doing everything wrong. And I thought, "It is always in the equipment. You can be in the best shape in the world but if you have the wrong equipment, you're toast! Just like in Greece with the boots and running shoes. I have known these truths all my life and here I am again at 65 being stupid. Will I ever learn? Why didn't I ask more questions vs. just showing up and thinking I could knock this thing out?" I was embarrassed again. I hadn't done my research. I hadn't a real strategy. I was over confident.

His shoes worked much better. I want to mention how grateful I was for him caring about me, and helping me.

He said with a big smile "No problem Mr. Owens. Then he took off on the rocks like a mountain goat. He was fast and agile. And I was faster too. The cuts and blisters didn't bother me as much and just as in Greece, my feet acclimated to the pain.

Going around Monarch you come to Three Arch Bay where I lived. The group kept following the easiest route and it took us up the rocks. These kids had done this before so I just followed.

As we got to the top of this rock section, we came to the end of our ability to go forward. We came to a cliff. This was the cliff we could see from the Three Arch Bay Beach from my house. No one has ever been on it that I knew of. I lived there on and off for 50 years and never saw anyone up on that cliff. We had come from the southern Monarch side which was really unusual. Here we were. Now I knew why they had climbed upward instead of swimming around the point. They wanted to jump off this 50-60 foot cliff. It was the highest jump of my life. I couldn't imagine I was there doing this. But one by one they just jumped and screamed all the way down and what was I to do? Act old or scared? I had to just step up and jump. It was not the time to act rational or old. So I took a deep breath and jumped.

One Thousand One.

One Thousand Two.

One Thousand Three.

One Thousand Four.

One Thousand Five.

Ca-Whooosh.

It was crazy high. Like you could barely hear the person before you hit the water below you it was so far down. But it was like pier jumping in high school and it was fun. Just higher. I was about the 15th person to jump and I was scared. But I was before the 20th. I did not want to be the last as the old guy.

I made it and it was a moment in time. I came up, acted like it was nothing and followed the others who were already swimming 5-10 minutes to shore. As I was swimming, the others behind me were jumping and screaming all the way down. Some landed better than others. You needed good form or you could get hurt. Some looked hurt but not badly. I was glad it was behind me. When they hit the water, it exploded like a hand grenade had gone off. I thought "Wow. That is a really high jump."

In all those years of lifeguarding Three Arch Bay and living there, I'd never seen anyone on the point or jumping those rocks. If anything, I would often stand and watch the winter storm waves come in and pound that point and those cliffs. In the winter, the waves would come in so hard and hit the cliffs that the spray would go up and block out the view of the houses above the cliff. It was a BIG cliff on a rocky point. The keys for me had been:

a.) Good form for the entry.

b.) I couldn't show any fear to any of them. I was to be a kid like them and do what kids do or I shouldn't be out there doing this. It was such a rush!

c.) My five kids would have been envious and proud of me. Dad did that cliff! Or... did Dad really do THAT cliff?

When we all gathered together on the beach we ran again until we were below my house and we ran out of sand. Then back on the rocks as it was a really long swim around the next shoreline of rocks.

We did rocks for the next 30 minutes until we reached the Blow Hole area. And this time we had a good three or four wave set swell hitting the rocks.

We didn't do the Blow Hole. They decided to keep going. However, each of us had to jump down into the swirling water that was about shoulder or chest high in the ravine and crawl up the other rocky side. The ravine was about four feet wide where we were to jump in. It got wider up the rocks and thinner towards the ocean.

The whole area is covered in barnacles, mussels and some thin seaweed so it was slippery and challenging. Those barnacles could cut you good if you weren't careful. They were really sharp on the edges. The key was to jump in and quickly find a place to put your hand for a hold on the other side that wasn't covered in barnacles and mussels. Then find a foothold and pull yourself out.

The waves would break on the rocks and then surge in everywhere and especially up the ravine. When the water subsided, after each surge of water, each guard had to time their jump down in this area and get up the other side before the next wave would surge in and wash you up into or on to the rocks. If you had to, you'd rather be washed up on to the rocks rather than hammered into the rocks. Or if you were really slow or couldn't find a hand and foothold, the waves would wash you out of that area and wash you back out to the ocean through the ravine.

If that happened then you'd be washed back up through the tunnel and ravine with the next wave... and so forth. All of us knew the longer you were in the ravine the more dangerous it was and the more cut up you could become.

It was just like guard training in high school. And that is why most these kids were so comfortable at it. Actually some of the younger kids got THE BIG EYES when they saw the Blow Hole area that day. It was alive!

Fortunately they had gone through guard training in the last few years so they weren't unaware of the dynamics. And the best part about rock training is that you observe and have to figure it out quickly. You must learn to read the ocean, the swells, the amount of waves per swell, watch the water patterns in the surges and how much time you had between the breaking waves and the water surges. The key was to watch the others. Some figured it out immediately and got through. Some tried different routes and couldn't find hand or foot holds. They were peeled off the rocks and into the ravine surging waters. No one got hurt that day but some knew they better figure it out quickly or they would be in trouble. I just watched and observed. I didn't want to be the first nor the last to jump in as those who had gone first had already left that area and moved on.

David went through OK as did some others. I watched a few get tumbled around. They got out with minor cuts.

So finally, I said I'd go next and jumped in. I got to the other side and got a hand hold and was climbing up the other side when the surge came through and hit me. It knocked me off and took me underwater and up the ravine. I surfaced and could see many staring at me like... "Oh my God, look at Mr. Owens. He's in trouble!" David's eyes and face showed he was really concerned. You could tell those who were watching were worried. I'd been the first to wash up the ravine.

Then the water ran back through the barnacled covered ravine to the ocean with me in it. I knew that the key to this moment was to not panic and stay fluid. Just flow with it. Don't fight it. If you get rigid, when you hit those rocks they can shred you. You need to stay limp underwater and above water and be as flexible you can. Try to think about protecting your head. Stay long and slide like a hot dog into and out of a long skinny bun. Try to glide over the rocks and barnacles and not get so cut up.

As I washed back in I looked up at David and smiled, then went underwater again. The next wave washed me back up past the staring onlookers and back to the end and top of the ravine. This happened a couple of times. They came in too fast for me to get a handhold. But finally, as one washed out, the water left slower than before because I was now in between sets of waves coming in. I grabbed for a rock hand hold and held on to it for a couple of seconds.

David's eyes were huge as he stood above me wondering if this old man was going to need rescuing. I smiled again and then lost the hand hold and slid back underwater with the receding water in the ravine. When the water came up the next time I went for the hand hold again and held on to it as the water surged up the ravine past me. And as the water receded I still had my handhold and then a got a foot hold and climbed out.

The guards just stared at me. David's eyes were glued to me. He was relieved. I just had a fun, exciting, nerve racking adventure. It was great. David said "Wow Mr. Owens, that was wild. I was really worried for you in there. I didn't know if you were going to need help."

I just said, "It was fun. Couldn't keep my handhold, but I got it finally." It was a moment for sure. But remember: Always smile under pressure and never show weakness.

He laughed and gave his big smile and said "Wow, that was great!" And we moved on.

The kids behind me still had to jump in and get through. I mentioned to David that back in lifeguard training in high school we had to jump in there. It was pretty much the same. It was fun. Then he said "But you're like 65! That is amazing...."

I said "Once you learn it, you never forget it. It's just the rocks." And he said "You're right. It's just the rocks. You never forget how to ride a bike or jump out of a plane. And you never forget the rocks."

I was cut a few places on my legs and hands but nothing big. I was a kid again! As I keep saying, "I am in the Game! This is way fun."

We moved on. We did rocks and short swims and ran the sand all through South Laguna until we hit Laguna Beach. Laguna was a longer run. We stopped at Aliso Beach for water and food then again at Main Beach Laguna for fueling and then ran to the rocks leaving Main Beach. It was about 11 a.m. and it was warming up. We did the rocks by "Rockpile", then Divers Cove, Shaw's Beach and Crescent Bay. Lots of swimming and rocks. Then finally we got around to Emerald Bay and into Irvine Cove. That had taken about two hours. When we climbed out of Irvine Cove, the kids were in the front again, and I thought we were supposed to take the easiest route. It happened though the "easier route" took us higher and higher on the rocks. As we came around the corner by Moro Bay, there was a shear drop off. It is where the big house sits out on the point. You can see it easily from PCH. The house was above us. Below us were four guys surfing the point.

The guards who arrived there first yelled down to them. They looked up and were shocked to see us way above them. We motioned for them to move out of the way. They couldn't believe 20 or so people were

Me in my red Speedo, it was a very fun day.
About 11 a.m. at Aliso Beach, which is where as
a 16 year old lifeguard I had my second person,
the lady, drown 50 years earlier in 1967.

going to jump down on top of them. I am sure they had never surfed that point before and had people above them much less people about to jump on top of them.

So they moved over on their boards and one by one, like back at Three Arch Bay, we jumped. And again, it was a really high jump. Probably as high as Three Arch. This time I just walked to the edge and jumped. "What the Hell?" I thought. "Just another jump. I have no choice." I thought, "Just get it over with and enjoy it. Remember to keep your legs tightly pressed together or it could really hurt." Again you probably had to count to six slowly before you'd hit the water. It exploded as before, like a hand grenade had gone off.

We all jumped and swam a good distance to shore. The guards acted like it was nothing. It probably was, except to me!

We gathered ourselves on the sand and then the longest run of the day began. It was Moro Beach to Crystal Cove to Little Corona. Halfway, parents were on the sand with Gatorade and bars. Sandy was there and said, "How's it going."

I said "OK. Had some wild jumps. Like that one back there." She said, "You jumped that one?" And I said "Yes and it was like the big one at Three Arch Bay."

She asked "Where did you jump Three Arch?" I told her. She said "You did the far point by the houses?"

I said "Yep" and she got the big eyes! She just looked at me with that, "I don't know about you sometimes" look. I told her I had to do what the guards were doing. I was with the kids.

It was hot by now and guys and girls were putting on a lot of sunscreen. I had a Pararescue t-shirt on and my speedos. I felt pretty good. I put some sunscreen on my face and ears and I kissed Sandy on the cheek and said, "Goodbye." We took off again running on the sand.

The run lasted maybe an hour on harder sand. There were a few places to jump over rocks, but mainly nice, clean, warm, hard sand.

We waved as we had all morning to the guards in the towers who knew what we were doing. It was an annual event in August. Some stood up, some waved and cheered us on and one saluted. There was a respect shown as it was for the lifeguard brotherhood, no matter which city you worked for.

Finally we ran out of sand and started on the rocks again. My feet were more sore on the rocks than on the sand. David's shoes worked but my thighs were really tired. Going up and over rocks on all fours a lot was hard. These were different angles in climbing than what I had trained for.

I could climb up, but climbing down was taxing. There were times when it was even hard to step down and find a rock as my thighs began to cramp up. But some other guards hurt worse than me, to my delight. Well sort of. I wasn't happy to see guys struggle but I loved that some who were almost 50 years younger than me were hurting. All those CrossFit squats, rowing machines and stairs were paying off for me.

We got through Little Corona and Big Corona Beach and came to the jetty. If you know the area, on the south side of the jetty is Big Corona Beach in Corona Del Mar. Then there is the channel for the boats to motor or sail in and out to the ocean. On the other side was the other jetty and "The Wedge" in Newport Beach. Then there was flat sandy beach all the way to Huntington Beach.

Of course I didn't know anything about what was next. But the next fueling spot was at the closest lifeguard tower near the jetty at Big Corona. Steve, the older guard who I had seen at 6 a.m. was here waiting for us along with some parents and Sandy. He had a jar of peanut butter and Gatorades waiting for us. Parents were there with stuff too. But here was Steve with his big infectious smile beaming with this big jar of peanut butter. He was asking anyone if they wanted some. It was 3:30 p.m. and I was cooked. We'd been going since 6 a.m. It had been a long day in the sun. He just smiled at me and congratulated me and said, "You only have a little more to go. You're almost there! You are doing great!"

Those were great words. He had such a huge smile on his face that it made his words believable. He said, "You need quick energy Robert. Here take some peanut butter" and he stuck out the jar to me." I looked at it and figured it was some sort of ritual and just stuck my two fingers deep into the creamy peanut butter and pulled out this big glob. He radiated joy and delight to see me stick my dirty sweaty fingers in my mouth and pull that glob off my fingers. He said, "Like it?" And honestly, it was really good. I couldn't talk right away but when I did I said, "Thanks, that was great!" It must have been the salt in my mouth connecting with the salt in the peanut butter. Then I got some Gatorade from Sandy and washed the rest down.

He then stuck the jar back out to me and I grabbed another, bigger glob of peanut butter and pulled those fingers out of my mouth again without much peanut butter on them. Sandy said, "That is so gross. That is terrible." I guess seeing all the other guys' fingers go in the peanut butter jar grossed her out. But I really thought it was great. I washed it down with orange Gatorade and said "Do you always have peanut butter at this point in the race" and he said "Yes, it was sort of a tradition." I shook my head in amusement. Sandy turned her head and said, "You boys are gross."

But it was a new experience that I had never thought of. I think it worked.

I didn't know if we were going to swim across the channel to "The Wedge" or what, but I wasn't going to ask. I was too tired to care. It would work out, whatever we did.

After a few minutes, Steve pointed to the Newport Beach Lifeguard Rescue Boat coming into Big Corona from Newport Beach and said, "There's the boat. Go swim to it." I thought "OK, I guess we are going by boat."

We all said goodbye. I kissed Sandy and waded through the Sunday crowds and swam out to a large, powerful, yellow and red rescue boat. It was designed to get to swimmers in the surf who couldn't get in to shore. It had an operator and a lifeguard who would jump off the back and swim to the swimmers if they needed help. The guard could either bring the swimmers back to the boat or pull them to shore on his long rubber orange buoy.

All of us swam out and one by one crawled out of the water. There was a wooden platform on the back of the boat in the water. All 20 or so of us fit in the back of the rescue boat. We just looked at each other without saying much. It was a really fun moment but it was nearly 4:00 p.m. and we were tired. The operator turned the boat around and gunned it and it took off. It took us about four minutes to get around the Big Corona Beach side of the jetty and over to Newport and "The Wedge."

There were some good size waves breaking at the Wedge like back in Laguna. It was a west or southwest swell and it was fun. The operator took us just outside the break, turned the boat around, lowered the engines and said, "OK, you're here. Have fun!" And one by one we hopped in and swam through the body surfers and breaking waves to shore. It was an unusual moment for people at The Wedge. All these guys jumping off the rescue boat, and swimming in only happens once a year. We were guards.

The Wedge is a world famous beach break for surfing and body surfing. I almost broke my neck there when I was living on Balboa Island going to Orange Coast College in 1971.

Back to the guards:

There usually is a pretty good sandy slope running down to the water from where the people watch. I climbed out of the water and climbed up the soft sand to where the people were watching. I just watched as all the guards who got out before me had climbed up the sand slope and were running away north towards Newport Pier. It took real leg strength. The Newport Pier was maybe two miles away.

I thought, "Unbelievable! This is nuts." This sand is so soft it is impossible to run in." But you run. I just put my head down and jogged the best I could along the top of the berm looking for any hard sand anywhere. There wasn't any. Not at the water's edge or on the berm or on the slope. I scanned the situation continuously as I jogged north. It was hopeless. Everyone just had to plow through.

I kept my head down and started counting my steps. It's a micro-goal technique to keep me going. At 100 left foot steps, I'd stop and walk 50 steps. And repeat. It was late afternoon about 4:00 p.m. in the hot sun. My legs felt tortured. But I kept going. I've been through this stuff before. I saw the Balboa Pier getting closer which was about halfway to the Newport Beach Pier. It didn't seem to be getting much closer very quickly. I'd been working to get there for a while.

I'd think about getting to the Newport Beach Pier later. I just wanted to get to the Balboa Pier as my next goal.

Then out of nowhere, David comes running towards me like he hadn't done anything all day. He had this big smile again. He says, "Hey, Mr. Owens. You are doing great! You've done it! You're finished. It is over! Just go up there by the snack bar and finish." I had my head down for so long that I didn't notice the progress I made.

Unbelievably, again I had the wrong information. It finished at the Balboa Pier, not the Newport Beach Pier!

I was so happy but tried not to show it. I smiled back and said "Thanks" and did what he said.

I went up the sand and into the snack bar area with outside showers and finished. No fanfare. No greeting. It was just over. Actually, I think some people thought I looked strange as a 65 year old semi-bald guy in my red speedos and blue Pararescue shirt. But I didn't care. What did they know about anything?

All the guards had found stuff to do, or were saying Hi to friends in other places.

I walked up, went to the showers, and washed the sand off my legs and then stepped onto the concrete walk way and froze. I couldn't walk. The bottoms of my feet were so tender and blistered that I couldn't walk and didn't want to. So I faked it like I was just observing the situation and slowly walked up to the base of the pier.

Gingerly I got up some steps and took off my water backpack that I had carried all day. I had run and swam with it, with no problems. I unwrapped my phone from my watertight homemade packaging and turned it on. It worked and was still dry. I called Sandy. She answered and I told her where I was. She said she'd be there in a few minutes, but there was a lot of traffic on the peninsula. I said "OK" and just stood there leaning against a pier railing. I didn't see any of our group but David came up to me again and congratulated me again and said what a great job I did. It was so nice. He is just a nice kid. David says nice things to everyone.

I thanked him for his encouragement all day and his loaning me his rubber rock shoes and he said "Forget it. No big deal. Keep the shoes until you don't need them anymore" as he saw that I still had them on. I asked if we could get a picture together. He had his phone and I had mine and we took pictures. That is the picture in the book.

Then he said that everyone is at the end of the pier having a milkshake at the hamburger place. He said they'd like to see me. I wasn't the last one to finish but close. I didn't tell him about my feet and that I barely could walk. Truthfully, the last thing I wanted to do was to walk out to the end of the pier and back for anybody. I said "I am waiting for Sandy then I'd come see everybody."

He said "OK" and left up the pier. Finally, Sandy arrived and pulled the car up as close as she could to me. Then I asked her to put it in park, since she was in a non-parking spot, and come up the pier stairs and help me. She did so and helped me down the stairs and into the car. She put a towel down on the seat and I plopped down into her seat. "Wow" I said, "that was a long way!" It was now 5 p.m.

And she took me home.

A little while later I got another call from David asking where I had disappeared to. I said Sandy and I had a few errands to run before the day was over so we couldn't stay. I had honestly been in the bath tub soaking my sunburned body and damaged feet. He said, "That is great. A bunch of us are going out for pizza back in San Clemente. Would Sandy and I please come and join them. Everyone wanted to see me."

I again thanked him but lied again and said that Sandy and I were stuck in Newport but wished them all a great time. Actually, I had moved from the bathtub to my old man recliner chair with ice bags on my thighs and really soft slippers on my feet like a really old person wears. He said "OK" and that he was disappointed. I told him I was really disappointed too but we could do it another time. And he hung up. I just smiled. I said, "San... I did it! I made it! If David only knew I was in this chair, he'd laugh. He thinks I am a stud. I am sooo done."

She said that she thought I'd done a good job and brought me a nice cold beverage. I didn't move for a long time. Then she was sweet enough to bring me dinner in that chair. What a great wife. I stayed there until I went to bed.

I was so cooked, but it was so much fun hanging out with that bunch of kids. I had made it. I was told I am the oldest guy to ever try this thing. I was amazed at the day and the peanut butter! Why didn't I think of that before? And those jumps were rad! They really unnerved me. But I jumped anyway and no one knew anything. Jumping is a trip whether it is out of a plane or with a bungee jump or off rocks. It always scares me. But you just do it!

It took me a few days to get my feet back but they always do. By Tuesday I was feeling pretty good and was at Crossfit by Wednesday at 8:00 a.m.

Now here is the fun part. Little did I know that David was a college graduate who had a brother being trained to be a Pararescueman. And

David had signed up to go in the Air Force as well in two months. He also was trying out to be a PJ. They both had slots from the 306th PJ Reserve Group in Tucson where a number of OC and San Diego Lifeguards guard were Reservists.

I had David and 11 other guys over for dinner about three weeks after The Quest. Some brought their parents and we talked about the military and about what the different military branches offered in the area of SOF or Special Operations Forces.

He went into the Air Force and is through basic training. Then he went through a BA (Basic Airman) Prep which is an eight week physical prep course to get him ready for Indoc and then went through Indoc. At Indoc graduation, he was given the Honor award by the instructors and is now in Jump School.

I was able to fly down to Lackland Air Force Base in San Antonio, and spend time with him and his BA Prep Class for a few days and then return for his Indoc graduation. He and his brother are great young leaders. The Air Force is fortunate to have them.

It was time to focus on Kokoro. It was two months away.

Two endurance events down, three to go.

David and I after The Quest run.
I can't walk, but he doesn't know it.
We're on the Balboa Pier after the race.

LEADERSHIP LESSONS

1. Research
2. Research
3. Research
4. Allow People to help you, which takes humility.
5. Develop mental Toughness and Confidence through experiences.
6. 20X Principle: Stay in "The Moment" and embrace mini-goals.

**The next chapter is about focus and humility.
There are times to just be quiet.
You are to be seen and not heard from.
Listen a lot, ask questions and learn.**

Saturday morning workout crew at SEALFIT.
Notice I'm training in military boots. I'm on the right.

CHAPTER 9

Training For Kokoro

When I began to work out at Eternity Crossfit in San Juan Capistrano in 2015, I knew I wanted to change the focus in my life. I was an 11 time IRONMAN finisher but knew there was a whole lot more in me than I was using. I got to Crossfit and I was challenged instantly.

Not since I was a Pararescueman had I been challenged the way Gary and the others challenged me. I considered myself a lazy IRONMAN and a recreational guy. I only worked as hard as I had to. People would always say, "Robert, if only you would train and buy a bike and ride it you could do great." But I was happy borrowing a bike for 11 years and just running on treadmills to get by. It worked for me in 1980 and it was still working for me. I wanted to just be a really well conditioned multi-purpose athlete who could surf and ski and do IRONMANs when I needed to. Crossfit radically affected me and I liked the way my body and strength levels were changing.

Then I heard about SEALFIT. I went online and read everything I could. I read about the academies, the 20x Principle and about his views on mental toughness. I read Mark's book about the 5 Spiritual Mountains.

In a sense, I found a second home. I looked forward every Saturday as I got up at 5 a.m. in Laguna Beach and drove down for the 8 a.m. class.

I had been working out for six months in Gary's Crossfit before I heard about Kokoro. And like the first IRONMAN in 1980 or the "The World Marathon Challenge" in 2016, I had to attempt it. It was audacious.

So I began to train only at SEALFIT. Kokoro took me two and a 1/2 years of five days a week training but I knew my "Why." I had to have that "oldest ever" record and be the first Pararescue and Air Force guy to accomplish it.

I endured that right shoulder surgery after the box jump competition which wrecked my shoulder. But it didn't deter me. It was a minor setback. I had time.

My workouts matured and I continued to do more of everything: push-ups, pull-ups, sit-ups, core work, stairs, squats, thrusters, runs etc.

When I finally got my shoulder back in January of 2017, I was discouraged that I'd lost so much strength but I was encouraged because I knew I could get it back. Plus, there was more in me. I could get better. I was 65 but I knew that there was more that had not been developed. I felt like a kid.

I had set my heart on the October, 2017 Kokoro. I was glad it was in the fall and not the summer or winter. Maybe it would not be too hot during the day, or too cold at night. I sweat a lot and long competitions in the heat have taken a toll on me before. I really disliked being any colder than I had to be, after doing rescue work in Alaska. I was hoping for a mild fall.

When I got back from Greece with a win, I started back again intensely. I did not want to just train but I wanted to be legendary at 65. I wanted to be an "old David Goggins". It seemed I was watching Kokoro YouTube videos daily. I wanted to be prepared. I added the weight vest to my daily routine to make it harder and began to do a lot of workouts with the vest.

What was really discouraging for me were my pull-ups. I came to Crossfit barely being able to do three dead arm pull-ups. I was still at six in June of 2017. I could do my 100 pull-ups kipping in the Murph, but not the dead arm ones. I've never been a strong guy, but I could go all day.

So I asked the men at SEALFIT how to increase my pull up gains in these last four months. Different guys gave me ideas which I tried. Fortunately, there were also YouTube videos on how to increase your pull-up strength. I gleaned a little insight everywhere I could. It worked. I got to 10 dead arm pull-ups by September and even got to 12 dead arm pull-ups by October. I was elated and stoked.

The people I trained with a SEALFIT were dedicated. Many of the men and women I worked out with on Saturday mornings did a Murph every Sunday morning. I didn't because I lived 40 minutes away and I owed Sandy some time. But I knew they were my standard.

A Murph every Sunday was crazy. But they enjoyed it and afterwards had breakfast together. Do you know many people like that? No trainers around, no one asking them to do it. They were just focused. And they had time standards for themselves. Dave Crandall and his son Matt were in that group.

There aren't a lot of compliments given out at SEALFIT. There wasn't much to compliment. We were in a culture where it was the norm to be quiet and do your work. Maybe you'd hear, "Nice run" or "Great job" for something but it wasn't expected.

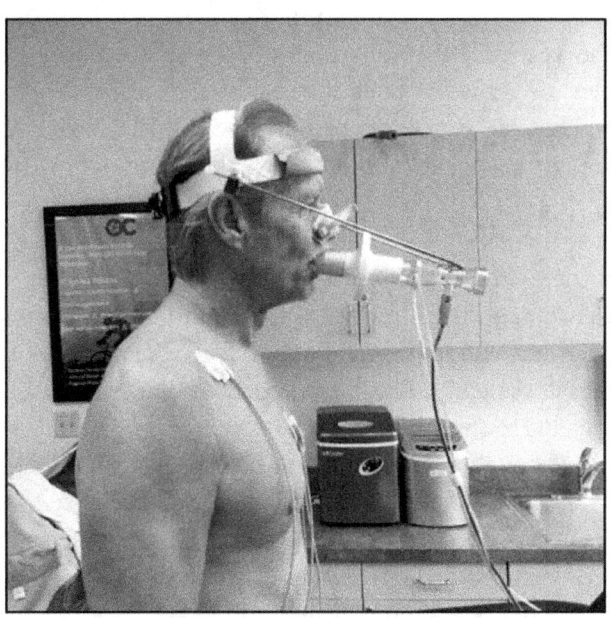

In the doctor's office for VO2 testing prior to Kokoro. I wanted every advantage I could find.

Occasionally an encouraging word would come my way or something. They were nice to receive. My goal was to watch and do everything Dave, a middle aged 50 year old guy named Trey and this tall, skinny 50 something guy named Chris would do each week. You would never guess if you saw them on the street that they were so tough. If I couldn't keep up with them, I shouldn't be attempting Kokoro. Trey had done Kokoro years ago.

By August 2017, I had stopped going to Gary's for the 8 a.m. class and had decided to drive most mornings to SEALFIT for their 6 a.m. class. That meant I had to get up at 4 a.m. I missed my friends at Gary's CrossFit but they didn't understand me. The SEALFIT people knew and understood my goals.

At 6 a.m. I'd do the SEALFIT class. At 7 a.m. I'd start my pull-up routine. Then I'd add in 100 burpees. Then I'd do 10 more for Kokoro. Hooyah! Then I'd do 20 more pull-ups in four sets of five. Then three more for Pararescue. Hooyah Again!

I'd follow that with my longer runs. I'd do the first run with the vest on. I wore one of three pair of my military boots I'd broken in. Then following the vest run, I'd run without my vest. I needed the different kinds of intensities. I really liked the runs there because I felt like I was in my zone. The runs were on a path alongside of PCH overlooking the ocean. I usually finished about 9 a.m. I was tired but not overwhelmed. I knew I was in a good zone and in a special time. My confidence was growing.

Let me mention something about my boots. In the three day Leadership Academy, they told us to show up in military type boots. I asked the other guys about this and they shared about the boots they had used in the past. Actually, Pat did his daily workout in his boots. After some talking and online research, I purchased a pair of desert sand colored Nikes. I bought them and filled them with water from a hose and put my feet in. I wore them for the next 8 hours so they would mold to my feet. Then I worked out in them and wore them for three weeks before the Leadership Academy to break them in. I wanted to 99% assure myself that I wouldn't have any blisters. It worked. But in the Academy, we were kept wet a lot. Whether it was with a hose or being in the lake, our boots were wet most of the time. I felt like I had made it through without blisters but I was lucky.

Going into Kokoro, I thought it would be wise to get another pair of boots as an alternate pair in case hot spots or something developed with my Nikes.

So I researched and decided on a pair of desert sand Rockies. Again, I looked for the lightest boot that I felt would work. I again soaked them with water on the first day so they would mold to my feet. These turned out to be great as well. After a few workouts they became like slippers. I couldn't believe how comfortable they were. I enjoyed working out in them as much as in my running shoes.

As we got closer to Kokoro, I kept thinking about the long ruck I'd be taking in Kokoro. It would be an all-night thing up a mountain and back down with my pack. Mike who worked at SEALFIT mentioned to me that there was a boot called Lalos. They were a tactical boot with a real strong metal shank in the sole for stability. He mentioned they were great for rucking. So I purchased a pair for $350 and broke them in with water and by training in them. I wanted to be as smart as possible and prepared for the unexpected. Didn't work, but at least I tried.

By the time October and Kokoro finally arrived, I was aware I was working out with at least five Kokoro finishers every Saturday. Two were Dave's son Ryan and his friend Matt. They did the May 2017 Kokoro while Dave and I were in Greece.

Matt was really strong and tough. He was crazy enough to come to a Saturday workout with a large apple. I thought, "What in the world is he going to do with that apple besides eat it afterwards." But as soon as the music was blaring and the one hour workout started, he bit into the apple and kept the apple in his teeth while doing the whole workout. Why? To make it harder to breath. Push-ups, sit-ups, wall balls, burpees and a run, he did them all with an apple in his mouth. The apple only had deep bite marks in it. He never took a bite.

I was told he crushed Kokoro.

Some of the guys would ask occasionally how my training was going and how I felt. I especially listened to the guys who had finished Kokoro before. I listened intently and searched their eyes, tone of voice and smiles for secrets. Those guys encouraged me to get more long rucking in. Like five to nine hour rucks up hills and mountains with at least 20 pounds or 30 pounds packs. I was not doing them, so I added them occasionally. It was challenging because I was tired from my other workouts. My dilemma was, "Should I stop doing something I was doing and add the rucks or just add the rucks?" I was doing about three hours a day as it was. In retrospect, I should have added the rucks.

A recap: It had been two and a half years of being up at 4:00 a.m. or 5 a.m. four to five times a week. Sometimes six. I was mentally tired. The trip to Greece and The Quest were nice breaks in the routine. But like anything you do the first time, I was training in fear. It isn't fun. It is fun, but it isn't fun. I could never do enough. It was just like training for the first 1980 IRONMAN. All fear. That is mentally challenging and occasionally draining.

The saving graces were the videos and podcasts that I had found. I listened to David Goggins over and over and over. I listened to Tom Bilyeu, and Tim Grover. His Book "Relentless" was so helpful. It took away my excuses. Choose to be good, or be great, or hopefully, legendary. Have epic moments and memories. It is my choice. And we play like we train. I wanted as Tim Grover said, "To be a closer."

I listened to Joe De Sena from Spartan Games and then Michael Phelps and other Olympians.

Every morning I did as Mark coached us at the three day Leadership Academy. I'd get up and swing my legs over the bed and breathe through my nose and begin to take on my feelings of tiredness. I was going to bed at 8:30 p.m. often and still waking up tired. I talked to myself all the way to a 5:30 or 6:00 a.m. workout.

Or I'd listen to Mike and Mike on ESPN Radio if they had a good conversation going on.

Why do I share this? Because I fought those daily voices in my head that wanted to lie to me and steal my dreams. I tried to feed my "Courage Wolf" as Mark Divine would call it. I envisioned myself being a strong 65 year old like Dave Crandall. I envisioned myself getting stronger and doing better wall balls. I envisioned myself being able to do 20 toes to bar with ease and doing repeats. And I just fought to become stronger. I did not want to be just a swim bike run weak endurance guy. In my big picture, this was still an experiment. I wanted to see myself getting into my 70's and 80's strong. The oldest man to have finished an IRONMAN is 83, I believe. I want to beat that.

Could I still be in the game at 84? Could I be strong into my 90's. It was a great vision to meditate on. At this point in my life, I didn't want to be a Crossfit guy nor a SEALFIT guy. I wanted a higher standard. I wanted to be a Kokoro finisher and a 12 time IRONMAN finisher. I wanted to finish 50 straight hours of this. And with no disrespect to Dave Crandall, I wanted the record of the oldest Kokoro finisher in history. We were going to be Class 48. That meant for 47 classes, no one:

1.) Had tried, or
2.) Could do, or
3.) Had the balls to attempt this at 65.

Plus, there had never had a PJ attempt Kokoro.

I was going to own this and stop taking nice subtle crap from these Navy guys around me. They always called me a fly-boy or gave me that laugh like... "It was nice that you were a PJ but you were only Air Force." I'd heard it often.

I wanted records. If Dave Crandall decided that he wanted the record back and made a comeback at 67, I would come back at 68. This Kokoro age record was going to be mine. I wanted to be legendary.

To add incentive, I was in contact with Josh Smith at USAF Pararescue Indoc. He was the Commandant of Training. He would be like the head Navy SEAL Trainer at BUD's.

He had read Mark Divine's books. He wanted to meet Mark and ask him Special Ops questions.

I emailed Mark and asked if Josh could come observe Kokoro. If so, he would go to Coronado and spend some time at the SEAL Naval Special Operations Compound. Mark emailed back saying, "Sure, glad to have him and meet him."

So Josh worked out a trip to observe Kokoro and my performance. I was 65 and representing the Air Force and Pararescue. It was epic. The Air Force Special Ops Training Commandant would be there watching. There should be a 25 year old PJ doing this for the Air Force. But it was me. I had to finish and drive my stake into the ground that Pararescueman were as tough as SEALS. Bring it on.

Then about three weeks before Kokoro, I was doing pull-up, push-up and air squat intervals with my vest on when my left shoulder tore. I was doing push-ups and straining with my hands wider than normal when I just felt that tear that you feel when you tear something. It was a moment. I went, "Crap..... I just tore my shoulder."

So I lowered myself onto my stomach and rolled over and got up on my knees. I moved my shoulder around and sure enough there was that pinch and sharp pain that I knew well from tearing my right shoulder 18 months earlier. I thought "OK, another challenge to figure out."

The last three weeks I took off my vest for push-ups and burpees and modified my hand placement when doing push-ups. It didn't hurt as much doing pull-ups fortunately but push-ups became a bear.

Looking back, the last few months were a blur. I was working some still as a business consultant, but not much. I was locked in. Sandy was nervous and scared for me as usual and wanted this done and behind us. She wondered what would happen if I had a heart attack.

And then I tore my shoulder. I would just have to figure out how to be smart and power though Kokoro with a torn rotator cuff. I was as ready as I knew how to be. The injury was just another challenge to make it interesting. What was I going to do? Quit and not show up? Are you kidding? There could be no excuses. Too much was on the line. I was ready to do this thing and get it behind me.

Added to this, my son Matt is a film producer and director who has been a cameraman at the Spartan World Championships in Lake Tahoe. I asked Geoff at SEALFIT if he needed another cameraman to help him over the 50 hours. Matt had a night vision camera that could be helpful since Geoff didn't film at night. He had to sleep sometime in those 50 hours. Geoff and Matt talked and decided that Matt would be allowed to come and help Geoff film. This was going to be a family affair.

I remember doing my last workout. It was on a Monday, Kokoro started on Friday. I was giggly. I was nervous. I was agitated. I was really intense. I didn't know how to "taper" for this but I stopped.

Now the wait...

LEADERSHIP LESSONS
SEVEN 20X PRINCIPLES

1. Pay the price. Don't cut corners. Suffer and Grow.

2. Cut everything out of your life you can to focus. Research, strategy, cost, change friends, find role models, ask for accountability. Start and Adjust.

3. Find a way to win, even with a torn shoulder. Adapt.

4. Visualize pain and practice going through it.

5. Talk to yourself: Feed the "Courage Wolf." All day.

6. Practice being overwhelmed and out of breath during all workouts, and staying in "The Moment"

7. Tell yourself, "I Love This!"

This next chapter is about the toughest experience in my life.

It lives up to its billing as "The Toughest Civilian Training In The World."

My personal experiment was to see if I could get stronger in my 60s as I got older. It took 3 years but my body responded. I changed from a lean Swim, Bike, Run guy to all that plus stronger. It worked. Seniors do not have to be frail.

Assisted handstands to strengthen those shoulders. I knew I was going to be challenged with Log PT at Kokoro.

Robert H. Owens

Thank God I love the ocean!

CHAPTER 10
Kokoro

I won't tell you everything about the beginning but it got your attention really quick. All 52 of us were waiting in the parking lot nervously. We had no idea what was about to happen. Being asked to be there an hour early gave us more time to live in fear. Then this white van drives out to us and no one gets out. It just stares at us. We don't know what we're supposed to do. So we just stood there trying to look ready and composed. We waited and waited. I began to sweat. After two or three minutes, an instructor gets out with his black hat on and his sunglasses on even though there wasn't any sun and asked us to get out our drivers licenses and tell a certain designated instructor if we had any medical issues going into Kokoro. The other instructor then marked the t-shirts for the guys with different issues like asthma, allergies or diabetes. Then guys gave the instructor anything they had brought with them like asthma inhalers.

Then he started yelling at us to get into lines or columns. Of course nobody could remember the difference. Many of the guys argued about what a column was so he just began to yell at us more for being fucking stupid. That went on for probably the next five minutes as he finally took control and got us into columns and inspected our clothing to see if we were wearing what they had told us to wear. Again, of course, almost everyone had something wrong with what they were wearing whether it was the T-shirt type or the stenciling on the T-shirt or the boots or the fatigue pants. We did nothing right, nor could we do anything right from the beginning. Then he'd see a guy smiling and say, "Get that fucking smile off your face fuckup. You don't have your shit together. Look at your T-shirt. Don't ever smile again. Do you understand fuckup?" A quick reply came, "Yes Sir." Then the instructor said, "I am not your Sir fuckup. I am your Coach. Don't ever say Sir to any of the instructors again. Do you understand me fuckup?" A quick, "Yes Coach" came back. We all just soaked it in. It had begun.

After he put the fear of God in us, he then said, "You guys better have your shit together. You haven't followed basic pre-event instructions so far. Some of you should never have shown up. Many of you will be gone quickly. You are not prepared. You think you are, but you haven't put in the time. You have lied to yourself." Then he just stared at us saying nothing for probably 30 seconds. Then he shook his head in disgust. He said, "God, this is going to be a long weekend. This class will be fun." Then he said, "Follow me and keep up with me" and took off running into some brush and into dry creek bed at the base of a dry scrub brush covered hill.

It was October and it looked like it had been a dry summer. Soon he yelled "Get down, get down, incoming fire. Crawl and keep your asses down." That's when we started crawling through gravel and thorns and ants and dry creek bed stuff. Of course, nobody could crawl correctly for them, so they yelled even more "Get your asses down!" The two coaches berated the guys who stood out to them. "What the fuck kind of crawl is that? You want to get your asses shot off?" After a minute or two they'd yell, "Get up. Let's go." And we'd start running again. After a minute or two we'd do it again. "Get down. Get down. They're shooting again!" We did that probably five or six times and it seemed like they'd always pick the worst places in the creek bed to have crawl.

Finally, we got through that and we followed the coach running up a hill. My heart was already jacked up with adrenaline so I had to quickly work on my breathing to get a hold of my emotions and focus. I needed to settle in and try to pace myself to surviving this test or "evolution."

We ran over the hill and down the other side.

At the bottom we ran to another hill up a road and were told to stop. We were broken up into Boat Crews or Teams and assigned a "Swim Buddy". Then the instructor pointed to the top of the hill in front of us and told as a group to start sprinting up it for time. Last guys get punished. "GO !"

At the top was an instructor watching with his dark sunglasses on. He said to different guys or the two women.... "What the fuck. Why did you even show up? Why are you so fucking slow?! You should never have come. What's your name fuck up ?" You'll be gone soon. GO! RUN FASTER!" And guys (and ladies) ran down this loose dirt rain rutted hill slipping and falling. At the bottom, that instructor was calling out the times. The last third of the guys were being berated as they got to him.

The first five or six hours they try to work you so hard that you quit. They hope half the class will quit. "Why have people here who don't deserve to be here?" one instructor said to all of us.

From noon to 11 p.m. they make you miserable and tired. I never knew that bear crawls and crawling in the dirt with my weapon could be so exhausting and painful. My hands and knees and elbows were scratched and cut.

The instructors just kept saying "This is the easy part. It only gets worse. Some of you should just quit now. You have lied to yourself. Go home and prepare and come back when you are ready. You need to leave." And my classmates started quitting.

About dusk, we had to do our first "Standards Test" as advertised. We had been going in wet clothes nonstop for six hours. It included pull-ups, push-ups and sit-ups for time which I passed.

My standards partner had flown in from Hong Kong. That is a long way! He paid his $2,500 entry fee. He had made his commitment. He failed all four of the push-ups, the pull-ups, the sit-ups and the air squats. He did 20 of the 40 push-ups required. I was embarrassed for him, having to call out his failing numbers. They asked him to leave. He was gone in a flash. I thought how could he have come all this way so unprepared?

We lost five in the first six hours then three or four more with standards test.

Then it was time to do the mile run test. It was dark now, and about 7:00 p.m., I was exhausted. They soaked us with the hose and told us to line up. My fatigues were sticking to my legs and my boots were full of water. They said "Up that road where we have been running up different hills was a truck. You have 9 minutes and 30 seconds to run up and around the truck and run back. Don't fail this."

The instructor said "Go" and off we went. It was a partial dirt road with sections of soft sand. It had little gullies in it from the rains. It was 1/2 a mile up and back. I was having a tough time getting traction and staying out of the ruts and soft sand. I knew I was screwed. There were only three behind me. My heart was beating out of my chest and I was struggling for air. So I concentrated on gaining control of my breathing and just focusing on my foot placement. Everyone it seemed was running downhill as I was still running up hill. I fought discouragement.

I had trained but it seemed worthless now.

I finally rounded the truck and took a deep through the nose breath three or four times as I began to run downhill. I knew it was now or never so I began to run almost out of control fast for me. I just focused on where I was stepping. I kept breathing deeply and concentrated on my legs and arms and sprinted. I don't know if I have ever pressed myself that hard before. Maybe in Crew in college at Orange Coast on the ergometer, or in the last 500 meters in the 2,000 meter race. But I was beside myself. I ran through the finish and Coach John was calling out times. 9:10 Owens. I had made it. And then I fought back puking, successfully.

I just kept walking down the road trying to be away from the others. I didn't care about them at that moment. My focus was in box breathing and getting my control back. I didn't want anyone to see me struggle, especially the instructors. As per my box breathing training, my emotions came back into check. I recovered relatively quickly. Those burpees and box jump repeats in training worked. And somehow, there were about seven others who finished behind me. How, I don't know.

Soberly, I reflected, I am six hours in and 44 hours more to go. I am in the game. Hooyah!

I can do this!

We continued as I will call it on "The Grinder." That is a PT place in the military. SEALFIT had its Grinder on a concrete parking lot surrounded my buildings. This Grinder was a dirt lot. It had pull up bars on one side for equipment and that was it. Except it also had water spigots with long hoses.

The point of the hoses was three fold:

1.) To keep us wet all day and all night.

2.) To harass us if you let it. Water isn't a big deal to me usually so I sort of enjoyed them coming around and spraying the water into my face while doing PT. Sometimes they got real close to my face with the hose but you just had to hold your breath a little bit. I'd just open my mouth and spit it back at the instructors. It was a calculated risk. It could make them mad and they'd punish me for it or they would get the idea that they were wasting their time harassing me.

Honestly, I sort of enjoyed it. It wasn't a big deal. Mostly over the 50 hours, when hosing guys down they left me alone. I just added a smile to the water I spit back at them. They would look into my eyes and see that I enjoyed it. A couple of instructors almost started smiling back. My challenge was that I had a contact in my right eye. I didn't want them to spray it out.

But some instructors didn't like my smiling. One in particular said, "Get that Fucking smile off your face. I don't want to see it ever again." That caused me to smile even more inside.

3) The water was to make the Grinder muddy. Therefore it made us wet and muddy too. Mud was a harassment feature to some. I learned back in Pararescue days, that anything external wasn't a big deal. Dirt, pee, crap, puke, mud were all externals. They wash off. You can get used to it. The strong do.

We stayed on the muddy Grinder from 6 p.m. until about 10:30 p.m. The Grinder was lit up with truck and car lights that were situated at different angles. At 9:30 p.m., it was time to do the next test: The Murph.

"The Murph" was a Crossfit test that was named in honor of Michael Murphy who died in Afghanistan. The Movie "Lone Survivor" is the story about Marcus Lutrell the Congressional Medal of Honor Recipient and his three teammates.

Michael was the officer who willingly sacrificed himself for his other three teammates. He died by making himself vulnerable to enemy fire while attempting to save his buddies. It is a tremendous story of heroism.

Everyone in any Crossfit Box knows what a Murph is and so do most military PT instructors. It is for time: a mile run, then 20 repeat sets of 5 pull-ups, 10 push-ups and 15 air squats and then another mile run. These instructors demand you do it in 70 minutes. Some places make you do it in 65 minutes and some in 60 minutes. Thank God, we had 70 minutes. We were in wet muddy fatigues and boots, plus we had backpacks with twenty pound sandbags and a full one gallon water bottle in our packs. They were like large round bleach bottles which made them unstable in the backpack while running or doing push-ups. They'd roll around if they weren't secured tightly.

I can't remember if we were broken up into two groups or we stayed in one but the Murph started after having done PT for nine and a half hours.

We were to run on the surrounding circular dirt road around the Grinder then come back and do our pull-ups, push-ups and air squats and then take off back down the dark rutted dirt road six times to finish. Part of the challenge was not twisting my ankles in the ruts in the road as there weren't any lights on portions of it. There were only three or four trucks with headlights lighting up the Grinder.

On the first mile you could hear yelps and groans as guys didn't see the ruts or drop offs. It was good to be slow and listen to where they were having problems before I got there. Since I couldn't see the guys but only hear them. I could remember the whereabouts by the sounds coming from the guys who went before me. I had to navigate those sections with great care. I thought I broke my ankle one time as it went into a hole but fortunately I went with the fall where I would drop and roll to avoid breaking anything. We knew that other guys in other classes had broken ankles and twisted ankles on this course before.

You'd ask, "Why would these Navy SEAL instructors do this with us?" It was to remind us that in war, things aren't neat and tidy. There would not be manicured roads by which to run away from the Taliban or Al Qaeda. Be aware and be smart. War is hell. Figure it out or die. You make a big, or little mistake, and you are out.

I got it and so did my classmates. Running in the dark took skill and a different form. Knees had to be flexible for the unexpected. Ankles needed to be ready to get twisted. You had to be alert and remember little things. Hands needed to open and poised for a fall.

I did my first mile and then headed onto the Grinder. There were instructors yelling and berating and challenging guys.

I had a fun time because I had a friend there. When I did Greece with

Dave Crandall, there was another guy there named Graham Dessert. He was from the Encinitas area. He was a buff stud and a Crossfit guy. He had made it through an earlier class of Kokoro. Sometimes in Greece, as we walked or ran we talked and hit it off. He was probably 35-40. Graham knew I was doing this and he had planned to volunteer for that weekend, which he could do as a Kokoro graduate.

As I ran onto the Grinder, Graham, along with another instructor were watching guys do their push-ups, pull-ups and air squats in the truck lights. They were the accountability guys that were stationed to watch each guy to assure that no one cheated but did all of the required reps - properly. If our form wasn't proper, they'd call us out and tell us it didn't count or start the count over.

I ran up to Graham and started doing pull-ups first then push-ups and then air squats. I did pull-ups first and air squats last because I would have fresher arms for the pull-ups if I did them after the air squats.

He had a green felt tip pen and after each completion of pull-ups, push-ups and air squats, he'd take the pen and make a line on the shoulder of my semi-white shirt. I needed twenty lines or four groups of five lines.

I'd do my pull-ups in front of him, then my push-ups and air squats next to him so as to save time in getting him to put a new line on my shoulder.

There were lots of guys needing lines and I didn't want to wait much for my line. I say guys because only one of the two women was left. The one who quit was a real athlete, 20-25 years old who flew in from Pittsburgh.

Graham would just smile, because he wasn't allowed to be my friend. But occasionally he'd smile and say, "You are doing great. Keep it up!"

When I got to my 20th line, he smiled and said "GO!"

Then I ran back out to the road and through the first unofficial obstacle section. I had almost twisted my ankle twice before on the first mile. There was a deep drop off into a ditch left by fast running rain water. I stopped and tippy toed through that section and made it through without incident six times, which was a victory for me. The second mile was easier because I had a pace, and some knowledge of the road and what to expect.

Finally, I turned the last turn and ran back on the lighted Grinder. An instructor called out my time. "Owens 63 minutes." YES!

I'd passed both my standards tests and now they couldn't flunk me out. And amazingly, there were guys still on the course behind me. Some more were eliminated after the Murph.

When I came into the Grinder, weirdly, some guys were still by Graham getting their lines on their shoulders. He looked up at me and whispered "You are a BEAST" with a big smile. It made my day and a rush of confidence surged through me. Here I was done and guys were way behind me! The next oldest guy in the class was 50! I was in the Game!

Guys finished and guys were gone. The instructors then told us to get ready to move out and get our weapons. Pretty soon we loaded into vans and we were going somewhere.

I knew in advance from asking around that one night you will be in the ocean, and one night you will ruck up a mountain. I wondered which one we would do now because the previous class did the ocean the first night.

We seemed nowhere close to an ocean after 30 or 45 minutes so I figured it was the ruck. Sure enough, these vans pulled onto some dirt road and drove a ways and stopped.

We were told to line up with packs and our twenty pound sandbags, (everyone had to carry a sand bag), our gallon water bottles and our weapon.

Then some guy said "Follow me and keep up." There was an instructor in the front and one in the back. And we started going up this dirt road.

The pace wasn't fast but it wasn't slow. I could do it but it took concentration and work.

Most of the guys weren't fazed at all. They were talking and laughing and having an easy go of it. It started about 12:30 or 1:00 a.m. I think. But after a while I was really struggling. I just couldn't keep up. You didn't want to be seen as struggling by an instructor. It was an invitation to being harassed or evaluated as weak. Instructors were able drop or kick candidates out on the spot.

At sunrise this dog came and was watching us as we were doing push-ups in the sand. On the beach we're wet "Sugar Cookies."

We had been told by Mark Divine that each of us would experience probably some dark moments in these 50 hours. He was correct. He said we would be tested severely. Mark Divine made it clear that most guys, if they quit, quit in the dark at night. Mark had admonished us, "Don't quit at night. What you are hearing in your heads at night are lies. Fight through until sunrise. It will get better at sunrise."

I was really struggling going up a steeper section. I just couldn't seem to keep the pace. I thought about dark places and had voices in my head telling me I hadn't rucked enough. The voices were having conversations about my plight and telling me I wasn't going to keep up. I was about to go into a dark place in the dark.

There was this tall lanky senior from Mission Viejo high school who was a beach lifeguard for "OC Lifeguards" by my house in Laguna. His name was Cody Harrison, he was also a lacrosse player. He wasn't fazed by anything so far. This whole experience seemed to him, and another 18 year old who was called "Q Tip" because of his bushy ball of curly blond hair, just a fun adventure.

I sped up to him in the pack of ruckers and humbled myself and said, "Do you mind if I held onto your arm for a while?" In the dark he looked at me and said, "Sure Mr. Owens. No problem. Hang on." I put my right hand around and inside his left arm and just held on. Wonderfully, he just sped up and pulled me with him. It was a new lease on life. The ruck up hill was three hours long. I held his arm for probably 20 minutes like an old man with a grandson and finally said "Thanks" and let it go.

It was a short lived euphoria. I began to fall back again in the next steep section, and I was too proud to ask him for help again but another guy had noticed that I had been helped before and he said, "Would you like to hold on Mr. Owens?" And I thanked him and quickly said "Yes."

I grabbed his left bicep and the same thing happened. I found myself again in the middle of the guys and then towards the front. That was amazing. Me in the front group. That lasted for probably 20 or 30 minutes until we came to level ground and I thanked him and let go. I wanted to give him a break. I was sweating even as it was getting colder the higher we climbed. Others were sweating too.

I did pretty well for a while because the dirt road flattened out, but then it became steep again, and I looked for my high school friend. I saw him and asked if I could get back on his arm and again he said "Sure! No problem." And I grabbed on and stayed on his arm until the road leveled off again. It must have been two or three in the morning by now but it was getting colder. I became aware of a light drizzle falling and we could see our sweaty breath. By the time we got to the top it was raining slightly. It wasn't a fun rainy moment. It was getting colder.

At the top the instructors handed out MRE's, those terrible military rations that were made 10 years ago. They demanded that we eat every morsel because they would help us. I squeezed out some semi-solid old crap from what was in the biggest pouch. Then I threw the rest away. I couldn't stomach it. The stew and the old saltine type crackers weren't any good. Nor was the chocolate. It was like eating semi-chocolate stuck together chalk dust. The whole experience left me deflated. If this was our food for the first time in 14 hours since we got there, I'd rather go without it. The instructors told us we had to eat all of it or else get in trouble. Then he asked, "Did everyone eat all your MRE?" I lied and said "Yes." I'd rather get in trouble than eat that crap.

The instructors made us sit down in the rain while we ate. We were all shivering and having a difficult time talking to each other. Guys were as close together as possible to try to conserve heat, which wasn't working but was a good survival try. I thought we looked like a bunch of shaking farm animals huddled together in fear of something.

Now, looking back, I felt and looked like one of those dogs on TV that have been mistreated and left out in the cold starving and shaking.

All of us did.

After 15-20 minutes this one instructor named Craig James who was sort of nice compared to the others said "Five minutes. Get yourselves together and throw away your trash over here. Let's get ready to go."

I had a tough time getting up. I was stiff and shivering. But I managed to roll over on my hands and knees and figured out how to stand up. He said "Let's go. It took us three hours to get up here but we are behind schedule". I had a tough time getting up. I was stiff and shivering. For the 50 hours we were always told we were "behind schedule" I needed to speed up. It was crap. They just played with your head to make us go faster. He said "We have to make it down in two. Let's go" and he started to run.

He headed down the hill and little by little we warmed up. I had brought a headlamp with me that I had bought at REI just in case they let me use it. And they did! I was amazed. No one got on my case.

We just kept hearing, "Come on you guys, we're late. We need to make up time. Let's go." And the pace quickened. This is when that 50-ish baldheaded personal trainer from New England made his first trip and fall. No one was allowed to stop for him, except a medic in the back who was to handle those issues. He was hurt but that was his problem. He tripped and fell a second time. When he got back with the group his face was a mess on the right side as were his hands. There was dirt and blood all over his face. He had tripped twice I guess when stepping into and around one of those ruts in the middle of the road that we were all navigating. When he got back with the group you could see he was tough but struggling. Then the medic pulled him off the course again. That was the last I saw of him. I was not sad to see him go. I thought he was a jerk and had an attitude. He was a short guy and seem like he wanted to let everybody know how tough he was. He also told everyone that he was an IRONMAN finisher. He was probably 50. I thought so what. I've done 11 of them and am 15 years older than you. Get over yourself. I just tried to stay away from him from the beginning. Now he was gone. Next.

I should say that there is a pastor nice guy side in me. But when you run into cocky guys, it can be enjoyable to see them humbled.

Back to the moment.

I had a tough time staying up with the group. Going downhill with my wet pants and my backpack was really difficult. An orthopedic surgeon from Tulsa asked me if he could carry my pack and I said "No". But he kindly persisted. He said he was a "rucker". He said he did 100 mile rucks with 60-80 pound packs in competitions. I was amazed and then said "Sure. Thanks." I didn't even know there was such a thing. I gave him my pack and he put it on backwards so that my backpack was on his chest. He just ran with mine on the front and his on his back. It didn't phase him a bit.

One of the instructors came by and asked what he was doing and he explained that he wanted to help his teammates. And he was helping me! The instructor said "OK." But a few minutes later another instructor came by us and said "What the fuck Doc? Give Owens back his fucking pack. He can carry his own weight and go home. Got it Owens?" The Doc argued a little but I got my backpack back.

Later, some other guys asked to carry my pack since the hardnosed instructor wasn't around. It was nice that the guys were looking out for me. However it was awkward as I wanted to carry my weight around these men. But guys would say, "Remember Rob, this is a team thing. Some of us are better a certain things compared to others. Let us help you. We have 30 hours to go! It was humbling to allow them to help me. I wondered where, if ever, I could help the team. How would that ever be possible? I agreed again. It was still really dark and no instructor would know unless they came by again. Most instructors stayed in the front or in the back of the group. I tried to stay in the upper middle section of the guys. Plus, all of us were used to getting yelled at and it wasn't that big a deal anymore. I let them. But later an instructor told the guys to give it back for me to carry. The good thing was that time was passing. Somehow that two hour run downhill kept me focused on not tripping and other stuff and kept those dark voices out of my head. I thought a lot about not being taken off the course like that other guy had. I didn't want to be like him. Mark Divine had said that different guys will have different dark moments over the course of 50 hours. Mine came quick that first night going up the hill. Fortunately I didn't have any per se going down the mountain.

Finally we made it to the bottom of the mountain and back to the vans. I was really tired as were the others. It had been an intense 5-6 hours. We were no longer cold at the bottom but sweating again. It was an intense 2 hour downhill run in the dark. Those high school guys still weren't phased. They were still loving it.

The instructors had us get back in the van and drove us back to Temecula and the Grinder. We marched into Vail Lake Campground about sun up. Staying awake in those vans was miserable. No one was allowed to sleep or it would mean team punishment. Most got busted for falling asleep at some point. Punishments were handed out to be done later. Once outside the campground area we marched quietly for 15 minutes past the sleeping campers and motorhomes and back to our secluded Grinder.

We were immediately hosed down and started PT again. Each of us during that PT time had to get back in the horse troughs of water. This was probably our fifth time so far. This time there wasn't ice in it. It was no big deal except the water had been sitting all night. It was cold.

Doing PT on the muddy Grinder with my backpack and a "weapon" that we all had to carry with us on the rucks.

However, once you're sprayed down with cold hose water the horse trough wasn't as shocking. Once you are wet you're wet.

I don't remember that morning much except that we had to check and refill our sandbags in our back pack, fill up our gallon water bottles and start our pushups with our back packs on in the mud. They also had us do a lot of squats with our sand filled PVC pipe "weapon" over our heads. It weighed maybe 5 pounds. They wanted to see how our thighs were doing after the ruck. I am not sure how I made it holding that squat position over and over. Most of the guys were suffering through them. But I do remember standing on the Grinder wet and muddy at attention at noon. Mark Divine commented how we had made it 24 hours.

Again we were given the opportunity to quit honorably. None would. We had about 20 of the 36 who had started still in the game.

That day is a blur. But I do remember doing PT in the mud and doing longer runs up different dirt roads. Just before dark we had to do "down pilot". It was a simulation of carrying a hurt pilot on a stretcher through incoming enemy fire. Of course, the goal was a team building exercise to get the guys on the stretcher to the top of a hill where a helicopter was supposed to come rescue him. Naturally, the team that did the best was rewarded and the team that lost was punished. The instructors picked steep hills with narrow dirt gravel paths of course. It was miserable. After that we ran back to the Grinder to be sprayed down again.

They fed us another MRE for dinner at dark and had us do more Grinder PT. I hadn't eaten hardly anything so far. Maybe a protein bar once or twice that they gave us and that lousy MRE on the mountain. Now another MRE. It was a little better but not much. I gave what I didn't eat to another guy. Then we were told to go get in the vans again. We all sat quietly as we were driven to the ocean. It was an hour away. No sleeping was allowed.

We arrived in Encinitas and unloaded at the beach parking lot where I trained. There were two different beach experiences or evolutions that night.

The first was at Swamis Beach. There were six flights of stairs of about 10 steps per flight going down to the beach. How do I know? Because they were a half a mile south of the SEALFIT Box. It was the turnaround point for our Saturday morning mile runs. I had run up and down the stairs at the end of my daily Monday-Friday workouts. One of our Saturday morning SEALFIT workouts was to run to the stairs and run down and up the stairs 10 times. At the top, we had to do 50 burpees each time. Then run a half a mile back to SEALFIT. I knew those stairs well.

We filled our water jugs at the top of the stairs and then were told to line up at attention facing the ocean. Coach John said to us "Well......... you made it through last night and you made it through today but I'm telling you the worst is ahead. Tonight will be nothing like what you've experienced so far. I want to give you a chance to stop now before this night begins. Usually, most guys make it the second 24 hours if they have made it this far. However I am just going to warning you: Most likely many of you will not make it through the night. Take a moment and talk to yourself. Are you sure you want to put yourself through this? You can quit now. You've done good to make It this far."

The last thing I wanted to do was talk to myself. I was tired and semi dry and I wondered if he was telling the truth. I thought to myself "I don't know if I can go through this. He may be right. Maybe I should call it quits if it's anything like last night." I felt numb. And then the other voice in my head said "You can't quit now! It's the beach! You've been waiting for this. This has to be a lot easier than last night because you'll be in and out of the ocean. That's not hard. That's easy. YOU ARE IN YOUR ELEMENT! Suck it up and go have fun. You knew this was coming and fortunately it is on the second night. The ruck is behind you. It's not going to be that hard. John is just bluffing again trying to get in everyone's head. Hooyah!"

He looked around and said "Are you sure you want to do this?" No one moved. So he just stared at us as we stared ahead at the ocean that was lit up with a half moon. Finally he said, "OK get your stuff and get down on the beach get your sandbags out and get them filled up again to 20 pounds. GO!

We put our water bottles back in our muddy crusty wet backpacks and ran down the stairs.

Wonderfully, there was a warm breeze on the low tide beach that night. It was so nice and unexpected. I had 40 years of beach moments go through my brain. I thought "This may be one of the nicest nights on the beach that I've ever had. This is a tremendous night! It a beautiful great night! Let's go!" I'm sure many of the others did not feel the same way.

The first evolution was team races up and down the stairs with our backpacks on. The winners got rewarded. The losers got punished. After one team won two or three times they mixed up the teams and made us race again. The goal was to just wear us out and keep the races competitive. The losing team usually had to do bear crawls or hold plank positions or do burpees while the winning team sat and watched.

One guy caught the eye of the instructors and they begin to verbally berate him and ride him really hard. He was having a tough time with the stairs and somehow they felt he had an attitude. He was getting slower and slower. But they didn't like something else he had done or said I guess on the stairs. The instructors kept talking amongst themselves about him. They didn't like him. Remember: every 10 or 12 hours we got new instructors. The rotating off instructors told the incoming instructors about the class. They would give their commentary on each guy to the fresh instructors. I don't know what the outgoing instructors said about this guy but this fresh group of instructors were on this guy quickly. It saddened me to hear them yell at him and cuss him out as they did. I thought they were being tremendously cruel. They were relentless. He'd made it this far and hadn't stood out before. I hadn't noticed him on the stairs as I was working hard just to keep myself together. For some reason, he now was in their crosshairs.

We were on the beach as he did one last going up and coming down. One instructor yelled at him to stop. He stopped halfway down the stairs. We just watched as an instructor went up the stairs to him. We all stood and listened as he just yelled at him and cussed him out for something. The instructor yelled at him that it was just a matter of time before he would quit because they were going to make his life more miserable. The guy didn't quit but went to the bottom of the stairs and rejoined us. Then our teams did another race up the stairs and this guy came down slowly. The instructors yelled at him some more. Then the guy finally quit. The instructor told him to get the fuck out of there. He walked back up the stairs in the dark and we never saw him again. We just looked at ourselves like "Wow.... that was intense." I wondered what had he done to get the instructors so mad at him? And for-sure I don't want them getting on me.

Then we started beach PT games and running in and out of the ocean. This was the part I was waiting for because I was a beach guy. It was so weird to be running in and out of the ocean with all your clothes on with those military boots. The water was sloshing around inside as I felt more and more sand getting into my boots. The front of my boots began to fill up with sand which was taking up my toe space. We would go in and submerge ourselves sometimes as two man teams and sometimes all together with our arms locked up as one big line. It was always different. And then we came out and did push-ups, burpees, bear crawls and forward and backward crabs over and over. Thank goodness it was low tide which meant the sand was hard versus soft.

We spent that first beach evolution finding out who was comfortable in the water and who wasn't. Some guys freaked out just going into a dark ocean with waves coming at them. Some guys got a little freaked having to go out as one big line of guys locked arm to arm and lay down in the surf. Sometimes we laid down arm in arm facing the incoming waves which meant you couldn't hold your nose or protect your face as the waves came on you. Some guys hated that. Other times, we faced the beach while being arm in arm and waited for the waves to submerge us. I looked for the guys with the most fear and rearranged them to be arm and arm with me so I could talk them through it. After a while, everyone did fine. You could figure this thing out. It was so much easier than running or burpees or holding our sandbags over our heads for long periods of time.

About three a.m. they told us to get up the stairs and get back in the vans. We did what we were told. We were wet and sandy and tired. Then they drove us about three miles south to a big wide open beach where I had turned around on my training runs on PCH.

They told us to get out and line up on the beach. This beach had lots of soft sand compared to the last beach which had hard sand with lots of pebbles in it.

They told us to hit the surf and get completely submerged then run back up and do a sugar cookie. A sugar cookie is where you have sand rubbed on you everywhere by your swim buddy. If they could find a non-sandy area on your face, head or body, you'd pay for it.

Of course they always found fault with someone so we had to go back into the ocean many times and re-cookie ourselves. Our swim buddies had a responsibility to make sure there wasn't a place on our bodies that didn't have sand on it. You can imagine your partner spreading handfuls of sand all over your head and body. The half moon wasn't up enough to see well, which is why the instructors used flashlights and always seemed to find those areas we missed.

I knew my son Matt was around filming because on his night vision video camera, he had a green light on the front. I could never see Matt but I'd see the green light off in the distance moving around both nights. He was not allowed to talk or communicate with me for the 50 hours. But it was good to know he was there. Actually after the second night, the instructors loosened up a little and let him be closer to me than before. It was fun to catch his smile occasionally.

Running and rolling around in the sand at 4 a.m. was quite an experience.

I remember seeing 15-20 guys doing lunges up and down the beach in the dark with our wet sandy twenty pound weighted backpacks on. I don't think I'll ever forget it. I say 15-20 because I don't know how many guys were still there. It didn't matter to me. It only mattered that I was still there and my swim buddy was somewhere close to me.

We would do 300 lunges in the soft sand south down the beach and then have to sprint back north to start them again. We did them over and over. Of course instructor John reminded me consistently that I was a fucking embarrassment to myself. He kept asking me "How could I be so fucking slow?" I didn't say a word or look at him. In a way I got used to him. He wasn't going to get in my head. I had enough voices arguing in my head already without letting his inside as well. The key was to just breathe and focus.

My legs and thighs were shot. They just weren't moving fast. Especially in those wet and sandy fatigues. I want to say… anymore as I'm not sure if they had moved fast in a long time. I could stay up with the guys in PT but I was cooked when I was running and doing lunges. I was so discouraged because I had done thousands of air squats and heavy squats at CrossFit and at SEALFIT in preparation for this. It was as if I'd never trained a day. Except I found a way to always do one more. The key was to stay "in the moment" and just think about the next lunge and breathe. Over and over I'd say out loud if an instructor wasn't standing next to me: "I can do this. I'm feeling good. I'm looking good. I am going to Hollywood. I paid for this! I love this. This moment is not too big for me. This evolution will be over soon. This is Epic. Just keep going. I am a BEAST." And then repeat.

Self talk kept the voices in my head at bay. They couldn't discourage me if I couldn't hear them. I had to fight them off. So I talked out loud to myself over and over. I also had the confidence that I knew this evolution would be over soon like all the rest. I had made the mountain ruck. This wasn't as bad. I knew I could survive this. Whenever an instructor came by I smiled even if they were cussing me out. It was a game. Just focus.

It was right after this that we did the stairs that I mentioned in the beginning of Hour 44. The instructor who would later be at the top of the stairs who called me a BEAST saw me at the end of this sand lunge evolution and just smiled. I thought it was a nice smile and he was just being nice. Maybe it was a nice encouraging smile or he was just looking at me and thinking what I was about to face. He knew what was coming. All those lunges were to prepare us for those backwards bear crawls up those stairs. It is like a dentist who smiles and is nice before he puts his mask on to do a root canal.

I mention this again because seeing a smile for any reason from anyone after 40 plus NON STOP Hours was a tremendous confidence builder for me. It helped remind me that it was a game. I knew the Instructors mental game was to try to discourage me and tear me down while they wore me down physically. They wanted to know if they could crush me and kill my "Why". So to see a smile or hear an encouraging word from anyone was huge. I chose to believe his smile was sincere. Maybe it was sadistic. I made it work for me.

I tried to again to stay in the moment and breathe. I had to keep my emotions in check and just do the work. I got the BEAST comment at the top which reset me.

After the stairs we went down to the sand again where the vans were parked. The sun had to be coming up soon. It had been a long night.

The group went back down the stairs and walked down the sand again to where the vans were parked. Instructor John called a team meeting so we all sat down in the sand and he began a talk with us. He became a nice John again for the first time in a long time. He told us we'd done good. And he asked us questions about what we were learning. Then he asked us questions about us personally.

Looking back, I think he was killing time. I believe we were to be back inland in Temecula at a certain time and we had a few minutes to kill. Whatever the reason, it was nice to have a reprieve from the shouting and yelling and PT for a few minutes. It was now maybe 4:30 a.m. We'd been up about 42 hours.

Finally, we were told to get into the vans again and not go to sleep on the hour ride back inland. The van drivers turned on the heaters up on high again to make staying awake really difficult and drove us back. The threat was made, "If any of you get caught sleeping the whole van will pay when we return in burpees."

I chose to sit as close to the instructors as possible so as to try to listen to them and stay awake. I knew if I went into the back of the van I would never be able to stay awake. It seemed the driver would turn on the van light every five minutes and would turn around while driving and half the van was asleep. He'd yell, "What the fuck do you guys think you are doing. That is 25 more burpees when we get back to camp!" I don't know if we didn't care or couldn't stay awake no matter what, but I think he stopped looking back at us at 200 burpees. He turned around directly at me and caught me three times nodding off. Of course he'd say, "Unfucking believable Owens. How stupid are you. Can't you follow directions ever? You are a shitty role model to these men. That is 25 extra for you old man." Then he'd shake his head and say to the instructor in the passenger seat. "Can you fucking believe Owens here? He can't do anything right. He hasn't done anything right all night. Unfucking believable." Then he'd turn around and look at me.

Strange as this was, on the way back, the two instructors were talking about starting businesses after getting out of the Navy. They were talking about internet strategies to attract people to their websites. I took a risk and made a comment about a strategy I'd used in the past and they both listened. I knew that if they'd break character with me and talk with me it would help keep me awake. As it turned out, the next 20 minutes turned into a conversation between us. They became nice again and we interacted about business. I shared some business consulting experience and they listened and asked me questions. It worked. They stopped calling me names and stopped turning the light on in the van. Guys slept and I was able to stay awake. It was so strange to have these Jekyll and Hyde moments with the instructors. I never knew what was going to happen next.

We finally made it back inland to Temecula and the Vail Lake Campground and Resort about daylight. We got out of the vans and were marched back into camp. Then we finally marched back into the Grinder area.

It was good to march quickly because it was cold. I could see my breath and we were still damp and sandy from the beach.

At the Grinder the yelling started again. We then were sprayed down with the hoses while in the push up position and started PT again. We had to do all kinds of weird push-ups and things in the mud. The key for me was to just budget my energy and emotions and just do whatever they demanded. They would usually pass you by quickly if you didn't stand out. It was dark and they could see a lot but they didn't see everything or everybody all the time.

They also weren't sure all the time who they were yelling at or giving orders to. Therefore I just tried to cruise and stay below their radar. We'd been through a lot of this already. I could do this. Usually, they would yell at you because you were a body. In a moment they'd move on to the next guy. If you could find an area where the instructors didn't come around as often, get there.

Somewhere in all that my name was yelled. I was told to come over to the horse trough that was filled with ice and water.

The instructor or volunteer said get in head first which meant you slid in head first on your stomach until all of you was in and underwater except your head.

Then they'd watch you and tell you when you could lift yourself out. What they are looking for is any hesitancy or fear. If you didn't give them any then they'd maybe let you get out of there quickly.

The water was chocolate colored from the mud that had washed off the previous guys. It was a sort of eerie fun. The night was really dark, with only the light from the cars and trucks headlights.

There was a shine on the mud on the Grinder when it wasn't being splashed around in. The ice water in the horse trough looked like the sea in the movie Titanic.

I stayed in until he said "Turn over Owens." It was a challenge to do so, as I am tall but I turned over and then he just stared at me. I smiled back and closed my eyes with my head leaning back like I was taking a bath. I wanted it to look like I was relaxing. I wanted to convey that all was good and I wasn't bugged by being in there.

He then yelled at me to get out then changed his mind again and said get back in and sit down with my legs hanging over the sides and out. Then he told another guy to get in with me.

All this ice water sloshed out with two of us in there. For both of us to fit, we had our arms and legs over each other's. We were crotch to crotch, pressed into each other. It actually took some flexibility, a little "Kama Sutra" and it would have been a real hot intimate moment if we were a couple, but it was just us. Our faces caked with mud, in our hair and everywhere. We just looked at each other. He wasn't smiling. I probably wasn't either. I don't remember who he was. Actually, it's not important. Just get through it and move on to whatever else was waiting for us.

The instructor just looked at us and smiled like he had found a new way to make men miserable.

Of course it wasn't a new thing, we had been in the horse trough a lot during the day to cool off from the hot 86 degree daytime weather.. He just wanted to play with us. He made some stupid comment like, "You loving this guys?"

I'd been in there awhile now. I will try to explain it, I was cold, but not real cold. The hose water was always cold at night. The spraying just brought an agitation to how you were going to be wet. The ice water just changed up how you were to be cold and wet. There was cold and colder. Now it was really cold with the ice. You couldn't let it bother you or get to you. The ice was just for effect. They wanted an emotional response from you.

Then I thought, here we go. I looked at the instructor and took some of that muddy ice water in my mouth and slowly spit it out like I was a fountain in someone's backyard. He just stared at me. Don't know if it worked per se, but in 30 more seconds he yelled at us and told us to get out. It was a challenge for both of us to disentangle and get out. As we were exiting, he grabbed the hose and started refilling the horse trough and putting more ice in the water for the next guy or guys.

Mud PT went on for a while. Then we were marched in silence to a pool area that turned out to be a large community pool with a cyclone fence around it.

We were told to take off our boots and line them up on the side of the pool. The instructors then led us into more PT on the pool deck. We did bear crawls and push-ups around the deck while the instructors hosed us down. We became pretty cold instantly. Then two by two he had us go over to an outdoor shower and wash the sand off ourselves. The instructor said the pool people didn't like dirt and mud in their pool and we needed to honor their desires. All the time the instructors looked warm with their jackets on.

Each team of two guys had 60 seconds to wash the sand off ourselves and get back to our place on the pool deck. We were all shivering. The showers were cold water but it didn't matter because the water from the hoses had been cold water. It was all the same.

Then we all had to get in the pool in the deep end and tread water with our hands out of the water. Again, we had our fatigues, shirts and socks on. Some really struggled. No one was kicked off the team but there was a lot of yelling. I think if we'd made it this far, they were not going to

We were sprayed down while in the Pushup position frequently.

kick anybody out now, but who knew? They weren't pleasant with us.

This pool PT and swimming lasted a seemingly long time. We had to swim relay races, do pool side PT and more swimming. Often, when we weren't in the pool we were doing bear crawls around the pool, or put in a plank position. The steam from the pool reminded us that it was chilly outside. Later we found out that before sunrise it was 47 degrees. As long as we kept moving we were OK. But the pool deck was cold as well as the water on it. My fingers began to become white.

The instructor liked tag team races with our clothes on. We all just thrashed around. We may have had four teams, of four or five guys. If one team won too much, he'd change the teams to see who would try to win the next time.

We'd be told to race. I was pronounced the 3rd fastest swimmer. The instructor finally began to say to me, "Owens, don't let that guy beat you. Go!" He made me race over and over as he did others. His goal was to just tire us out. It didn't really matter who won in the pool. I finally figured out that he wanted to wear the ones who weren't so struggling, out. So more races. It worked on me. I was finally getting tired of swimming. Then when he felt satisfied, he lined us on the pool deck and told us to go get our boots and put them back on. Getting my wet muddy boots on over my wet socks was a challenge. I had super "pruned" feet that were white and stiff.

I had been informed and warned about this next evolution. It was called the second morning's breakfast.

I mentioned in Hour 44 in the beginning about enjoying my face in the mud puddle with my swim buddy Grant Langham. You can see us in the picture. He is a 45 year old or something businessman who is a great guy. He was from Denver and was planning on going into Seminary in the next year or so. He felt he was called to go into the ministry. Somehow, as we were standing in the parking lot waiting for the Kokoro instructors to come bring us in to the Grinder, that information leaked out. We were told to be in the parking lot an hour early to get ourselves ready. So 36 of us just introduced ourselves and talked, waiting for the onslaught from the instructors begin. Somehow we were made swim buddies after 6 hours and after the "Standards Test". It was sort of fun being randomly paired together. He called me Pastor and I called him Christian or something. We were a strange team in this setting of f-bombs. He said he had always wanted to try out to be a Navy SEAL but it just didn't happen. He liked that I was a PJ and then a Pastor.

I had been informed and warned about this next evolution. It was called the second morning's breakfast.

Sure enough, while dripping wet we were told to line up. We were now informed that we were going to be given a treat: a warm breakfast of bacon, eggs and hash browns. Some were thrilled. I wasn't. We were all really hungry because we hadn't had anything to eat except two terrible MRE's since we started. But I was told by previous Kokoro finishers the nice breakfast was a set up. They'd let us eat, then work us out again to throw it up. It was a test on our emotions and self-discipline.

Knowing the upcoming test, when the plate came to me, I ate the bacon and scrambled eggs but hardly any of the hash browns. I thought I could hold down the eggs and bacon but didn't want to chance it with the heavy hash browns. All the guys were different. Some only ate a little and some ate everything on their plate. Others ate what wasn't eaten on another guy's plate. You could even ask for seconds. We told it was a reward for making it through another night.

The challenge for me was that I was shivering and my fingers were now white. They had us sit down on the wet, muddy, cold, tall 4" thick, uncut grass. I remember it perfectly. You sank down into it and into the mud below it. Someone had watered the grass during the night.

We were allowed to sit back to back for support. However, the longer I sat, the more I shivered.

The sun was just beginning to come up but it hadn't brought any heat with it. It was now the coldest part of the night. Finally, I went to move and my whole lower back seized up. I can't remember ever in my life having it happen. It was like someone cinched up a belt of knives around my waist. I gave a yelp but no one noticed. Each guy was in their own state of discomfort or was half asleep.

But I was in real pain. I thought, "Is this a deal breaker like Dave got in his first Kokoro attempt?"

After a minute or two of trying to move my way out of pain, I called to the medic who was over by himself eating.

He came over and I told him my predicament. My back was spasming. He put down his food and reached out his arms to me and pulled me up to my feet. But I couldn't walk or move. I just stood there shivering in pain. I don't remember how but he led me to a concrete block restroom building. There was a concrete slab around the building and he had me lay down on it.

The cold concrete wasn't a break from pain. It just like putting my back on ice. That increased my shivering. He then got out a metal blanket and tucked it around my wet shivering body.

I noticed with excitement that the sun was just peeking up over the tops of the trees in the distance. It had to be about 6 a.m. It had to be about the 44 hour mark. We had six hours to go until about noon when this thing would be over. We had made it through the second night! Now

Pool PT in the mid 40 degrees, and yes, even though we were wet, they kept spaying us down! That is steam coming off the pool.

I needed to make it through this.

Somehow the metal blanket didn't work immediately but maybe the shivering gave it life. It was one of those dark moments when my hope of finishing began to fade. Laying on the cold concrete shivering and shaking harder than I'd ever experienced rocked me. The blanket began to warm me up everywhere except my back. The medic talked to me a little and tried to stretch me out but it didn't work. Movements meant pain. He then said I was done. I had to quit. I was disqualified. He was taking me out of Kokoro on a medical issue.

I told him he was crazy and I wasn't out. He was some short Hawaiian Army guy. His name was "K". He thought he owned the world and talked like he was God's representative. F him. He finally left me alone on the concrete shivering but came back with the super intense instructor who led the pool PT and the breakfast experience.

This guy now came out of intense mode. It was Coach Rob Ord (co-founder of Kokoro). He knelt down like a guy who really cared and shocked me by saying, "How are you doing Owens?" I told him I was fine except my back was locked up. He smiled and said he understood. He then took the metal blanket off me and began to stretch me slowly on that cold concrete. But at least the sun was coming up.

He did that for two or three minutes then said, "Just stay here and warm up." So I laid there and the sun hit that blanket and felt like a million dollars. He turned around and left me with the medic. I didn't say anything to him and he didn't say anything to me. He just stood there writing something down on a clipboard.

After a few minutes that now nice instructor came back and checked on me again. I was shivering but not as much. He stretched me again. I heard my teammates doing PT in the distance. They were doing jumping jacks and other stuff probably trying to get warm.

I said to the instructor, "How much time do I have before I get dropped?" He said he'd go check. About three minutes later he came back and said I had two minutes to be with my team. And then he smiled. "Can you do that Owens?"

I said, "Yes, if you'd help me up." And then an amazing thing happened. I heard my team calling out my name in the distance on the grass by the pool. They were yelling, "Come back Owens. Come back Owens. Come back Owens....."

They probably all yelled that 8-10 times. Then Coach Ord looked at me smiling and said "They need you to come back." I asked him, "Who told them to do that?" He said "Nobody. They miss you. You are the old guy. You are the leader. They respect you and want you back with them." Tears came to my eyes. As you might imagine, that was an amazing moment.

The medic stood off to the side and Coach Ord helped me to my feet. I sort of ran back around the corner to where I could see the guys doing relay races. They stopped and started shouting words of encouragement to me. When I got to them they cheered. They were smiling and happy for at least a moment and so was I. It was back in the game. It was like in the movies for me. Then I started running relays with them.

I think I missed about 20-30 minutes of PT. Soon an instructor told me to go see a different instructor about 30 yards away. That was instructor Scott Jones. He seemingly always had his sunglasses and his black hat on whether it was day or night. Coach Jones said to me, "Owens how's your back?" I said "Good coach". Then he gave me one of those fun sadistic smiles. He said "Owens, I want you to run as fast as you can and give me 16 somersaults in a row. Got it?" I knew immediately that he was testing me to see if this would take me out. I also knew it was throw up test time. I thought to myself, "He's coming after me. He's trying to take me out. How dare he! That is mean. He could cut me a little slack, couldn't he?" The muddy grass was cold and wet. With each somersault would be a splash. It was a moment.

I said "Got it" with confidence. In a split second, I thought to myself, "This is about technique. Just get the angles right when rolling on your back. You've got to protect your back. Figure this out! Breathe!"

I ran and jump-rolled on the grass and then rolled again and again. All the time thinking about the splashing mud, hearing Coach Jones yelling "Faster", and counting the rolls. I also tried to figure where was the best place to start each roll was with my head and neck. The head and neck is the first contact point in the roll. I hadn't done any in probably 50 years but I knew from somewhere what I was doing. Isn't that weird!

I missed a few times and it hurt. But after a few I sort of figured how to start each roll. When I got to 16 I slowly got to my feet. I was really dizzy. I located Coach Jones with my blurry eyes and yelled, "16 Coach! Hooyah!"

Then I just stared at him to see what he'd do. He and the other instructor also just stared at me. He said, "Run back here NOW!" I ran back to him and the other instructor who were enjoying this way too much. Coach Jones said to me, "How do you feel Owens?" I wanted to own the moment and not let them enjoy seeing any pain in me and said, "Great Coach. Thank you. How many this time?" He just stared in my eyes to see what he could see and said, "Good. Give me 16 fucking more! GO! This time you better be faster!" So I did them again but they weren't faster. He just got 16 more. It was now fun and easy being outside rolling around and being a little dizzy after 45 non-stop hours.

Everything they hoped would happen in that test didn't. I didn't break down and I wasn't overwhelmed. Like being sprayed in the face with the hose or the ice baths in the horse troughs; they didn't faze me and this, like the stairs, didn't break me.

I had this overwhelming amazing moment thinking: Here I am two days away from my 66th birthday running and doing somersaults on this wet muddy cold grass at sunrise after being on that concrete slab and told that I was out and being dropped by that cocky Army medic. This is tremendous!

I thought, "I am in the Game! I am living life. I am alive! Wow!"

Euphoria came over me. I was thrilled and so happy. I felt like this whole thing was just getting started. I didn't feel tired or sore anymore. I was overcoming and going to make it.

Then Coach Jones told me to stop doing somersaults and we were now going to have log rolling games. I was to lay down in the cold wet grass and put my arms above my head with my hands clasped and roll like a log away from two other guys doing the same thing. It took a lot of core.

They were going to roll and try to tag or touch me. If they did, it would be burpees for me. If they didn't tag me in a certain amount of time, it was burpees for them.

Back on the muddy cold grass we went. They separated us and the game began. I found that I could roll pretty fast. It took about a minute for them to catch me the first time. But I didn't have to do burpees.

Then we did it again. It took longer the second time for them to box me in. But there wasn't anyone puking. We were laughing. The other two guys were in their 30s. I was doing a respectable job of staying away. No burpees again for being caught.

Then they did it again but this time I joined one of those guys in rolling and chasing his ex-partner. All this time the other 13 were running PT drills of some sort about 20 yards away from us. We could hear some of our teammates puking breakfast as we did our log rolling. They paid for that nice warm meal.

I guess the three of us missed what the other 13 had already done here in the mud. I was sad when the games stopped because it was way easier than PT.

By now the sun was up and it was warming up. For the next three hours we did tug of war contests, running games where we had to carry guys on our backs, dizzy team games, sit-ups and push-ups.

I felt like we were cruising to the 50 hour finish line. I had a great time in the sit-ups. The instructor said, "I think you should do 50 sit-ups. Don't you?"

"Yes Coach", we yelled back. So we counted out 50. "Up 1, Up 2, Up 3" and so on. We got to fifty and the instructor said "Great, you looked good. Let's do another 50." We did. Then another 50, for 150. And he kept going. We got to 350 sit-ups and the instructor says, "What the fuck" he said to one of my classmates. "Can't you keep up with this fucking old man?" "Good job Owens." We then rolled over and started another 50 push-ups.

I was again elated because I was in the Game. All those extra morning sit-ups and core work at Gary's and at SEALFIT had paid off. I was crushing it. Back in training no one understood why I was putting in that extra time, but I did. Group think would have left me unprepared for this moment 45 hours into this test. Thank goodness for those videos of David Goggins and Tim Grover and others. My fingers and parts of my hands were still numb and a few of my toes were still numb but it wasn't a big deal now. They were small side issues that weren't deal breakers.

We stayed on the grass doing PT by the pool area until about 10 a.m. I think. We had been there since before sunrise. Being at the beach seemed like a long time ago. Then they lined us up to go back to the Grinder.

We marched back to the Grinder. I was coming to really dislike that part of the 50 hours, to PT or to the vans or whatever. Somehow, I developed AN ATTITUDE in this running and speedwalking thing.

Log PT - it's a team building exercise made all the more fun since we were being sprayed down.

From Scott Jones, SEALFIT Instructor:

People who choose to test themselves in the most severe manner achieve the highest levels of success. I have the honor of putting people in positions to recognize their own weakness and either push through it or succumb to it. I will prompt them to overcome an obstacle, but that is on them. The obstacle remains and I will not cheat them by removing it.

What may seem "sadistic" at first glance, is embraced and relished by those who know the reward found on the other side. Lots of times people compare our coaches to "sharks who smell blood in the water" when someone is struggling. I assure you, their approach is to promote growth. Struggle is the fertilizer of mental toughness.

Take your experience, what you initially saw as sadistic actually wasn't. You were struggling because your body was giving out. It wasn't a mental lapse and you weren't looking for a way out. When I told you to do the 16 summersaults again and again, it was because your back was weak at that point. The best way to work through that weakness and pain was to address it directly, not with rest, but with movement. I knew that if you could do the tasks I gave you, you would begin to trust your body again. As you know, where the mind goes, the body will follow. You took that and used it as further mental fuel to drive yourself to continue.

Today, there are too many people looking to have challenges removed for them and too many people who truly believe they are serving others by doing so. I disagree.

Respectfully,

Scott Jones

We got to the Grinder and they started hosing us down again. The Grinder wasn't muddy enough anymore. Then we had a an exercise called "Will to Win" rock carry for a couple of hours, then started Log PT. The point of Log PT is a team building exercise on following directions perfectly or a teammate suffers when one guy can't do his part.

I am not going to go on with all the last 2-3 hours of stuff because some things need to be not talked about. But it became as miserable as anything before. Maybe because we were at the 47+ hour mark but the Grinder became hot and muddy and miserable.

Mark Divine and his coaches have some closing rituals that are unique to say the least. But every time you thought it was about over, it wasn't. There was always another surprise awaiting you to assault your senses and mental condition. It was again mentally draining and challenging. They wanted to crush us a few more times.

One of the things that really stood out to me was when Mark Divine asked us towards the end, "How many of you could go another day or 24 hours?" We all looked around at each other and most raised their hands. It was a surreal moment. He talked a little more about that. He said that there is more in all of us than we ever allow to come out. He said he knew we could do another 24 hours. That is why the kids in Navy SEAL Hell Week go from Sunday at 5 p.m. until Friday at 5 p.m. It was to prove to those young men that they could if they had to.

We learned over the 50 hours, that time became irrelevant. It wasn't the driving factor in this test. 50 hours could have been 30 hours or 70 hours. It wasn't about time. We were tired from the first hour on. But we pressed ourselves beyond our mental limitations which was the point. We could do far more than we had ever expected. Mark said, "Knowing that, will change your lives." And in many ways it did, and has.

That experience set me up for the challenges that were coming in 8 weeks during the 777.

Finally, the real end happened. Mark stood before us and said, "Class 48. You are secured. Congratulations."

We were elated! I turned to some guy and just hugged him. Others screamed for joy and kissed each other. I couldn't believe that this time, it was really over. For me: The Game finally stopped.

I was stunned that it was really over. I thought they were faking us out again. But it was done. We'd finished and I'd finished.

Class 48 jumped up and down and hugged each other for about four to five minutes. We had made it. 24 others hadn't for one reason or another.

It was a magic moment for me because my son Matt was there. He had been so engrossed with filming this thing that he stayed up the whole 50 hours. He said it was like filming a reality show. He was so caught up with the different guy's sagas and issues, he couldn't pull away to miss whatever came next. He also wondered which guys would get dropped or injured.

After Mark "secured" the class and told us it was finally over, he then addressed us as a group as we stood "at attention". He then told us he was proud of us. He said we had gone through a lot the last 50 hours mentally, emotionally, physically and together as a class. He said "we all will recover and reflect on this experience differently. You have all experienced the reality of the 20X Principle. Your lives will never be the same. You'll head into life from this more confident and mentally stronger." Then he said "All of you will handle this experience differently. Some of you will be normal and move on just like your scabs and your bodies will heal. Some of you will be more emotional than you're used to and might find yourself crying out of nowhere the next few days. You have been through deeper trauma than maybe ever before in your life but you will be fine. You have felt things and wrestled with your mind deeper than ever before. Any questions?" A few of the guys asked Mark questions.

Then Mark had us line up in a single line and come by all the instructors so the instructors could shake our hands. That was a nice experience except I did not enjoy shaking some of the instructors hands who had been the most demeaning and negative. I just shook their hand and said thank you and moved on.

Mark Divine was the last one to shake our hands. When I got to Mark, he congratulated me with his big smile. I'd seen and / or talked with him occasionally for almost 3 years, getting ready for this moment.

I had remembered when he had offhandedly said back in training, "You will crush it Owens." I thanked him for those previous kind words and for at least acting like he believed in me. I am sure he said that to everyone who he watched training for Kokoro. They meant a lot to me especially as I struggled to see myself able to do it.

Then I said to Mark in a semi-delirious state, "Mark, that is three down and two to go. I did Greece with Lance and Dave, and The Quest. I have IRONMAN Mexico in three weeks and then the 777. I am now the oldest Kokoro finisher."

He just looked at me speechless with my hand in his hand. I'll never forget that look.

He looked like he was staring at and listening to a delirious crazy man who was out of his mind who had just finished Kokoro. He was right. I probably was out of my mind. But I had thought about that moment for three years. I'd been training for three years thinking about the day Mark Divine would congratulate me. It was part of my "Why". It worked. The concept and mental picture of that moment had kept me in the game more than once. I could care less that I had ever finished an IRONMAN. They were nothing in comparison. I had finished Kokoro, "the hardest civilian training in the world."

Off to the side was Pararescue Commandant Josh Smith. I walked over to him and he gave me a big bear hug and shook my hand. He was there at the start and on and off the whole time checking out the Navy SEAL instructors and watching me. It encouraged me to see him off to the side with sunglasses on staring at us. It always reminded me to perform well and be a leader.

I introduced Josh to Matt and we all reflected on what the last 50 hours was like.

He said "Congratulations. You did it!" We talked for a few minutes and he told me how I had made the PJ Community proud. He smiled and talked a lot and called me a "true badass!" He said "Watching the 50 hours was amazing." He was there at the start, at pool PT, and at the finish. It always encouraged me to see him off to the side with his sunglasses on, just staring at us.

I loved the moment with Josh and Matt.

It was mine.

I owned it.

My Class. Secured.

Robert H. Owens

Relaxing and recovering from "the Games!" I didn't say much for a week. I had some cigars, wrote in my journal and stared out into space. Tears just appeared and rolled down my cheeks for no reason.

CHAPTER 11

Post Kokoro

There is an unspoken rule about Kokoro that you just don't talk much about Kokoro after you do it. At least as of two years ago. I didn't realize that the guys weren't telling me a lot about it beforehand for a reason. They'd share bits and pieces but not everything. But I understand why now.

Why? Because it is something that you really can't explain. You have to experience it. Everything you need to know about Kokoro prior to attempting it, you can find on the Internet through YouTube SEALFIT videos or in Mark Divine's books. It is all there if you're just looking for basic information and training suggestions. Actually though, it isn't all there too.

What I can say is that it crushed me mentally emotionally and physically. It took everything I had to finish. I was mentally tormented the last 6 hours. I was holding on for dear life much of the time. It was just as Mark Divine had said to me early on in my training. "Robert this thing is 80% mental and 20% physical."

The SEALFIT instructors played their roles very well. I respect our SEALS and Special Ops Communities now more than ever. I didn't appreciate the way they handled us often during the 50 hours but they had a purpose for everything they did. They made us remember that SEALS are trained for war not for an athletic event. It is not fun and games. Navy SEAL training is training to learn how to become mentally stronger to overcome and survive people who relentlessly want to kill you. Being in that type of atmosphere and environment was interesting for an old PJ. It seemed way different than when I went through intense Pararescue training in my 20s. Maybe it was just my age. I knew stuff was coming and could anticipate some things. However, this is a Navy thing. It was fun to be in their environment. I was reminded that the Air Force, in its own way, is different than the Navy. Our culture is different than the Navy, Army and Marines. Not harder or less difficult. Just different. I was excited to be in and survive the Navy's most difficult type civilian training and proud to be an Air Force guy. Surviving Kokoro made me smile to think back to when I was in my 20s in the Air Force. I wondered, knowing David Goggins story who tried to be a Pararescueman, if I would have made it as a SEAL back then.

The week after Kokoro was surreal for me. I didn't talk or move much. I did a podcast for MODe Nutrition on Kokoro and I was very emotional. Internally I was a mess. I was asked a lot of questions and when I talked I found myself being choked up over and over. The involuntary tears just came out often before I could speak. I wasn't used to being like this. I just sat at home and stared into nothing a lot of the week. My mind was reliving each part of the 50 hours.

Occasionally, Matt and I would relive the moments from his perspective as he was filming it and was with the coaches the whole time. He filled in the blanks to many of my thoughts and situations about the different things that happened. Can you imagine that he stayed up the whole 50 hours! He said it was the best reality show you could ever imagine. He heard the coach's critique of my classmates and me in real time. He also heard who they thought shouldn't be there or who they wanted to quit.

On the outside, I had scabs everywhere. My hands, elbows, knees and shins were bloody and slowly healing. My first three toes were numb on both feet as were my fingertips. The second morning in Kokoro was so cold from being wet at pool PT it reminded me of my Alaska frostbite days. I remember vividly the morning at the pool when my fingers turn blue and then white and numb. It was a trip to have them stiff and unresponsive. But I figured they would heal in time as they had in Alaska. Off and on the whole week I would stick pins in my fingers, to see if my feeling had come back yet. And to my amazement, I could stick a pin in my finger a long way with no feeling at all for the first week.

Same with my toes.

And most of all, I didn't want to train or do Ironman Mexico in three weeks. I was cooked. My brain and ego wanted to continue on with my quest for all five endurance events but someone else inside me couldn't care less. That person was done.

Kokoro was over at noon on Saturday and by Saturday night, congratulatory phone calls came in from many places which was really nice.

I remember having a voice message from Dave Crandall about two days later. It was "Hey Rob. It's Dave. I hear you made it. Congratulations. When you have time, give me a call. I'd like to hear about it." Click.

I smiled and thought, "What a great guy." We had grown closer in Greece and it was good to hear his voice.

So I called him. "Hi Dave, it's Rob."

"Hey Rob. Congratulations. You made it. How was it?"

"Dave you didn't tell me about it before. It was brutal. It crushed me. You didn't tell me it would be like that! It was wild."

He replied, "It is really hard to talk about it. You just have to experience it. Right?"

"Yes. Nothing you would have said would have helped. I am just glad it is over and I made it. I think the instructors could have driven me out if they wanted to. But they let me stay. I was often the slowest. I am just glad I made it."

He said, "Me too Rob. You hurt?" I said "No, just banged up."

"I understand. How many finished?"

"52 signed up and I guess paid. 39 showed up and 15 finished. There were guys from Canada, Switzerland, Hong Kong. There were two girls who showed up and didn't make it. It was wild. There was a really tough 50 something IRONMAN guy who was doing great until he fell twice on the downhill ruck in the dark the first night. The first time he braced himself with his hands as we were running downhill. The gravel took the skin off his hands. The second time he fell on his face as he couldn't use his hands to break his fall when he tripped. He ended up falling on the right side of his face ripped that side off his face off in the gravel. He didn't want to quit. He was pissed. They took him away."

"Yep, I get it," Dave said.

"Congratulations on finishing it Rob."

"Thanks Dave."

In that first conversation there really wasn't much to talk about. Just congratulations and a chuckle. In subsequent conversations, we told stories and laughed some. There were special moments we both shared about our classes and experiences. But honestly, you just have to experience it.

But what I can say are these thoughts.

I wasn't ready. But I may have never been ready.

I visited Gary's Eternity Crossfit Box in San Juan Capistrano the next Wednesday and they had me tell stories. I thought my stories would inspire and encourage some of them to want to try it. However, the more I talked the more they looked at each other and didn't want to have anything to do with it. They looked at all my scabs and bruises and just shook their heads. They thought I was nuts. I said more than once, "It was fun. You could do it. You would like it!" They just laughed. I couldn't understand why they didn't find it a great fun challenge. ALL OF THEM were better athletes than me.

But most of all, I just spaced out. Out of nowhere, two or three times a day, I had tears rolling down my cheeks. I contacted some of my finishing Kokoro 48 classmates and they had a variety of experiences. Some had a normal week and just went back to work. Some took a few days off. I'm sure the two high school kids wrote it off as just another fun weekend.

Mainly, I slept a lot and talked with Sandy. She was a good listener. She knew I'd been through trauma. She understood it as best she could. She reminded me more than once that I wanted it to be difficult and that I wanted to be tested. It was more than I could have imagined. I was just glad that I hadn't quit or been dropped by the instructors for being slow in the runs and lunges. Sandy was glad I wasn't hurt more than I was. I was relieved I hadn't died like that 40-year-old in great shape finisher a few classes before me.

I reflected a lot on the finish of Kokoro and all the kind words the instructors said to me as we shook hands at the end of the class as we file by the instructors like after a game. Somehow I needed to replay those moments in my head often. It was weird to remember the way they yelled at me and berated us and to then see their smiles and hear their kind words.

A number of the instructors said very nice things to me which was kind of them. Somehow, I needed to hear them. Being told over and over for 50 hours that I was a fucking embarrassment and a fucking loser and that I should never have shown up to begin with had got to me. It bothered me that they had won and penetrated my mental defenses. They had gotten to my "Why" and rocked me. They didn't know it but they had. I had worked hard before and during Kokoro to not let that happen. But they got in. That was scary. Thank God they didn't know it and Thank God for deep breathing training and staying "in the moment". I just wondered how many times they were close to getting on my case the way they did to that kid on the stairs at the beach the second night.

One of the best comments I received came from one of the harder more intense retired Navy SEAL instructors, Rob Ord. I shook his hand and thanked him for allowing me to finish and stretching me out when my back had gone out. He said to me, "Robert, you did great. You have nothing to be ashamed about. You were slow in some areas but others had difficult times in other areas. You did great in PT. You were stronger in your sit ups and core work than any of them the last morning. You did 350 sit ups in the grass like it was nothing. Others were struggling. Everyone got through the 50 hours differently. You were older by 25 years than any of your classmates who finished. You were amazing. Your classmates wanted you to finish."

Then he continued by saying, "We the instructors just said, 'If Robert doesn't quit, we will let him continue. He made it through the Standards Test and he made it through Murph and he made it through the first day. We will just watch and see what happens. As long as he doesn't quit, he's good. And we knew you'd never give up. You are a PJ. PJ's never quit. We are proud of you. Robert, you were a BEAST! Congratulations." What was nice was the genuine big smile on his face. It was real.

Again, why I needed that affirmation I don't know. Being affirmed as a beast was meaningful. It meant that they thought I hadn't just survived but I held my own. And it meant to me that I hadn't been crushed. In retrospect, I needed that because I never considered there was a beast inside me until then. Not in my 20s, 30s, 40s, 50s had I ever conceived of the concept of being a beast. I was an average guy who worked hard on doing non-average things. I'd been doing it since high school. It was satisfying hearing it from a well-respected Navy SEAL and Kokoro co-founder like Rob. To hear those words at 66 years old put a quiet smile on my face. We seniors still had game in us. I wanted to be like David Goggins. I felt the experiment of attempting to get older and stronger was validated. I had trained for almost 3 years to change my body from an aerobic swim bike run guy to an aerobic and anaerobic strength and endurance guy. It happened.

The guys at SEALFIT who I had trained with said there had never been an IRONMAN complete Kokoro the first time they attempted it. That thought motivated me greatly. I focused on that fact daily. I wasn't going to be in that category. I believed that if I put in the time and hard work, I could hang with stronger fitter younger people. I had proved it at my CrossFit and on Saturdays at SEALFIT. I was experiencing the 20X Principle. I didn't want to just survive Kokoro. I wanted to be legendary. Like in Tim Grover's book "Relentless." He writes, "Cooler, Closer, Cleaner… good, great, unstoppable. You can be whichever you want. If you want to be unstoppable, you've got to make the commitment." I wanted to be a 66 year old "Cleaner."

Something that bothered me was that I couldn't get out of my mind the one instructor's repeated comments that we were the worst class they had ever had, and that I was a fucking embarrassment. He said it more than once. He said lots of things to lots of guys, but I took it personally. He really never came out of character. He enjoyed being an asshole way too much. It bothered me then and still bothers me.

I texted Graham Dessert, the instructor volunteer who put green lines on my shirt during the first night while doing Murph. I say volunteer coach because officially you could not be an instructor unless you had been a Navy SEAL.

I called and asked if we could have coffee and process this thing. I needed answers. I met with him in Encinitas.

We had an illuminating talk. He filled in some of the blanks on the 50 hours. A lot had happened to so many. Some quit, some had been hurt and some were asked to drop out. And he mentioned that by the first 24 hours mark, they pretty well knew who was going to make it.

I asked him about the one guy who was driven out of Kokoro on the beach stairs that second night. He replied that he hadn't been cutting it for a while so they finally got tired of his attitude and excuses and eliminated him. I said they got on his case until they broke him. And Graham said, "OK." I mentioned I'd never want them to do that to me. It was cruel. Graham said, "That guy needed to go." Then he told me we weren't the worst class ever. He said, "Let it go."

I really appreciated being able to talk about the experience and get his perspectives on the whole thing. As we sat at a little round coffee table, I was bleeding from my arm on to the table. He just smiled as I wiped the blood off the table a few times. My leg was also bleeding again for some reason. There was blood running down my calf onto my flip flop and dripping on the clean polished concrete floor. The restaurant owner and waitress looked curiously at me as I bent down with a paper napkin to wipe up the blood drips. Graham just smiled. It wasn't any big thing to us. It was all part of the experience. War wounds.

I have since talked with Rob Ord who had stretched me out that last morning and he also said we weren't the worst class ever. He encouraged me a lot. I have vivid memories of Rob's intensity during different sets of the evolutions. He always had his dark sunglasses on and his arms folded as he told us what to do. He never raised his voice much or yelled but he was stern and made his points clear.

It's amazing how clearly I can see the different instructors faces today in my mind.

I said to one instructor, "Hey, thanks for the smiles. Were those real smiles, or sadistic smiles?" He smiled and wouldn't answer. "They really came at the right time. You were a little nicer than the others, and I appreciated it, and you." We talked some more and laughed about certain instances and he said "Bless you" which shocked me. I didn't expect that from him. I asked "Are you a church guy?" And he replied, "Yep" and we talked about that a little. That spun me. I said, "How could you go to church on Sunday and say Praise the Lord, and be so sadistic and mean those with F bombs?" He just looked at me and smiled again – but didn't say a word.

Here was a Navy SEAL instructor who was a church guy. He could be so cold and severe then flip the switch and be the nicest guy like Rob Ord. I knew there was something different about him. When he yelled at me he still had a kindness in his eyes. I sort of enjoyed being yelled at by him.

And I want to say this. It applies to all of our lives: The instructors could be brutal. And it could go on for hours. But that was because war could be brutal. It wasn't an athletic event. It was a Navy SEAL military preparation event. They wanted to know if we could stay positive and in the moment in a totally negative environment. Military battles are not usually positive experiences. There is a ton of stress and mental challenges to work through. But every once in a while, one of them or a volunteer would say something nice or encouraging like, "Good job" or "Owens, that's the way to go." I'll never forget at the top of the stairs after the bear crawls up backwards on the second night. I was constantly being put down as the last guy, and the slow guy. And when I finally got to the top, the one instructor who had been on my case disappeared, but another said quietly on the side, "Way to go Owens, you are a BEAST. Good job!"

Those words gave me hope and a surge of strength that carried me through the rest of that miserable night. No matter what came next I had hope and confidence that I could get through anything they threw at me. It was strengthening to know that some instructors and volunteers viewed me as worthy to be out there. I had voices in my head the whole time debating and arguing about my abilities.

It is amazing what an encouraging word can do at the right moment for all of us. Encouragement is life giving. It reminded me to try to daily give encouraging words to people because I know we all need them in this world.

LEADERSHIP LESSONS

1. Encourage your team when they least expect it.

2. Debrief after tough times.

3. Remove team members who are toxic quickly.

4. Are you an encourager?

5. Remember time is usually a healer. Give recovery time to work for you. You will see things differently with time.

6. 20X Principle: There was more in me than I could have imagined. I needed the instructors and teammates to pull it out of me.

**This next chapter is about perseverance and getting past your emotions.
We have to do this every day of our lives.**

Riding my annual bike ride!

CHAPTER 12

Training For 12th IRONMAN - Mexico

The first week after Kokoro was a tired blur. By the start of week two, I knew I needed to do something to get ready for IRONMAN. I had gone a few times to a Masters Swim Team workout in Irvine with the NOVA Swim Team. They had an experienced IRONMAN finisher coach named John Collins. I called Sherry, an ocean swimmer I knew who worked out there and asked, "What was happening with NOVA these days?" She filled me in and invited me back to swim with them.

The challenge for me was that I was in shape, but not swimming shape. It had been a year since I'd swam at my last IRONMAN and I don't swim in between. I went over and stood on the deck with John and told him I had just finished this military thing and had less than two weeks before IRONMAN. I think he thought I was a bit strange. But I asked him for a swim critique of my stroke. He said, "OK, it will be $125."

I met him at a private community pool and he filmed my stroke underwater and above water. He said I was swimming with old techniques and to make these certain changes to my arms and head. Then he counted the amount of strokes it took me to get across the pool. Then he made the adjustments to get me longer in the water and said, "Now let's see how many strokes it takes you! Over the next 30 minutes, I went from 21 strokes across the pool to 17. And my times were now faster with 17 than they had been with 21. I was amazed. Just a few adjustments and I was faster and more efficient in the water. It was my first swim instruction since high school.

Then he told me to come swim at NOVA for a workout the next morning.

I did and he put me in the relatively slow lane at end of the pool and I started the swim workout. It was difficult. I was out of breath from the beginning. I was swimming with these 35-50 year old women and I couldn't stay up. One lady was getting ready for her IRONMAN somewhere and she knew I had an IRONMAN coming up. She just looked at me like, "Really...you are doing an IRONMAN?"

When I crawled out of the pool at the end, I thanked him and left. I went over around the corner by the outside showers and sat there for 30 minutes. I was done. I was defeated and discouraged. I knew I was mentally fragile and not in a good place. I felt crushed. And I never went back. I wasn't ready to train again. He probably thought, "What's the deal with that Owens guy. He talks a good line then he disappears. Probably another all talk guy."

I thought about calling him a number of times but never did. I found myself dealing with the voices in my head instead.

Two weeks had passed and I had eleven days to swim before we were to fly out to Mexico on a Thanksgiving Thursday. Finally as the mental pressure mounted, I went back to my 24 Hour Fitness pool in Dana Point on that Monday and started again. Starting hard things can be hard. I wanted to procrastinate. I had been procrastinating for 10 days. It seems like all my life there are days when I have to start hard things. You probably do to.

This time I went back to my old training ways that had served me pretty well for 11 IRONMANs.

I put my old two and a half pound wrist weights on and stuck my pull buoy between my legs and just began to swim. I never train with my legs because they don't give me a lot of extra speed. I train with my upper body using my pull buoy because I need to be strong in the water. This won't be a pool swim in Mexico. The weights make it more difficult. This time though I practiced counting my strokes and getting longer as John had pointed out.

My wrist weights make training harder, so I'm stronger in the actual race.

Monday, 20 lengths or 10 laps. Tuesday 20 laps. Wednesday 36 laps. A mile. Thursday 45 laps. Friday 72 laps. Two miles. Saturday 45 laps. My stroke count was around 17 to 18 but I added only breathing every four strokes to wean myself off oxygen.

I was back in the Game.

I took Sunday off and relaxed. I had four days left. We flew out late in the morning on Thursday so I could get in an early morning swim before flying out.

Monday 72 laps with breathing games. I got up to eight strokes without breathing consistently.

Tuesday 72 laps again repeating the breathing games. And I added four laps of kicking with a pull board. My legs kept cramping up and it was hard work for me. I was "in shape" but not in swimming shape.

Wednesday, 72 laps or two miles.

Time for a new game: Push off the wall and take a deep breath then eight strokes without breathing then a breath then six strokes without breathing. I did that for 32 laps. Then kicking again and I threw in swimming 'underwaters' - the length of the pool a number of times.

Why? Because I want confidence that I can survive without air in case I get run over by a pack of swimmers as I had in the 2003 Kona IRONMAN. My goggles were kicked off and I lost one of my contacts. It was a tough day that didn't start well in the swim.

The weights always tax my shoulders. That is old Pararescue training stuff. Be tougher than is required. When I take those weights off and start swimming, my arms always feel like they are floating through the air as I reach out in my stroke. And when pulling the water, it just seems so much easier as I am not pulling those weights any more. It is unconventional but it works for me for the ocean swims. As well, I didn't ride my bike once on the street before the IRONMAN, it was my 12th time tradition.

We hopped on a 12 p.m. American flight from Orange County airport on Thanksgiving Day and flew to Dallas where we spent the night. On Friday we were on American's only Dallas-Cozumel flight at noon and landed in Cozumel at 3:00 p.m. The shuttle to the Cozumel Palace Hotel picked us up. We like it because it's very nice and at the finish line. After checking in, I walked across the street to the Convention Center and registered with one hour to spare. Registration closed at 5 p.m., and Sandy went to our room to unpack and start loving her waterfront room with a balcony.

I then go down the street to the TriBike Transport bike holding pen. I pick up my bike, have them check the tires and roll it back to our hotel room on the 2nd floor. There is all kinds of activity going on in the streets, but we are pretty disinterested. We unpack some more and sit on our balcony. It has a wonderful view. We can see the pool below, the swimmers in the ocean and the two to four weekly cruise ships filling up to leave around 7 p.m.

It is an all-inclusive hotel which is a shame because I don't eat much nor do I have a glass of wine. I am focused. Sandy is relaxing and probably reading and maybe having a glass of wine.

My thoughts always wander to the swim and the bike.

My nightmare is that the Caribbean water could be choppy and rough on Sunday morning which would be a terrible and miserable experience for the swimmers. Or it could be a glassy, smooth, beautiful Caribbean warm clear swim for two and a half miles. Often, one morning looks choppy and windy and terrible but the next is smooth. We never know. I've done IRONMAN Mexico 5 times.

The bike ride could be extremely windy on the other side of the island as it often is, or we could get a miracle day with no winds. If there are winds, the backside of the island could be a real workout. I have had really difficult rides there before. That is where I go mentally to prepare.

We eat about 6 p.m. outside by the ocean and just relax. It is beautiful and fun, except, I am somewhat uptight. In 36 hours or so I will be doing an IRONMAN. During the race she will be making friends on the sidewalk in front of the hotel wondering how I did in the swim and where I am on the bike. They all will be wondering the same thing about the people they are supporting. I will hope to see her about 10:30 in front of the hotel as I plan to be coming by there at the end of my first of three bike loops.

We get to bed early, and rise Saturday to a wonderful relaxed buffet breakfast. Then I put all my Race Day stuff on my bed and sort which things go into my Race Day Competitor Bags. There is a Swim to Bike Bag, a Bike to Run Bag and if I choose to use them two Special Needs bags for the Bike half-way point and the Run half-way point.

I check my bags again before I take my bike around 4 p.m. to the bike start. When it is time to go check in, I grab my Swim to Bike Bag and my bike, and my Bike to Run bag, I go downstairs with everything and find a large taxi van for my bike, and travel the 15 minutes to the check in area. Workers check me in on a computer and remind me of my number. Then with a black marking pen they put numbers on my arms and legs and the letter "J" on my left calf to signify that I am in the 66-70 age group. There aren't many of us. I check the air in my tires and put my bike in its assigned numbered slot. Usually I walk around a little to see what new things might be there compared to last year and take some pictures. Then I head back to the entrance to the check in area to catch a taxi back to the hotel.

All that takes about 90 minutes. Sandy is usually relaxing. We talk and head down to dinner about 6 p.m. again and call it an early night. I'm anxious, excited, curious and a dozen other emotions – but not bored.

I try to be in bed by 8:30 p.m. as 4:30 a.m. comes quickly. In the morning, I get up, have my coffee and maybe a banana, put in my one right contact and head out about 5:30 a.m. to catch a taxi to the Swim Exit area which is the start meeting point, where my bike is located. Some athletes are talking a lot to others, and others are super focused and quiet. It's here!

LEADERSHIP LESSONS

1. Get professional advice – a little change can make a huge difference.

2. Have a routine for your pre-event to keep your head in the game.

3. 20X Principle: Train harder than you expect the real test to be.

Next up is the actual experience, and what it's like to do an IRONMAN. I find myself coaching a first timer and we become great friends as a result.

BEYOND AVERAGE

The excitement is building and I'm ready for #12.

CHAPTER 13

12th IRONMAN Mexico
Race Day

The air is thick with the excitement of 2,000 - 2,500 highly strung athletes all tuned up and ready to hit the water in the "Swim to Bike" transition area. It is a zoo. There are all types of people. Last year there were people from 27 nations. Some look fit while others look like they shouldn't be attempting this. However, inevitably, they will pass me on the bike ride later today.

I can't wait for a 5:30 a.m. bus with all the others on the dark street out in front of my hotel and the other hotels. I decide to grab a taxi. It costs $10, but is worth it. When I get to the check in area where my bike is, there is loud classic rock and roll blaring and huge lights beaming everywhere in the dark. This morning I step out of the cab to the music of Journey, AC/DC, and Boston. The atmosphere is teeming and alive. There is an announcer loudly saying, "Good morning everyone. Welcome to IRONMAN Mexico. You have 90 minutes to go. It is a beautiful morning for a great day. We are excited for you. Check your bikes and get your transition bags to the bus with your number on it. Let's go!" He will be talking almost non-stop up to race time with updated instructions. I love the people watching. It is fun to observe them nervously mingling around, getting their stuff ready.

There are nervous and non-nervous athletes scurrying excitedly everywhere. The busses leave for the start line at 6 a.m. The pros start at 6:30 a.m., It used to be a 7 a.m. for the age group start. This year they moved the age group start to 7:30 for the first time.

The first thing to do is go to my bike and wipe the dew off and check my GUs situated on my main frame bar that runs between my legs to the handle bars. I taped six liquid gel GUs to the frame for eating during the six to seven hour ride. Sometimes when I come before the bike race like this, the tape holding the GUs to the frame has given way and the GUs are hanging over the right or left side of the frame. It is a big deal. If the frame is covered with dew, I can't re-tape until the moisture is off the

Me dropping my bag off, at the Bike To Run bag area.
During the race, it's kinda chaotic...

frame and dry. And that might not happen even if I wipe the frame down. Humidity is 80% that morning.

It sounds like a little thing but it can turn into a time eater, when I don't have the time to mess with it. I try to eat a GU every 20 miles in the bike race. There are aid stations every 10 miles. I have six GUs in 112 miles. If I have done this GU thing right, I just rip the GU away from the tape and slide the GU into my mouth. It is an easy thing. If I've messed the GU thing up, then they are falling off during the race and my knees may be hitting them. That is irritating. Then ripping them away from the tape doesn't always work and becomes a sticky challenging mess. I hate that sticky stuff on my hands mixed with my salty, sweaty fingers. So each race morning getting this GU thing right is a necessity. Some triathletes have a different system for nutrition during the ride.

After I get that squared away I get my tires checked for air one last time, and disperse my Special Needs bags to the right busses that will take them to the proper locations. Then we all head out to the starting line.

The bus ride to the start line is usually quiet. All the men and women are in their swimming attire, carrying their goggles and whatever. Most are barefoot. There is some nervous talk occasionally. This year there is a 60 year old guy talking to a 40 year old woman that is fun to listen to. He sounds more like he wants to take her out to dinner, than get to the race start. He is working hard to get her attention. But most athletes are just staring straight ahead thinking about the long day ahead of them.

We arrive at the starting area 10 minutes later searching for clues as to the weather on the water. It can change quickly. Was it going to be windy and choppy or smooth water? It is the huge question. One year it was so choppy that they canceled the swim leg altogether.

They've changed the starting procedure three times over the six years I've been going down there. These last few years we get in the water at a hotel about two and a half miles north of the exit point. It will be a point to point race down the coast.

Often there is a nice current running down the length of the swim, past the exit point, to make for a nice, warm, and fast swim.

I think that when the conditions are right and normal, it is the best IRONMAN swim in the world. I say that because my previous swims have been two Hawaii, two Florida, one South Africa, one Australia and five Mexico swims. Being in the Caribbean, the water will be about 83 degrees, clear and hopefully smooth.

That also means it will be a non-wetsuit race which I prefer. For some reason, I didn't like swimming in a wetsuit in South Africa and Australia. It was constricting both times. Everyone else seems to like them. They help you with buoyancy and help make your swim times faster. But I keep going back to Mexico specifically because it is a non-wetsuit race and because of the warm water. I'll sacrifice the wetsuit advantages any day for a warm outside temperature, and a warm, smooth Caribbean swim. It's wonderful. Plus, some years you get a current working for you the whole way.

As we all walk towards the starting area, the loudspeakers are booming with rock and roll, the race organizers have strategically placed signs like 1 hour, 1:05, 1:10, 1:15, 1:20, all the way up to 2 hours posted in front of the swim start area. Those are to tell the swimmers where they should line up. I usually do my two and a half mile swim in 1 hour and 5 to 15 minutes so I go to the 1:05 section with about 40 other swimmers. We are all bunched in together like sardines. Men and women with their swim caps on and maybe holding their goggles nervously wait. They are all looking very intense and like they wish they were first place finishers. I don't put my cap or goggles on until I have to which is one minute before I jump in the water. Why have your cap on for 20 minutes before the race? Or even five minutes before. To me it is stupid but I am not an IRONMAN. I am just a guy going out to have a nice long day. For me the race doesn't begin until the bike ride, it just a long swim before that. The whole thing is quite an experience.

You hear many languages around you which is heartwarming. I am standing with athletes ranging from 20 to 75 years old. They are all focused on getting in the water and getting going. What really hypes the atmosphere is the blasting music. I love AC/DC, Guns and Roses and Lynyrd Skynyrd getting the swimmers pumped up and even more excited to get going. The IRONMAN announcer keeps talking the whole time over the music getting the swimmers into their starting spots.

Finally, the announcer's voice over the loudspeaker says, "Good morning everyone! Are you ready?!" The swimmers roar back all sorts of things. He says, "In 10 minutes the first swimmers will be the water. Are you ready?" And there will be another big roar from the 2,000 - 2,500 plus swimmers. It helps with the atmosphere to have a helicopter circling overhead with cameramen hanging out of the side door. Then the announcement comes, "You have five minutes swimmers. Ok, let's have the first swimmers get in the water."

It is a staggered start which is smart and kind. In the old days, we all hopped in the water together. Those who got in first could tread water for up to 15-20 minutes waiting for everybody to jump in or wade in. Then the fun would happen. The air horn would go off and all 2,000 plus swimmers headed to the same buoy. It was crazy and many people got hurt. Slower swimmers were swum over by faster swimmers. People collided together. Swimmers would get too close to others feet. Those swimmers were irritated and pissed off so they kicked hard to tell them to get off their feet. That resulted in broken noses, lost goggles, contacts being lost and all kinds of stuff. Arms could hit arms which wasn't good if you were a little lady getting hit by a big man.

Also, it is hard to breathe in all the chop of 2,000 plus swimmers starting the race bunched so closely together. It was crazy. I started IRONMANs in Hawaii, Florida, Australia, South Africa and Mexico like that.

In most of those races I would do one of two things: I'd position myself on the farthest side of the pack and try not to be next to anybody. The old lifeguard trials trick. On the outside you'd have to swim longer to the first buoy if it wasn't a straight swim course but you had smoother water. It still worked.

Or I would get in the back of the 2,000 plus swimmers and let them take off at the air horn. I'd tread water with a number of smart people and wait until the swimmers in front of me were gone. Then I'd start. It would maybe cost us 30 seconds or a minute in time but what is that over 12 to 15 hours?

Mexico used to have a rectangular swim course. You made four left hand turns on the course. You'd get in the water and have to swim up the shoreline to the first buoy. 2,000 plus swimmers wanting to swim around a single buoy? It was insane. And so was the second buoy. It wasn't so bad later as the swimmers became spaced out for the third and fourth buoys.

I just stayed wide on the first two turns and let the others beat themselves up at the buoys. It cost me time, but it was worth it. I wasn't in all that thrashing around and hitting each other. I think I did the course like that three times.

The last time I used that strategy was a wild year. It was the worst, and that is why they changed the course the next year to a point to point race. That year the current was really strong. As the starting horn blew we swam directly into the strong current which was really hard. The best of the 2,000 plus swimmers made that first left hand turn pretty quickly.

But many struggled to get to that first buoy. Once they made that first left hand turn, the water was pushing us off course to the left while we tried to swim straight out to the second buoy.

People were swimming against the current just trying to get to that second left hand turn. Plus others were still beating themselves up as they were bunched up. But once you got around that second left hand turn in the rectangle you flew down the course. That leg is the longest and it was fun to be in that current. It was like being on an escalator or having a small motor on.

But then you got to the next left hand turn and you hit that current again pushing you off the course to the right. Swimmers had to fight to swim straight towards the shore. If they made it to the last buoy there was the final left turn that put you back swimming against the current. Again, many were really tired and had a tough time making it back along the shoreline to the starting area.

Obviously, to some, it seemed like a really hard swim. I was never bothered by any of it. Even though I trained in a pool with my wrist weights, I was an ocean guy at heart. To me, it was just another day swimming out to rescue someone in the ocean with tides and currents and dragging them in. I really didn't have any problems.

I was told after the race that day that over 300 swimmers had to be pulled out of the water by stand-up paddle boarders guys. They couldn't make it in. Their IRONMAN aspirations were over for that day. And the IRONMAN organizers changed the course from then on to a point to point swim with the current.

In Kona in 2003 on my fourth IRONMAN, I was in that starting mayhem. I positioned myself at the front as I was swimming those in about 1:05 to 1:15.

In my first two Florida IRONMANs in 2000 and 2001, I didn't have any problems on the start. The air horn blew and we all ran down the beach and jumped in the water. Somehow I'd managed to not be in the madness. It was an out and back twice course. You would finish the first loop get out of the water and run up the beach around something and then run back down into the water and start the second loop.

It seemed easy enough.

So in my rookie Kona debut, and my one and only Kona race, I didn't think about being run over. I checked the previous year's swim start times of the 1,500 entrants and I was in the top 10%.

To me, I figured I'd be in the first 100 to exit the water which was OK. However, about 30 seconds into the swim. I got kicked hard in the face. It knocked my goggles down around my neck. As I stopped to grab my goggles and empty them of water and put them back on. I had probably 20-30 swimmers swim right over me. There were elbows, bodies, arms, legs and feet all banging into me. It was like being run over by a pack of fleeing animals. Plus, it was hard to breathe. I just tried to tread water with my face underwater to avoid getting hit, until the last of the swimmers swam over me. Then I gathered myself by breathing deeply which controls your emotions and your quality of air. Finally, I got my goggles on. I treaded water with my egg beater kick for a few seconds, relaxed and started over. The whole time I tried to not get flustered or mentally panic. It was really difficult to maintain composure as the other racers were swimming over me.

Many triathletes feared those swim starts in the early days. And in a couple of races, swimmers had heart attacks and drowned. That is when I started training by doing those pool length underwaters. I never wanted to be desperate for air again. Now, if something happens I just hold my breath under water for 30 seconds until the swimmers pass. No problem.

In Kona I lost one of my contacts during all that chaos. I really didn't notice it until I exited the water. Everything was off. I had never worn only one contact before. I had heard of people only wearing one contact and liking it full time but it was weird for me. All that day, my vision was off. I'd go to grab a water bottle on the bike and almost miss it. Riding a bike with one contact the first time was challenging. Interestingly, because of that experience, I have only trained with one contact for the last seven IRONMANs or any sports. It is one less thing that can go wrong as my brain has adapted to it. I've never allowed that kind of thing to happen to me again.

In this 12th IRONMAN the one hour swimmers jump off a small makeshift dock and tread water while music is playing to amp the crowd. They tread water maybe two minutes while we watch. Then the air horn sets them free. There is a roar from the onlooking crowd and the waiting swimmers. The next group then inches forward.

Dating back to Pararescue days, I have my own ritual for the start. When I get up, I have a coffee. It is 120 minutes before the swim start. By start time I probably need to pee or should pee to empty my bladder for the next hour of swimming. So as we are standing like sardines tightly together shoulder to shoulder with my Tri Shorts or Speedo on, I think of this moment and just softly pee in my suit and feel that nice warm pee run down one of my legs and on to my feet. It is a signature moment. No one else knows or cares. No one is moving. No one is looking down. The music just blares and it's a signature moment at the end of that long training period to say to myself, "Sweet. It is over. It has been a long intense number of weeks. OK. Let the Games begin!"

I also wear sunglasses to the start after I get off the bus. No one has them on but me. It is fun. I figure I am one of the oldest competitors out there with my "J" designation on my right calf. Some people see it and just stare at me probably thinking "What is a J? So I've decided to have my own fun. Let's be different than all the spunky, egoed out, super buffed younger people.

I carry my mandatory colored swim cap and goggles until just before I get in. I pee with my sunglasses on like a rock star, then take them off and stick them in my swimsuit. They are long and fit inside the swimsuit just fine. Then I put my cap and goggles on, and hop in.

When I finish the swim, as soon as I crawl out of the water and onto the five or six steps that take you up onto dry land, I reach down and pull them out of my suit and put them back on. It is my James Bond coming out of the ocean in a tuxedo moment.

The loudspeaker crackles to life, "OK, 1:05 swimmers get in the water if you haven't already. It is time to go!" We shuffle up which is an interesting process. We are all packed in together inching forward but no one wants to touch each other. It is sort of an unwritten code. If you do happen to have your shoulder touch the man or lady next to you, you say, "Excuse me" with a smile like you've violated their space. It is weird. It takes some work to keep that from happening.

I smile from ear to ear at nobody. I put on my cap and my goggles, get to the end of the dock and jump in. Swoosh! I am in the Caribbean!

I look around through my goggles and everything is a blur above water. Then the loudspeaker goes off as does the starter's air horn and my group begins the swim. I just start to swim, focused on getting long and relaxed in the water. It is a mental discipline. It takes work to get out of the adrenaline zone and into your rhythm.

I choose a swim line that keeps me away from others. This also helps me find smoother water. I just begin to breathe and think about John Collins coaching me on getting long in the water. I am wondering if I can really use less strokes and less energy over two and a half miles and swim it faster. It is a good puzzle to meditate on. Kokoro seems long ago and I am excited again. I think about all this and talk to myself the whole swim: "It is a new day. It is an easy day. It is a fun day. It is number four out of five achievements. I am going to be legendary. I am a cleaner. I can do this. It is only an hour or so. It is a fun day. It is an easy day....!"

My race number and "J" designation on my right calf - means I'm in the 66-70 age group and one of the oldest competitors out there.

It takes me about 10 minutes to get through the adrenaline stage and get my heart rate down. My arms feel great. It is just a wonderful feeling to start the swim with these light, strong arms. Imagine no wrist weights this time. My goal is to get from breathing every other stroke to breathing every four strokes and then every six strokes.

In the beginning though, it is every other stroke.

As I swim I am looking around underwater and above the water. Under the water I can see fish, rock formations, white sand and seaweed. Occasionally there is a sunken small boat or something. The water is about 30 to 50 yards deep, sometimes though it's only five or six feet deep, depending on the swim line. Along the course are big six feet high orange or yellow triangle shaped buoys which are anchored to the bottom by a rope. It is fun to see the rope as you come up on the buoys. When I look up while swimming I can see the buoys floating. When I look underwater, I like to see what kind of rope they used or what the anchor looks like or how far away it is. One year I had so much fun looking at all the underwater statues in a statuary area that I forgot that I was racing. There were all kinds of beautiful Caribbean fish swimming in and through the statues.

The buoys seem to be spaced pretty evenly apart so I settle in wondering how many strokes it takes to get from buoy to buoy. I begin to count my strokes. I say to myself, "That looks like a 300 stroke distance" and then challenge myself to make it in 300 strokes. If I am wrong, then I look two or three times at the next one and try to guess better and start counting again. Truthfully, I am always wrong in my stroke perception. But by the end, I am getting closer.

My goal is to make a boring swim, turn into fun games. I've learned that the way you eat an elephant, as the saying goes in this endurance thing, is one bite at a time. So I break this swim into manageable goals. I am not swimming two and a half miles, but from buoy to buoy. Occasionally I see other swimmers. I study their styles a lot. Sometimes I get passed by others. No big deal. It is a long day.

A few years ago the Mexico race was known for having small jellyfish in the water and small barracudas. The swimmers in the front seemed to be stung more than those in the middle or back of the pack so I appreciated those swimmers clearing the lanes for the rest of us.

As for the barracudas, they are maybe a foot long and would just nip at swimmers. No big deal unless you were from Minnesota or South Dakota, or some non-ocean area. If they bit you, it was usually in the arm pit area or on your side it seemed. I always wonder, if this is the year I'll get bit.

Fortunately, I've never had either bother me in my six IRONMANs there. But it keeps me alert. I have seen some IRONMAN riders with little blood marks on the side of their shirts on the bike ride, but it wasn't a big deal. The best thing for jellyfish stings is to put urine on them but that can be a challenge. The sting can be irritating for a couple of hours.

So the swim progressed from buoy to buoy down the coast. I think point to point swims are the best. You get to watch the hotels go by as well as hillsides. I think, "How long will it take to go from one end of the hotel to the other?" Then I count those strokes to see if I am correct. I am usually wrong here too. Occasionally during the swim, I see a scuba diver sitting on the bottom taking pictures. It can be fun. Everything around me is changing all the time.

This year it took longer for some reason to get to breathing every four strokes. I wondered when I would mellow out and not work so hard with every other stroke breathing. I had planned to work less this year. But it didn't go according to my plans.

And then for some reason it happens. It becomes easy to go from breathing every two strokes to every four strokes. Then I begin to practice breathing every six strokes. It is like for some unknown reason, my lungs just open up. My lungs are like new balloons. When you blow into one it takes work to get the balloon to inflate. But then it does and you stretch it bigger and bigger. Same thought with my lungs.

They just seem to stretch in time. Pretty soon I am swimming long in the water, breathing easier. I am breathing less and still counting my strokes. The buoys fly by.

Finally I see the yellow buoys in the distance and believe that I am closing in on the end of the swim. There are three in a row and I can make out the finish area buildings.

I have a swimmer about five feet in front of me, and one off to my right about 10 feet away. We are all cruising. We have been near each other for about 30 minutes. They have become like my swim friends. You know how porpoises swim together? It feels like that a little bit. One is a woman and one is a big guy. The woman has a shorter stroke with a great kick. The guy is longer and rotates his body less than she does. His legs look like mine. Just flowing behind me. She looks like a swimmer to me.

Sure enough the end is coming. Wow, this thing flew by. The buoy to buoy thing worked. I did about eight to ten small races. I felt really long in the water. I was reaching out trying to be more streamlined than ever. I was breathing looking down, with the water line hitting me in the middle of my head versus the water hitting me on my forehead as I used to swim. Technique is everything. It is funny to me. I had my first swimming lesson since I was 15 with John Collins and it worked.

There were stand up paddlers ushering the swimmers closer to land which was encouraging. And I finally got to the last yellow buoy and turned left to the shore.

The bottom is all sandy white. The sand is rising under me as I swim along a short pier toward the shore. The swimmers are sizing up the situation. The five or six swimmers are bunching together to make it to the shore. We are all aiming for the steps at the end of the pier where it meets the shore. We will have to take turns climbing out if there are too many of us. And that is fine with me. I can be polite. I am not in a huge hurry. My sunglasses are ready for their yearly debut!

Pleasantly, there are four of us who arrive at the same time at the stairs. I say pleasantly because sometimes there can be 10 - 15 swimmers arriving at once. They are usually not focused on helping others. They can push and shove to be the first ones out of the water. I'd call them jerks.

It is a shallow area about four feet deep. It's still too deep to stand. I slide my goggles up onto my forehead and look for the right side of the stairs closest to the shore. Others aim for the middle or the left.

We all go up and down a little with the water level as it is surging off the shoreline. I get a handhold on the wet slippery wooden steps. The key is to wait for the water to rise up underneath me and then grab a handrail and put my knees on a step before the water recedes. It is the hardest and most dangerous part of the morning.

The steps are four or five feet wide and the corners of the steps are sharp and slippery. They seem like they've been under water for years. If you don't deal with the steps correctly, you can slip and fall, getting cut and bruised up. I always think of this water exit like: "Gosh, this is like a third world situation. This getting out of the water could have been designed better. But who cares. It's Mexico. There isn't an ADA (Americans With Disability Act) inspector approving the exit anyway." We just find a way to win while someone else is being pushed by the water into me.

Anyway, I figure it out, stand up somehow without slipping, and climb the steps out of the water. Then I take my goggles and cap off and stick my hand into my trunks to see if my sunglasses are where I left them. Sure enough they are there. I walk slowly to give myself time to get my goggles and cap situated and into one hand and put my sunglasses on with the other.

Then I walk towards the screaming crowds. It is so fun. The planning worked. Women are pointing at me and men are just staring with smiles on their faces. It is an Academy Awards moment on the red carpet. I act unfazed and choose to smile at a few lucky people that I choose to acknowledge. It usually is the kids. Occasionally it will be an older man who likes me and thinks it is great to see an older guy doing this.

All the swimmers have a choice to run this section towards the Swim to Bike Change Tent to change into the bike stuff or to walk. I think each year, "What's the hurry. It is going to be a long day. Relax, catch your breath and gather yourself. The first part is done. Enjoy the moment."

If time is your big issue then you are running hard past the crowds. The whole thing lasts maybe five or six minutes if you walk like me and is really fun. I slap a few high fives and make it to the showers. I enjoy the showers, and wash the sand and salt water off. I just stand in them for maybe one minute, and wash off really well with my sunglasses on. Others swimmers don't even come in them. They run around them. They are in a hurry. This is a race.

What is hard to believe is that when I get out of the water my watch says I swam it in one hour. There had to be a mistake. Years ago in my 50s, my fastest time was a 1:06. Last year was a 1:15.

I find out later that I did a 59 minute swim. Unbelievable! That is wild. There must have been a strong current. It was so easy. I choose to believe my training and swim lessons worked. Plus, I was really strong coming off Kokoro.

Then I walk to my Swim to Bike Bag hanging up and take it into the

My James Bond moment at the end of the swim.

Change Tent.

The walk is supposed to be on rubber mats but by now, the rubber mats are wet and have separated. The dirt underneath the mats has turned to mud and we are walking in shallow mud or on muddy mats. Imagine what happens with the 2,000 swimmers behind me. It will be a real mess soon.

I am usually in the top 10%. It is only semi-muddy.

I go in the tent and look for an isolated spot. I dump my bike stuff onto a chair next to me. Then I stuff my goggles and cap into the Transition bag. I keep my speedos on this year for padding under my tri shorts. Every year, my bicycle seat eats my crotch up in this once a year bicycle adventure.

The changing into dry bike clothes and socks goes smoothly because I put a hand towel from the hotel in my bag to wipe off my feet and legs. The towel is tremendous.

Guys like me learn some tricks along the way. It is hard to get tight socks on wet feet plus, you don't want to have pebbles and dirt in your socks. They can eat up your feet over 112 miles. I've read the pros don't use socks at all,

I dry off my sunglasses at the start. It is nice to start the bike ride with clean lenses. Knowledge is power. It is what everybody else knows that you don't, that will frustrate you. The towel is golden. There are new guys often frustrated with getting the mud and dirt off their feet.

I drop my bag off with my wet swim stuff and walk to my bike while others are running by me. I take that time to get my helmet and bike gloves on. I am eating a banana that I had placed in my Swim to Bike Bag.

I get to my bike and walk it to where you are allowed to get on. Here again people are five deep, leaning against a separation fence, screaming for their loved ones and friends. Sandy used to come but she is over it. She'd have to get there about 7 a.m. to find an open spot on the fence where she could see me. In the past, even if she would yell at me, I often couldn't hear her above the crowd noise.

The last time she went somehow I found her. I came over and we talked for about a minute about the swim. Then she kissed me and I'd roll my bike away. But it was a lot of work for her to make that one minute happen.

I mount the bike and feel great as I always do. The swim isn't even part of the IRONMAN for me. It is a warm up. I enjoy it when it is over. Every year, the real IRONMAN starts with the bike.

On the bike, it is a trip to put my feet in the pedals and start riding. I haven't been on a bicycle since the previous year's IRONMAN. It takes a few minutes to get acclimated. Then I attempt to settle onto my aero bars. It can be wobbly. It is a balance thing. But it all works out in the first three or four minutes.

I find a gear that looks like what the others are using and see how I can perform compared to them. Off we go. I'll see if my hamstring is going to act up. My goal is to be at about 20 mph for the day but it never happens.

As usual, it is a beautiful day in Cozumel. The temperature is about 80 degrees on its way to 85. It hasn't become hot yet with that intense humidity. When I get to the windy side of the island it is calm. No wind. Again, unbelievable. Maybe it will last past noon.

I have two empty Gatorade bottles right behind me. I've learned to put electrolyte powder in them to mix with water later in the day.

I eat two GUs, two bars and drink four bottles of Gatorade on the first loop. I am back in the town by now and come by the hotel and finish line. Sandy is waiting and talking to her new friends who are all waiting for someone. I slow down and stop and say Hi. It is a fun moment because all these riders come zooming by me as if they were on the Tour de France. And here I am talking to my wife, eating a candy bar she gives me and taking pictures. I finally tell her I'll be back in two hours and get on my bike again and ride away.

I get around to the other side of the island and amazingly there is still no headwind. This is the first time in six rides with no headwinds. I make it to the halfway point in the ride where the Bike Special Needs Bags are located. This year for the first time, I talked myself into putting some supplies in one. I pull over at the place that has the racks with all the Bike Special Needs Bags

There is this big, black, good looking guy standing in the shade of the building eating a sandwich like he was taking a break on a day hike. He looked to be about 6'4" and 240 pounds. You don't usually see anyone this large in an IRONMAN. Not black, white or Hispanic. He was a big boy. We talked a little and I just enjoyed watching him. He seemed like he didn't have a care in the world.

And he said it was his first IRONMAN. I said, "Great. You enjoying it?" And he replied, "Yep, swim was good and ride is good so far." How many IRONMANs is this for you? I replied, "This is my 12th. And his eyes got big. "Wow.... that is a lot!" I smiled and said they were fun. We finished the small talk and I said, "Enjoy your sandwich!"

I turned away from him and laid down in the shade because I wanted to max out this experience. I had never allowed myself to ever stop half way before. It almost felt illegal. If I was going to stop, I might as well take full advantage of it. My thoughts were, "I am going to enjoy myself today. It is number four. Next is the 777 so be more relaxed than normal. When this day is done I have one more big one to go."

I ate my candy bar and then got up to leave. I asked him his name and he said "Carmen." I said he looked great and wished him a nice ride. He lifted up his sandwich to me and said, "Thanks, you too!"

I went back to my bike, and started again. I was leaving the beach and headed back towards the hotel.

I saw Sandy again, then headed around for my third and final loop of the island. I was so excited because the wind had never come up on the windy side but it had come up on the calm side of the island. It didn't matter because it wasn't as bad as usual. Normally, I get inner thigh cramps somewhere in this thing. They are severe and almost incapacitating. When they come in it is like someone takes a hammer to my inner thighs. Every year they show up. This year they didn't show up until the last five miles of the ride. Tremendous.

I rode with one leg for a while and then the other but I could make it to the end. When I finished, almost 2,250 riders had finished before me. I am not a bike guy. Friends say that if I trained and rode the bike between IRONMANs I'd surprise myself. Probably so.

But this year I had taken a different kind of salts for cramping and they worked. And interestingly, I ate less than ever.

I got to the Bike to Run change tent and was able to get off the bike without my legs seizing up. The deal is that when you finish your bike, you ride up and a helper grabs the handle bars, hopefully gently, to help you stop. Then they steady the bike as you get off. Some people fall over on their bikes as they try to dismount. That is an awkward moment as you fall on the asphalt with your bike on top off you in front of 50 cheering people.

They usually try to hold the bike upright but that doesn't help me. It hurts me. I need them to slowly lay the bicycle over on its side so I don't have to lift my leg high to swing it off. They think I am crazy but we negotiate. My English to their Spanish somehow works. Then we go through the dance and I thank them. If done right, that inner thigh muscle doesn't cramp up anymore and scream at me.

I waddle to pick up my Bike to Run Bag and then I go into a really hot tent to change. Last year it took me over an hour to get out of it as both my thighs seized up at the same time. I somehow laid across the plastic small chairs and fell asleep. But I finally woke up when people surrounded me and asked if I needed an ambulance. I said, "no" and found a way to get up and stumble out of the tent. Sandy was really worried because she saw me go in and not come out.

But I came out and told her I had leg problems. She just shook her head and smiled and said, "OK Baby, now what?" I just kissed her and told her about my yearly predicament and walked away. Then I ran my marathon.

This year, I went in and felt way better. I was stiff but not crushed. I saw a nice young man and smiled at him and asked for his help. There are guys in the tent to help riders who needed care. That is a great thing. I hope they get paid well. Some riders never make it out of the tent. They are done in by that humidity and heat. These guys try to assist them or go get medics.

I put my hand on his shoulder and we went to a corner of the tent where, if there was a breeze possible, it would be there. Some years it is unbearable in there.

Then I slowly sat down. I asked him to please take off my shoes as I couldn't bend over. He did and I was so grateful!

Then I pulled out clean socks from my Bike to Run bag and asked him to take my old socks off and put on my clean socks. The 20 year old looking kid was so kind and he did it. Then I gave him my shoes and asked him to put them on my feet and again, he smiled and did it. Eureka! I was done.

He helped me to my feet and took my bag with dirty bike stuff like my helmet, gloves, socks and bike shoes, and I walked out of the tent while thanking him a lot. What a savior he was. Bending over to get those shoes off can be a killer.

Then I walked out. Sandy was back on the observer fence looking amazed. I wasn't in there 10 minutes this year. I came slowly walking out drinking something and eating something. I was happy and whole. She just yelled, "Baby.... I am here!"

The crowds on this fence had thinned out because the good guys and ladies had already been through earlier in the day. It was now 3:30 and I had started riding at 8:15 a.m. Long day for a non- bike guy.

Sandy had a lady friend standing next to her who looked happy and fun so we talked a little. She was waiting for someone too and she took our picture for us. I said all was good and stayed a few minutes then said I probably ought to start the marathon. They agreed. I kissed Sandy and thanked the lady and walked away still drinking something. I opened my little Base salts and licked my thumb, shook some salts onto my wet and sticky thumb licked it, and started running. Badda Bing.... Easy Day.

I try to run my first loop of about nine miles, then see how I feel. There isn't a gun to my head, so it is my way to figure it out. I saw Sandy again at the end of the first loop as I usually do in five and a half hours to six hour marathons if I am cruising. That means I am back in two hours on a three loop course. I do loop one, then do loop two. This year I start loop three and finished slower than normal. I was razzed about it on Facebook about it by my friend Jeremy, so I had to explain what happened. Jeremy always follows me on his computer. I wear a chip so everyone can trace me. Here's the backstory I posted:

"Hi Jeremy,

I have this bad left upper hamstring. I tore it training for Kokoro. It started to act up and I knew I could press through but it felt like a knife point jabbing under my butt each step.

My question was: Do I want to rehab a worse hamstring afterwards or rein in my ego to finish better? I decided to slow down.

Beginning my third loop in the marathon, that big 6'4" black guy is ahead of me. I am not sure how that happened, but there he was. He must have motored by me on the bike somewhere.

Turns out he is a really nice, maybe forty year old, Jamaican man who went to Bucknell University on a Water Polo Scholarship named Carmen. He also was on the National Jamaican Water Polo team. No wonder he had such a fast swim.

He was really struggling now. He was now dizzy and wobbly and looking really bad. Like almost delirious bad.

I asked him how he was. He said he didn't know if he could make it. I said, "Sure you can. You can do a lot more than you think you can." Then he told me again how bad he felt. It was dehydration. I'd been there many times.

He was so likable, I started coaching him. I said, "Do what I say and you will make it." He smiled and said, "OK."

It gave me a reason to walk. We walked the last nine miles or third loop and I tried to coach him out of his emotions. I showed him how to breathe through his nose with deep breaths. I gave him some salts, and told him how to walk. Then I encouraged him to keep his head up and straight, with his hands going out in front of him so as to lengthen his

Sandy and I in this pic, as I come out of Bike To Run Tent.
It is behind me 25 yards. A nice pic and then the marathon.

stride. And we got him fluids.

He asked me about my USAF shirt and Pararescue. So I began to tell him about learning to press through suffering. As Mark Divine would say at SEALFIT and Kokoro: *You have a 20X capacity inside you.*

I had him say out loud the whole way, "Easy day, good day, fun day, looking good, feeling good, I am Hollywood! I will do this, I am an IRONMAN, I can do anything, Easy day, fun day, looking good, feeling good." It went on for two and a half hours.

He'd ask, "Can I eat this banana from the aid station?" I said, "I don't care. Taste it and spit it out if you don't like it." He drank small cups of water and we just talked. We talked about everything to keep his mind off his suffering.

I had him smile at a few people and raise his hands like going over the finish line starting with six miles left. I'd get him to say to the

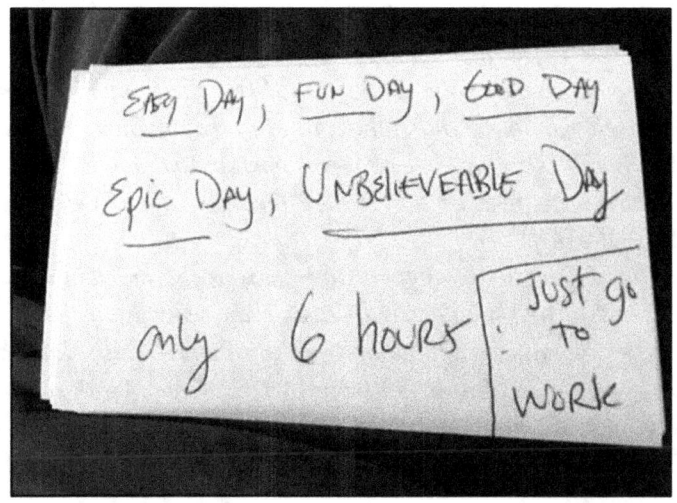

bystanders, "I am practicing my finish!" They'd all laugh and cheer him on. Then he'd put his arms down and ask, "Do you think I will make this?" I'd say, "No doubt in my mind" and make him laugh. He thought it was fun and crazy while not feeling well.

I taught him how to wave like a Rose Parade Queen on her float with the elbow, elbow, wrist, wrist style. I'd make him smile and wave to the people on the side of the road. And then I begin to have him say out loud more often "I am Carmen...I am an IRONMAN" to all the watchers we passed. "I am doing great. I can do this!" They all clapped and cheered him on. He did that over and over to stop focusing on how miserable he was.

The last two miles, his adrenaline kicked in and he said "let's go faster!" He got so excited. But he was really wobbly and faint and I hoped he'd make it. But he could hear the announcer in the distance *calling out people's names at the finish line. I said, "Carmen, that is you! You're almost there!"*

At the end, Sandy came out to find us on the course and she was successful. I introduced her to Carmen and she told him he looked great! She did a wonderful job of encouraging him. Then she walked with us.

At the end, he was alive. Wobbly but elated.

About 50 yards short of the finish line I said, "Now, go finish." He said "No..." but I made him run to the finish line ahead of me. I pointed to him where to raise his hands and smile for that everlasting picture of this biggest victory in his life. The IRONMAN official picture of him had to be EPIC. He ran to the finish line and with the announcer shouting his name. His hands were up and he stood upright and smiled and crushed it. The crowd went nuts as they called out his name: "Carmen... YOU ARE AN IRONMAN!"

I just stood back and watched and enjoyed the moment. He was so happy. Then I turned the corner to run up the runway to the finish line and raised my hands and smiled and ran through as well. Not a big deal to me as it was # 12. But it is always a BIG deal. It was so satisfying because he got his win and I finished my fourth major endurance event on my list. Often it is more fun to see someone else get a win than getting my own.

When I ran through, he saw me and grabbed me, shaking. He sort of collapsed on my shoulder and hugged me and sobbed and wouldn't let go. Then he continued to cry on my neck like a baby shaking convulsively. All the people went nuts.

So we just stood there. I am 6' tall and he is 6'4", two grown men having a victory moment. It was great.

He had worked hard to get that win in his life. He had lost 60 pounds to do that. He mentioned over and over on the run that he had been discouraged by his work life, and personal life and just let himself go. He said he wanted a new start and this was his first goal.

It was a classic IRONMAN moment.

An IRONMAN official and medical person came up to me and asked me what all that was about...

I said he made his first IRONMAN. That should explain it all.

I told the medical people to grab him and take him in the Med tent because he was out of it. They did. I looked for Sandy but didn't see her. So I went and sat down and faked that I was passing out to get in the Med tent too. I had been in that Med tent five times at the end of that race before. This time, I looked in pretty good shape from walking. They don't let you in the Med tent if you look good. You need to look like you are really needy and maybe going into shock or something. I wanted to see him and make sure he was OK. Also, I needed to get my IV as I always do.

I sat in my chair and when I felt the time was right I fell off and got in a fetal position, shaking. Some guy ran over with a wheelchair. When I faked being half-dead, they picked me off the ground, took me in a wheelchair and pushed me to the tent. Inside they found a cot for me.

Carmen was across from me. I received my two and a half IV bags and finally got off my cot after they took the needle out. I told him he was my hero. He had an IV in him also and he started to cry again. I shook his hand.

He was in pretty bad shape but he finished. He didn't quit. He was an IRONMAN! It was a huge win in his life. Many people never get those moments. He risked a lot and worked hard. Then something good happened along the way. Faith is getting out there and risking.

So Jeremy, that's why I was slow.

Carmen was taken from the Med tent to the hospital for the rest of the night. They let him out on Monday. It was the best thing as he came alone, which is never wise. He was a zealot, though not a wise one. But it worked out. We all need someone to watch over us, after that all day event. The hospital was his protector.

I remember being in the Med tent and smiling at him and saying, "Easy day, looking good, feeling good, YOU ARE AN IRONMAN!" And he faintly smiled back. He was so happy in his suffering. He said back to me as he lay on his cot, "Easy Day, Fun Day. I am now an IRONMAN" with a big smile on his face.

"We never get there alone. There is always someone. Go be that, for someone else down the road." He smiled and said "I will."

That is what it is all about...

I'd left him my phone number and email at the tent and wouldn't you know it, two days later he texted me and wanted to see me. He drove down from Playa del Carmen to Secrets at Maroma Beach and Sandy and I visited with him. He was so happy and grateful for everything. He hugged me again like I was his rescuer. We were excited for him too! Sandy loves this stuff.

I still stay in contact with him. He calls me Dad. He and his wife have reconciled to become friends and worked out their situation with the children. His life has turned around!

Why do I share all this? Because everybody wants a testimony but few want the test. But overcomers love a challenge to overcome. He saw he had the 20X in him – he didn't know it was within him. The happiest people in life are those with a significant purpose and regular wins.

Sandy and I had a fun vacation, recuperating in Mexico. We went to the Zoetry Villa Rolandi on Isla Mujeres. It is a boutique hotel on a small island with great food and ocean sunsets.

She puts up with a lot, she deserves a great time often.

Then we got on the plane and came back for the last big audacious test: "The World Marathon Challenge" or as it is known the 777: 7 Marathons in, 7 Days on, 7 Continents.

I have six weeks to get ready.

How am I going to do this?

Carmen was a happy man. We were catching up, after the Mexico IRONMAN. He came to see Sandy and me at Secrets in Playa Del Maroma, Mexico.

LETTER FROM CARMEN JONES

Five years. That's how long I had been chasing the dream of finishing a full Ironman. In 2012 I was 35 and weighed 340 pounds. Pre-diabetic, high cholesterol with chest pains and a bunch of other problems. The standard tests returned negative; nothing urgent. However, deep in my gut I had an uneasy feeling that if I didn't change, something terrible was going to happen. I promised myself to set a goal so high that I would surprise even myself.

My goal? I decided to complete an Ironman. In 2012, completing and Ironman was physically an impossibility for me. My family has always been extremely supportive of me, but in the end, this would be entirely up to me.

Fast forward 5 years to Sunday, November 26th, 2017. Race day. I met Robert at the first rest stop on the bicycle route where we could open our food packets. Riders huddled and sat on the sandy bank under the shade of a small almond tree trying to escape the tropical heat, refuel and rest. Robert was one of the few riders that was standing. He looked fresh, with a huge smile. An unusual sight. Our conversation was brief, and his parting words, "Let me know how it goes." have stuck with me. For me, running is the hardest of the three triathlon disciplines. Being overweight for that long took its toll on my knees and back. With only 8 kilometers to go to finish, I was completely exhausted, with nothing left in the tank. Barely able to walk, the thought of not finishing was crushing me. Anger. Desperation. Tears. From behind me out of the darkness, I see Robert. I was sure he had finished ages ago. With slurred speech I mumble, "Can you help me?"

"Easy day." "Just takin' a stroll." "Keep your chin up." "Swing your arms." "Breathe." Robert keeps repeating as we walk and chip away at the final 8-kilometer stretch. He does not leave my side. It's painful for me and I'm dizzy but Robert keeps me going. Somehow. We pass the airstrip and we hit the Malecon where the sea meets the main road. The sea breeze is crisp and

cold. I can barely see the lights in the distance. The finish line is nowhere in sight. Robert says "When you cross that finish line, raise your hands up in the air and smile." "Think about hearing 'Cameron Jones from Jamaica, you are an Ironman' when you cross." "Think about your son. His dad is a champion." We turn onto the last stretch and I can see the finish line. My pace quickens. My dream is within reach... "Hands up, big smile!" are the last things I hear from Robert as I break into a jog and head towards the finish. I cross the finish line, hands raised, big smile. Just like Robert said. When Robert finishes right after we embrace deeply. I'm still in disbelief, and extremely grateful.

Robert brought out the best in me when I had nothing left. What can you say to someone who helps you achieve a dream that means so much to you? Robert is a blessing and it's an honor to call him a friend. I recall this experience for inspiration when things get tough, and it also reminds me to pay it forward by helping others wherever I can.

Thanks Robert for all you have done for me.

I love a good cigar, and here I am having a custom made one, just for me! How cool is that?!?

Sandy and I, enjoying the post-race recuperation at a resort we love.

LEADERSHIP LESSONS

1. Knowledge is power. It is what everybody else knows that you don't, that will frustrate you.

2. Equipment is important – but don't let it stop you from trying to achieve.

3. Ask for help when you need it.

4. No one gets ahead alone.

5. When you've achieved, turn around and help someone else.

6. 20X Principle: You can drive out your negative thoughts with positive thoughts and positive self-talk to get through your pain and win.

Finally, the last big challenge of my year of challenges: The 777. I would have to dig deep mentally and physically again. But Thank God, for the Greece learning lessons. Enjoy!

The starting line of the World Marathon Challenge in Antarctica.

CHAPTER 14

The World Marathon Challenge - The 777

Sandy had a wonderful week relaxing, after the IRONMAN in Mexico. It is a yearly ritual. We usually spend seven days at a resort or two and just reconnect. I've been pressing now for nearly three years with early morning workouts and being physically tired. She has been a good trooper to support me in every way. It has been great. This is her payback. Whatever she wants us to do we do. She brings all sorts of reading that she has saved up for a month or so and I take one or two books that I've been saving up to read. It is a special time because we can relax all day on the beach or around a pool. For me, there is nothing like accomplishing your goal and then treating yourself to something special.

We fly home, and now the last big training period begins. I have from December 7th until January 22nd to get ready for:

7 Marathons in

7 Days on

7 Continents

I am not a runner, haven't been since Pararescue days. But I can run. There is a huge difference. Runners make running look effortless. They are smooth. They are fluid. They look so natural. Non-runners look like their running is a workout. Their faces express focused effort. Often they exhibit pain and struggle. I am a guy who makes a workout out of running. I start slowly and gradually warm up and then push until the end. It becomes fun some days, but it isn't always easy. Sometimes it is just a job and an act of my will. I make running look like work – which is how I approach it, like a job.

My weight is always an issue. My body always carries extra fluid in my midsection. The older I get, it just seems to want to blow up in my body. It is a weird thing. It just happens. When I run on a treadmill my body stays about the same. However, when I get out on the asphalt, the fluid and pounds begin to shed. After five days out on the street my body sheds much of the midsection fluid. Never fails.

My parents purchased a house in South Laguna in 1969 near the Pacific Coast Highway. It was down the street from where my father's parents had purchased property in the 1920s. I brought my family back to Grandpa's house three or four times a year to surf and see the grandparents. While there, I'd also work out and run the highway south towards San Clemente.

I remember getting ready for IRONMAN #3 in 1980 running that highway.

During the recession of 2009, 29 years later, I moved home and in with, my 92 year old father. My 91 year old mother had just died. They were married for 65 years. He was depressed and so was I after my divorce. He offered for me to move home and heal up. It seemed like a good idea especially since he was alone. When I arrived home, I needed something to focus on and it only seemed natural that I'd start to train for IRONMAN Western Australia in 2009. I loved Australia and it would be great to have a reason to go back and visit. It was healing and encouraging to get back on the training course that I'd run since high school.

The World Marathon Challenge was daunting. It takes me a lot of work to do one marathon. Seven was going to be more than challenging. I'd done the Sparta race as way to see what it was like to do eight days of 30 miles a day. But that was a run/walk with mountain climbs. This was a run.

How in the world do you train for that as a non-runner?

So I set out a plan. I searched the internet for testimonials by the three previous years 777 finishers to hear how they trained and came across one, real good suggestion from a middle aged man. He said he got to the end of his training being able to do five days in a row of 20 mile days. The race was seven days of 26 miles. But he felt confident that if he could do five days at 20 miles it would work, and it worked for him.

So that became my six week goal. I'd only ever run one marathon outside of an IRONMAN before. It was in 2015 when I flew back to Dayton Ohio for the Air Force marathon. It was sort of a bucket list deal and I'd always wanted to see Wright Patterson Air Force base. The marathon was to run around it. It was fun. My time was 4:55 because I stuck with the 5:00 hour pacesetter and just did what he said. But it was hard for me.

I wasn't sure what times to shoot for on this 777.

When we got back from Mexico, I began to run the highway. I know the distance points that I've used for years. The farthest distance I'd run, was to the 7 Eleven in north San Clemente at 8.5 miles which made for a 17 mile run. Within a week and a half I was back doing those runs three days a week. My training for Kokoro was still with me.

The challenge I set for myself was to do interval sprints at various sections during those long runs to get my heart up. It was my aerobic and anaerobic training. Usually, they would be sprints while counting 100 left foot steps. Then I'd go back to a normal pace for a few minutes then sprint 100 left foot steps again. Why left foot steps and not right? I don't know. They just seem easier to remember while counting. I think it is like the one contact thing. My brain just gets used to it.

After a couple weeks of that my hamstring really flared up again. I usually don't know how I do these things but I knew about this left thigh upper hamstring tear really well. One morning while doing my Kokoro training, I had my weight vest on and was doing 100 step sprints with my military boots on. I was training in fear of what they might expect me to do with that 20 pounds pack I was going to have to carry for 50 hours. That morning I was feeling great. I was pressing in my sprint repeats when I just felt this little bite on an inside spot of my bottom of my left butt cheek. I shut down the sprints and running immediately and tried to walk it off. It didn't go away. It didn't hurt very badly, but it was there.

I'd had one in my right butt cheek before I started training at CrossFit three years earlier. Fortunately, somehow I'd worked through it and it disappeared over time. The hamstring problems were stupid things in that I could do my runs with no problems until I tried to step up a curb or run up a hill. Then it would bite.

It was funny because, I'd run, but when I got to a curb, I'd have to stop, and then slowly step up on the curb with my other foot. Then I'd start running again. IRONMAN marathons were easy as there weren't any curbs.

Thankfully, that earlier right hamstring problem went away at CrossFit. I believe it was from doing all the squats and deadlifts which stretched and strengthened it.

But this one was different. It really hurt to stretch it. When I bent over to touch my toes with my legs straight, I'd lost about six inches of flexibility. I ran with this new pain, and thought about it every training run.

From the very beginning of this session of training, I really was tired of training. I'd been at it for three years as I prepared for Kokoro.

I'd trained some for Greece. I trained a little for The Quest. But I had trained so differently, and so intensely for Kokoro. Then I did the IRONMAN. And now came this. I was experiencing mental exhaustion.

People ask me, "How did you stay focused for those three years?" This was my mindset:

Every day I had to have the right mind frame. I said to myself, "I just have to go to work today. I am a semi-retiree and this is my other work. This is not a hobby, nor a fun thing. Everybody has to go to work whether they feel like it or not. No different for me. Get up and go to work. You get fired if you don't go to work. There can be no excuses. You can do this if you don't wimp out. Go to work and train. This experience is not too big for you. This will be EPIC and Legendary. NO ONE would ever try this at any age. You will be one of the greatest endurance athletes ever. You aren't just going to be the oldest Kokoro finisher ever. You are going to run seven marathons in seven days. You knocked out your 12th IRONMAN. You are attempting the unbelievable. Just go to work and train. You can do this. Live Legendary! Anyone can be average!"

I had to say this to myself every day. Some days were good. Some I just survived. But after every day, I knew I'd gone to work and put a deposit in the bank.

As I worked on the 777, I increased the amount of YouTube videos that I watched. I watched David Goggins over and over. I'd searched for new athletes doing unbelievable things. I watched Tim Grover in his interview with Tom Bilyeu many times, even though I knew what he was going to say. I just needed to see Grover's face and hear his voice as he explained Michael Jordan's obsessiveness to be the greatest.

And there were times when I didn't work out. I'd cut myself some slack and just sit in a chair most of a day. I'd just be mentally and physically empty. Also I was training in fear, which is the worst kind of training. It is the fear of the unknown. Sitting in that chair not relaxing, I counted the hours until I had to go to work again at 5:30 a.m.

Let me go a little deeper on that. Let me share with you some confidence building stories. There must be a foundation of confidence and mental toughness that an athlete has tucked away to know they can do these things. One of those confidence builders was when I did year three of IRONMAN, that year I trained in complete fear. I trained intensely for six months. I read the Sports Illustrated Article and started the next day. The way Sports Illustrated told the IRONMAN story it seemed to be a daunting undertaking. Nobody in their right mind should or would want to attempt it. It humbled the strongest competitors.

So I trained in fear. And I was fighting the event the whole time mentally. Like...how many more walls will I hit? How do I get through this one? Should I slow down, or speed up to the others guys? Am I drinking enough? Which I wasn't. Was 90 miles a week enough? No. So I went for 100 a few times in six days plus all my other training. Then I experienced it.

Another confidence builder was my third IRONMAN. It was at the 25th World Championships in 2003, that I said to myself. "I will again find a way to get through the walls or unexpected adversities." And I did.

I got sick from working too hard on my bike up to Hawi which is the halfway point on the bike portion. When I turned around at the orange cone in the middle of the street, I went over under to a shade tree and threw up. The sun had been hot and I got excited pedaling up the hill 17 miles and didn't drink enough. I felt so fresh and good, I just drove myself up the hill. But I had the wrong water system. I had bottles only on my bike frame.

The smart guys and ladies had a water bottle between the handlebars in the middle with large straws coming out. They didn't need to let go of the handlebars for fluids. They just bent over and sucked the water or fluids out while riding hard.

I'd never seen those before. Not having the center water bottle and straw meant I had to take one hand off my handlebars to grab my bottles. However, I was pulling so hard going up the hill to Hawi with my legs and arms while holding on the handlebars that I couldn't ever let go of them. Consequently I cooked myself by not drinking enough in the humid heat to replenish the sweat I was losing.

As soon as I entered Hawi, I threw up probably three times while standing under that tree, straddling my bike. All yellow bile. It wasn't fun and it confused me. I didn't know I had worked that hard during the hill climb. It didn't feel that tough. But I guess I was excited and way too into it. I had pushed myself harder than I should have. I stood under the big green leafy tree in the shade thinking, "This is not good. I wonder what will happen now." After a few minutes assessing my situation, I knew I had to start back for the 55 miles to Kona.

Now the challenge was that I was going downhill with a hot uphill wind in my face. Nothing is more discouraging than not being able to enjoy a downhill ride. A slow downhill ride is really discouraging. When it flattened out, the wind was still in my face and was a crosswind towards the ocean. It was life sucking and punishing.

Those 55 miles were miserable. I was dizzy, weak and thirsty. I'd drink, but I couldn't keep the fluids down. My internal stomach chemicals were shot. Once you start throwing up it becomes a whole new game. Nothing is right or normal. Only time and fluids can heal you. But I couldn't drink or eat. It became a new ballgame. I hadn't trained for this.

I barely made it back. I remember thinking, "You can't be going much slower than this. I am not making any progress. How much longer can this take? My legs are gone."

Obviously, I limped in. I was so grateful to get off that bike. You talk about "hitting walls." It was a mental challenge. Looking back, it was a mental toughness moment.

When I got onto the marathon course I had to walk a lot. I sipped a mouthful of fluids and I finally got some fluids to stay down. I also began to count 100 steps then walk 100 steps then repeat for the first 10 miles. The "win" was that I kept being able to repeat this. I thought, "Just do it over and over. Don't look up. Just focus." 100 running paces then walk.

By dusk it was cooling off, Thank God. Ambulances had been on the highway all afternoon taking athletes off because it was soooo hot. I would urge you to take a break from reading this and go Google the Julie Moss 1982 IRONMAN finish, it changed the respect for the IRONMAN forever. You can see the toll the heat can take over there. I must have seen 10-15 ambulances drive by as we ran. Some of the pro triathletes were in those early ambulances. 2003 was a really hot year for IRONMAN.

I made it to the Energy Lab, which is about mile 14, I made the turn and started the slight uphill back to the highway. But at the highway, I began to run out of steam and get dizzy again. It became another war of wills; mine vs. the voices in my head. The longer I went, the dizzier I became. I stopped all drinking and had stopped all eating hours ago.

Finally, while jogging or running slow, I fixated on the lady's shoulders in front of me and just stared at her. I mimicked her with my shoulders straight and head up. It was "just do what she does step for step." It worked. I was able to block out everything and do what she did. It worked for maybe a mile or two.

But out of nowhere, I had to pee. Unbelievable. I remembered IRONMAN 1980 and my dark brown pee at mile 14 out on Diamond Head. This couldn't be happening again. "Get control of yourself, Robert" I kept saying. I didn't have my wife following me in a van this time. I was on my own. I slowed to a walk and let the lady leave me behind. And finally I stopped. My thought was, "How am I going to do this? I am dizzy and weak and unstable. But I have this strong urge to pee."

Then I slowly turned to my left and to the shoulder of the road. We were running on the 'against the traffic' side of the closed down road.

As I turned, the equilibrium in my ears changed. I was pretty good as long as I did the same linear movements with no change. But this change did it. When I looked down as I was pulling down my pants, I crumpled like having a bag of potatoes drop out of the back of a pickup truck at slow speed and passed out.

It was sunset at that time. When I woke up, I had this wonderful hot asphalt warming my back. The sky was black with beautiful stars above me. I wasn't near a streetlight on the highway so it was a pretty Hawaii darkness. My head was still out of it. The asphalt felt so good.

I also had three ambulances attendees with me: two on their knees, one on each side and one standing over me. A medic was trying to talk to me like.... "Hey, what is your name? Can you see me?" They were doing the blood pressure thing and pulse thing again like in Florida except I wasn't in my hotel room.

The blur in my vision cleared a bit and it was two men and a woman. I said "Hi."

They said as they always do stupidly, "How do you feel?" How stupid is that! How do I feel? And I replied "Great...This is sooo comfortable. The asphalt feels tremendous under me, and the stars are beautiful out here in the dark! How long have I been here?"

They said they were not sure. I was reported to the officials about being out on the highway about 20 minutes ago. They said, "We had to drop off another runner at the hospital so we were slow getting to you."

I said something like…"Great. Nice to meet you." You finding my blood pressure OK and my pulse?" And they said, "Yes, you are alive and OK." I said "Great. Gosh this feels good to lay here."

Then this kid leans over and says, "Here Mr. Owens, drink this Gatorade." He stuck his right arm under my neck and lifted me up the way the Army guy did it in 1980 and I began to enjoy the fluids that seemed to want to stay down. The fluids didn't have much taste. Why didn't they have much taste? Because I had so much salt in my mouth and my tongue was covered with a white salty film. No taste was possible as the taste buds were covered.

Then the paramedic kid says to me after a bottle goes in, "Mr. Owens...Do you want to finish?"

I responded, "Sure.... I think so. I can probably do this." Just let me get my fluids. I'll be OK. I just need to replenish my fluids. The sponge needs water to work."

I remember being disappointed with my response. Why did I say "I think so." That was a cheesy weak unconfident answer. But I was a little mentally crushed. This moment had gotten in my head.

Then the kid starts to tear up. And I say to him, "Why are you emotional about this?" and he replied "Mr. Owens, I'd give anything to be you! I was in a car crash a few years ago and I am missing a lot of things internally and my legs have problems. I was in a wheelchair for a while but I made it out. I just wish I could do an IRONMAN. You are so fortunate."

Then the other two paramedics chimed in about this young man and how he had fought through a lot to be walking and now he's a paramedic. I said to him whatever his name was, "You are a good man. Most paramedics would try to put me in the ambulance. You are a special young man. You asked me if I wanted to finish. You are not a normal paramedic. I know you. I was a Special Ops Pararescueman paramedic back at your age. You are an IRONMAN paramedic! You are wonderful. You believe in helping people to overcome their challenges like we did!"

By this time it was a touching scene for all of us. The other two older paramedics knew this kid's struggle to get out of his wheelchair and fight to get his life back. They honored this kid. And all the while, the kid just kept his arm under my neck and giving me fluids. Finally one of the other paramedics asked if I was ready to try to stand up?

I said, like back in 1980, "Yes. Could you help me up?"

They stood me up on the highway and it all began to come back. The water was in the sponge. This thing would not beat me nor take me out. I was having a moment again. I would pass out again if I have to, but I will finish this 25th Anniversary World Championships.

So they walked me around for 5-10 minutes and then two paramedics walked with towards Makala Street.

I said thank you and goodbye and walked by myself towards the far lamppost on the corner of Makala Street. Then I began to jog. I turned the corner to the right and down the little hill and I started jogging, then running. Like seven minute miles running. My body seemed fresh.

There weren't many still on the course as it was late. They allow you to do it in 17 hours or until midnight. It was about 11:00 p.m.

Within a few minutes, I entered into the crowds. I was the only finisher coming in at that time. The crowds were still on both sides of the street and the announcers voice said, "Here comes Robert Owens from

I look pretty good, but inside I was dying.
Notice the cell phone in my speedos.
Illegal but who cares.

Nevada. Look at him! He looks fresh and great! Where have you been Robert Owens?"

I run through the finish with him saying loudly over the fun blaring background music, "Good job Robert Owens! YOU ARE AN IRONMAN!!!

The crowd went nuts clapping in sync to the beat of the music. I threw my hands up and the picture shows me with this huge smile on my face. I looked gaunt but good. An official came up to me and commented, "You finished strong for this time of night. What happened out there?" My response was, "I had a nice nap on the asphalt for awhile. Feel great now!" He laughed and congratulated me.

I kissed my wife and kids and friends who had come to watch from the mainland. Had my picture taken with them and then went into the hospital tent and took my two and a half IV bags and a massage.

It was the worst IRONMAN of the four I'd done, and remains the worst I have ever endured. Having the goggles kicked off my face in the beginning, losing one of my contacts, riding the bike with one contact for the first time, throwing up at Hawi, and not being able to eat or drink on the ride back to Kona, finding a way to get to the Energy Lab and then fighting dizziness until I fell over. It made for a long day. But I did it. I finished. I tapped into the 20X Principle within me.

Why do I tell that story? I don't train in fear of IRONMANs anymore. I can do them. In a sense I own them. They have thrown their best at me and I still finished. Humidity still kicks my butt as I train in a non-humid climate. But humidity won't take me out. I don't have fears. I've learned that when you hit walls just figure them out. They are to be expected.

And I now know Kokoro. I had trained in fear for two and a half years but I did it. I finished. I did it with a wrecked left rotator cuff and a bad hamstring. And I was fearful of not being able to keep up on the runs with the younger men. I made it. I didn't quit. Now I understand the adventure. The question to you is: have you developed your craft? Have you put in the time to develop deep confidence in taking on big challenges? It takes time and consistency. You've got to pay your dues.

I have grown my confidence over time, but I didn't know how to anticipate the toll seven marathons in seven days would take on me. I knew that unknown fear again. What I knew was:

I feared it.

I feared it as an athlete and non-runner.

I feared it at 66 years old.

I feared the unknown of my body taking that pounding.

I feared it for my feet. If I blow up my feet like I did in Greece, all my training will go out the window. I will have to just survive it like Greece in terrible bloody pain. I don't ever want that to happen again. Equipment will make or break all my training and good intentions.

I feared the weather in the Antarctic. It would be so unpredictable and potentially so cold. I hate the cold.

I feared doing the first two marathons within 24 hours.

I feared Dubai's potential heat.

I feared completing the last two marathons in under 24 hours.

There were so many unknowns. What I did know was :

The only way to train for unknowns is to research as much as possible, then train as smart and as hard as you can, and finally build mental confidence.

I knew again, that the only way to get ready for this mentally and physically, was to train harder than the seven marathons in seven days would test me. You play like you train.

Who cares if it is on seven continents? I will deal with it when whatever happens comes up! If the three previous years runners had made it on seven continents, I believed I could figure it out too.

So in the last three weeks, I went back to what I knew. I went military. I put that Kokoro weight vest back on and began to do my runs with it. You ask me "Why?"

There is more to know about mental and physical pain.

Matt Fitzgerald wrote a book entitled "How Bad Do You Want It?" It is a Ph.D study on the difference between the chemicals released in your brain between physical pain and mental pain.

Most think pain is pain. But it is not. There is a major difference in the chemicals released within your brain when experiencing mental pain and when experiencing physical pain. I needed to practice going into in through the walls and I'd most likely hit. I believed it would be a different pain than the pain in Greece with my feet and overall pain I experienced in Kokoro. I needed to experience the mental pain and physical pain of running every day 26 miles probably often by myself. That would be a head game for me. I never anticipated what it would be like to be running in the dark at night alone four nights in a row because I didn't know it was going to happen. It was a curve ball that happened as stuff always does.

When I read Matt's book, it reframed my lifelong experiences of hitting walls while running. I knew there were two walls, the mental pain and the physical pain. However, I am not a runner. I am not a loper, but not a fluid runner either. I have never been told I am pretty runner. I had to visualize myself pressing through the monotony of running. Again, there are four keys to overcoming this next test:

1.) Breathing correctly
2.) Positive self-talk where I would talk to myself out loud a lot
3.) Breaking each day's run into micro goals
4.) Positive internal images in my visualization.

This would have to happen each day as I trained. I had to visualize me suffering and working through it. I would feel the moment and visualize it happening every day and practice working through it somehow. To me it would be wall after wall after another wall. Every day.

Some people ask me "Robert, what do you think about when you're out there running those marathons?" And I usually respond "I'm thinking about every step I'm taking. I am thinking about the swivel in my hips. I am thinking the way my feet are hitting the ground, where my hands are and how my neck and head are positioned. I am thinking how I can make the next step better. I visualize what it should be like compared to what I'm doing. I have an ideal picture in my mind that I am visualizing and thinking on. I am wondering if the next wall is close. I guess you would say I'm pretty intense out there even though most people would not know it. I hate those walls but relish going through them.

My mindset for this training period was I wanted to run fatigued. Really fatigued. I wanted to practice pressing through the mental and physical pain. I wanted my body to adapt to strain.

I extended my runs to 20 miles a day with the vest on. Then I chose to do what I'd never done in my previous IRONMAN training. I'd run past the 7-Eleven which is my normal turnaround point for my previous IRONMAN training 17 mile runs. I chose to go further to the San Clemente Pier. That is where the Quest started back in August. That is the dirt path that I ran on in my Speedos and those crazy rubber water/rock shoes with those lifeguard kids. I had thought for years about running all the way to the pier but never had. This was an epic move in my psyche. I was now doing it, but also wearing a 20 pound weight vest.

On these runs, I couldn't run uphill because of my left hamstring but I could speed walk it. So I practiced how fast I could speed walk up hills, and then get back to a run.

My training had to be epic and legendary. At least to me! It had to be the hardest thing I'd ever done.

I'm fortunate, being semi-retired, my expenses are low, my kids are grown, and I have a wife who works, so I can train more intensely. The timing just seemed right. By the last week I was up to four days a week, with my twenty pound vest. On the fifth day, I treated myself with a speed run without the vest. I got to five days a week at 20 miles. My attitude was: I need to go to work every day. There weren't any emotions allowed. No feelings. Just focused commitment. Therefore, I just went to work every day.

It was wild to pick up my black vest each morning and see it layered in white salt sweat from the day before. I ran past the gated guard guy to where I lived each morning and he just stared. I left at 7 a.m. from my house and had a goal to be back by 10:30. He didn't smile or frown but just stared as I rounded the corner. I'd say, "Hi Leo!" And he'd finally smile and say, "Hi Mr. Owens." I'd comment, "Another 20 miles Leo. Not bad for 66." Then he'd break into a big smile and still just stare at me. My vest was white, covered in sweat salt.

I had visible results of hard work.

I was having my mental treat. I was pushing my limits. Being 66 turned from being a disappointment and a bummer to a badge of honor. Hooyah!

In my head, I dared anyone to do what I was doing.

I want to be the greatest athlete in the world in my mind!

I thought about Tom Brady. If he can, I can! I am young at 66. Shut the pundits up.

Finally, it was over. The last training day came and I ran my 20 mile speed run which wasn't fast. But it would do. I sat in my yard in the shade, giggly with excitement. I had two cokes and didn't move. I was sooooo tired but I had made my deposits.

Weirdly, I'd lost all my muscle mass from the previous three years. It was all gone. I tried and could barely do three pull-ups now. I was weak again.

The running five days a week had caused me to shed everything. I was skinny. Thank God I did Kokoro before this. All that hard work was a memory. It really bothered me, but I had this last challenge to tackle. Therefore it was worth it in a satisfying way. This training was hard but in a different way. It was so mental and sort of lonely. But I had been alone in my head already for three years. That had been a unique experience. It would take me now two or three years to train for Kokoro again if I had to. Which leads to the following questions:

1. What makes for the greatest endurance athlete?

2. Is the aerobic or anaerobic athlete the fittest? To me they are still apples and oranges. People say, "You look like you're in shape." But for what?

That is why I want to see if I can do both aerobic and anaerobic endurance events in the same time period. Putting the other three events in the same period just added spice.

Jets on the frozen continent as we prepare for the first marathon day.

The World Marathon Challenge would start in Antarctica, so I had to get to Cape Town to meet the runners and staff on Saturday night January 27th, 2018. Sandy flies mainly to Asia or Australia. So back in March of 2017 I called American Airlines about using miles that I have in my account to get a trip to Cape Town. I thought for sure that would be enough advance time to secure a good Business Class seat. I wanted to get those legs and feet up if possible for 25 hours of flying.

I'd been to Cape Town 15 times before as a speaker and consultant and I'd always flown to London on American then down to Cape Town on British Airways, or from Atlanta to Johannesburg on South African Airways then down to Cape Town. This was sort of like old times for me as I've flown four million miles on American Airlines and its One World partners to 30 nations. That doesn't include my flights on Delta, United, Southwest and European and Asian Airlines. However I haven't flown much since the Great Recession of 2009.

All those normal mileage flying options were already gone. The only way on miles for me to get to Cape Town was to go L.A. to Hong Kong for 14 hours then to Johannesburg for nine hours and to Cape Town in two hours. It didn't really matter which way I went. The challenge was that I'd have to leave on Monday January 22nd. I wondered if that would be my "taper." Take a week off. It wasn't an option, so that became my strategic taper.

Sandy booked her January flight schedule to be the Purser on the L.A. to Hong Kong leg so we could fly together. We had a great flight and then had a fun 24 hours in Hong Kong together. I was going nuts at the hotel, and got on the treadmill for an hour to work off my nervous energy. Then, I took her to one of my favorite restaurants, went to bed and then she flew home. I flew on to Johannesburg and Cape Town. I arrived on Thursday and was picked up by my good friend Gareth Stead. It was so good to be back in my favorite city in the world! We had dinner with his daughter and my good friend Carven Issaks from Namibia.

I spoke on Saturday morning to a group of men and then flew to Windhoek, Namibia for Saturday night and Sunday a.m. I spoke again to some businessmen, and then in Carven's Church and flew back to Cape Town.

My friends Nils Hinrichsen and Willem Du Tuit picked me up. They took me to the hotel and then to the first meeting of all the runners. It was really exciting as everyone was excited and nervous to embark on this 777 Challenge.

After the meeting, Nils, Willem and I went out to dinner and had a great time talking about our pasts and our futures. I had been coming to Cape Town since 1996, so we had lots to reminisce about. They dropped me off, and I tried to sleep that night. But it was nearly impossible. I tossed and turned, knowing in less than 48 hours my debut on the Antarctic icy course would be finished.

In the morning, I was so antsy again that I went in the Westin's Hotel workout room and ran for an hour. I hadn't run much in a week and it was driving me a little crazy.

I met with another good friend Bill Bennot for Monday's breakfast. Again, fun times seeing friends all of whom thought I was attempting something amazing. I concurred. All said, "You're 66. You really up for this?" I said confidently "Yes..... I think." They asked, "How many standalone marathons have you ever run?" My reply was one. But I had done 12 within IRONMANs."

It made for some nervous laughing. Bill hugged me and shook his head with his big smile and said "Go IRONMAN!" And we parted.

I had met Dorn, a Walmart Executive from Mexico City who was also running and we sort of hung out on Monday walking around getting things we might need at the last minute. We both wondered about electrolytes for replenishing ourselves. He bought some new salts and a size bigger pair of shoes. I had mentioned to him about my feet swelling in Greece.

I had to be up by 4 a.m. on Tuesday morning and be in the lobby by 5 a.m. to be bussed to the airport.

I don't remember much about dinner but I remember setting two alarms for 4 a.m. I don't know if I slept that night but I was up at 4 a.m. and double checking all my stuff. It had been recommended that we put our daily run stuff in seven different zip lock bags. There wouldn't be any laundry along the way.

So I had seven large Ziploc bags: Seven sets of shirts, seven sets of running shorts, seven underbody shorts to guard against chafing and seven sets of socks. For Antarctica, I had a bag of shirts for layering. I'd gone to North Face and REI and asked them about what cross-country skiers wear when racing. I purchased a wonderful light wool long sleeve shirt as well as another sweat wicking shirt that I hoped would work. Those shirts were in a Ziploc bags, as were four different types of gloves.

I had bags for three different types of hats and neck gear. I had three different jackets as I didn't know if the weather would be +20 degrees F or -20 degrees F. And I had four pairs of shoes: size 11, 11 1/2, 12 and 12 1/2. I didn't want Greece to happen again.

I'd wear the 12s for Antarctica because of the double sock selection

I'd chosen. For those of you who care, I chose an Altura Paradigm shoe for my size 11 and 12 because of its wide toe box and lowered heel. It feels like you are in a Birkenstock sandal. They can be great. "Iron Cowboy" in Greece had them and was sponsored by Altura. He loved his shoes.

I picked HOKAs which are just the opposite of Alturas for sizes 11 1/2 and 12 1/2. They have a really high soft heel which gives a different rolling heel placement. I wanted to give my hamstrings and balls of my feet a different torque and fight possible muscle fatigue. Mainly, I wanted options. It worked great. I ultimately used them all.

I purchased some REI rubber and metal snow shoe crampons for my 12s that I desperately hoped would work. I hadn't run on snow and ice since Alaska in the '70s. I didn't know if we would run on ice or hard pack or powder or what. I was most concerned about my feet sweating and freezing. All this was in a carry-on bag and a small roller check-in bag. I wanted wheels for my stuff. No straps and carrying anything except my backpack with phone cords, books and little stuff. Again, it was a good decision.

Tuesday: Antarctica

The alarms went off just fine. My adrenaline came the moment I opened my eyes. "This is it! It's here!" I thought. Oh my God. I broke into a nervous sweat. About 6:00 a.m. we were taken to Cape Town's airport and bussed to a private charter Boeing 757. We were told to keep our running stuff with us as when we landed in the Antarctic. We would be putting on our running stuff in the aisles of the plane before deplaning. 15 women and 45 men. Sounds like a unique experience. We got on and I chose to sit as far front as I could. I didn't know anyone except Dorn. I sat down and this guy comes and motions that he would like to sit next to me. Come to find out he was a 67 year old French man and didn't speak any English. As I saw during the week, he was tough as nails. And I found out he had finished two "Badwaters" in the last few years. Badwater is a 135 mile run from below sea level to over 8,300 feet in the California desert.

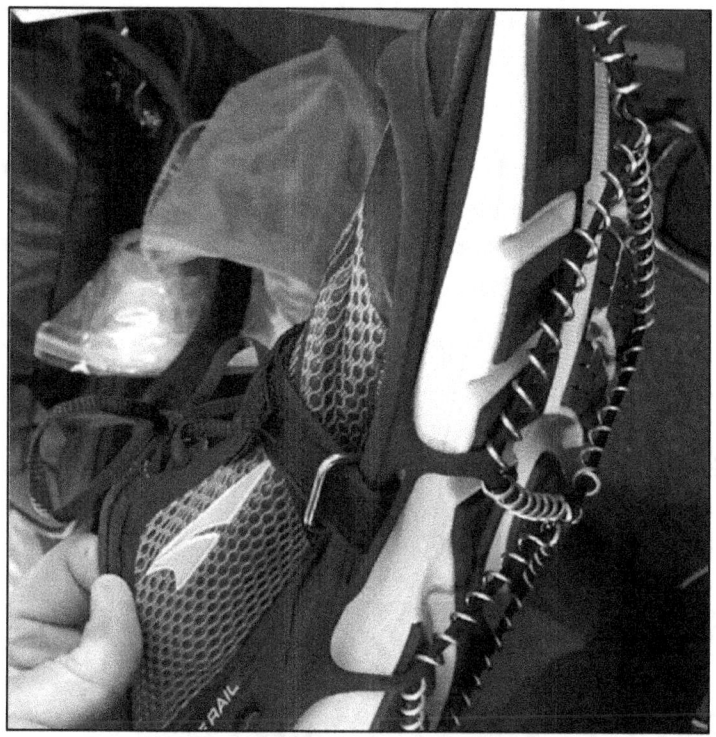

**Rubber and metal Crampons from REI.
I prayed they worked well. They did!**

    The flight attendants served us breakfast, but I didn't know how much to eat. We'd be in the air five and a half hours. Get off the plane and supposedly start running. It didn't work out that way but that is what I was thinking. So I ate my eggs and bacon and toast hesitantly.

    Maybe three hours into the flight I went up to the cockpit and was invited to sit in the co-pilots seat and talk a bit. The Captain was really interested and wanted to know more about us and me. So we talked and had a great time. He was amazed that I was older than him and doing this thing. He was about 63 and was the co-owner of the charter airline. I'd never been in a charter like this so I had many questions. He had landed in the Antarctic many times in this 757 which I found amazing. We took pictures together and I went back to my seat. He said on the way back, to come up and tell him all about it. He told me that after we got back to Cape Town and ran the Cape Town marathon, we switch to an Airbus

300-400 which is Airbus's biggest four engine plane. I think he said the charter airline had five different jets flying people and groups around the world all the time.

The back restroom of this 757 was done in black and gold and reminded me of a restroom that would be on Hugh Hefner's private Playboy jet. It was big and cool.

The plane only had about 75 business class seats. They fly all over the world picking up different groups from the band U2 to Bon Jovi to European soccer and rugby teams. The flight attendants were from all over the world too. They had flown in from somewhere to Cape Town. They'd be with us for three days, then another crew would come in for the last four days, at Dubai.

We had a good time talking. It was great fun being in the co-pilot's seat with no pressure to get out until I wanted to. Actually, the co-pilot came back in for the last 30 minutes.

Having my Kokoro Class 48 banner with me for
my inspiration as I'm getting ready for the first marathon.

With 30 minutes to go, we were told to get changed into our running stuff. We'd land, and the staff, who had flown in two hours earlier on a

Russian cargo jet, would have the course prepared.

I was tense and so excited. The weather was to be a tremendous +20 degrees! I had watched the Steelers play a game the week before in the 20s. They made 20 degree weather look easy. For the whole game I just watched the breath coming out of the player's mouths. Some of them didn't eve wear sleeves! +20 degrees was way doable.

Starting out on the first loop of the first marathon on Antarctica. The big guy on my right is Michael Hill, the President of the Florida Marlins baseball team. He did a great job and finished faster than me most days.

We went from flying across water, to coming in over snow with white snowy mountains in the distance. Unbelievable! I was in Antarctica. We all got to our windows snapping pictures when the Captain said, "Get in your seats we are landing."

He put that 757 down on a long, smooth open landing strip. Not sure if it was an open space or a real airport landing strip. It was just long and flat. There wasn't an airport tower or any signs of it being an airport. All we saw was a row of maybe 10 temporary prefabricated one story buildings or oversized sheds. We were told that there were Russians and Argentinians working there.

We disembarked and that cold air hit you clearly in the chest. Wow, this is Antarctica! It was a surreal sight. A long row of huts and these two jets parked in front of them with all this open space going in every direction.

Our marathon leader was Richard Donovan from Ireland. He is an interesting guy. When I first emailed him about participating in the 777, I didn't get an answer. Then a few weeks later, I emailed him again. Nothing. Then I got an email.

"Sorry Rob, thanks for writing me. Been running across South America. No WiFi. Glad to have you with us! Will contact you when I get done here."

Come to find out, the guy had run across America, Europe and all over the world. He puts on a North Pole Marathon and a number of these unique marathons. He put this thing together four years ago as a unique challenge.

Richard says to us, "The staff is still setting up the course. The course will be like an oval racetrack. It will be around the landing strip. Each long side will be three miles and all the way around will be six miles. Go get ready and stay warm. Men go in these certain metal buildings and the ladies go in these other buildings. Wait for us to notify you that we will start. So we find our buildings and go in and sit or lay on some bunk beds. The outhouse is in another building that is on stilts near us.

We wait and wait and wait. For some reason it is taking more time than expected to set up the course. I can't believe we are waiting like this. What the hell! Let's get going. I lay on this barren wooden bunk bed when finally someone sticks their head in our building and says to maybe 10 of us, "Let's go. Time to run."

Whoa... here we go!

We shuffle outside and walk on hard crunchy snow crackling under our feet about 50 yards to where the jets are parked. It is a beautiful blue sky because it was summertime and there is 24 hours of sunshine. We get lucky and it's a "warm day" with perfect conditions for a run. Richard points to the temporary starting point and gives us directions. We will do four, six mile loops plus a special shorter loop to fill out our 26.3 miles. I can't tell if the course has been plowed or is just windblown. I get my REI rubber crampons on and try to figure out which jacket, which gloves and which hat to wear. It is clear, no wind and probably +20 above zero. I finally decide on my layering clothing plan. After my first short starting loop, I am warm enough to have my light weight windbreaker open to my chest, no hat and gloves off.

Finally, we all line up for a picture and then an air horn goes off! We run through the makeshift start and finish line and everyone is talking. We are finally doing it. Some of the people have talked a big game, so now we see what everyone's got.

I am giddy, as is everyone else. We hear the crunch, crunch of snow under our feet and I try to breathe and get my pace going. It becomes obvious that there are patches of ice on the course as well as a light snow pack, and some deeper snow on the course. I focus on finding the ice and running on it as it demands less energy. My snow crampons work great. No slippage.

About 10 minutes into the run, I shed my outer jacket. I was heating up as I'm a guy who sweats a lot. I drop it at a wooden stake in the snow showing where the course runs. I know I can pick it up later on in the race if I need it. I am the only person who drops clothes on the course which seems strange because I think others would have warmed up as well. Nope, just me.

I unbutton my next windbreaker and unzip my long sleeve wool sweater. I am beginning to get into my sweat mode. I want to get that cold air onto my chest and try to find that clothing sweet spot where I stop sweating. I feel the beads of sweat come up on my forehead and I knew that if I sweat, later it will freeze.

I am thinking, "I am glad that I am wearing what I chose to wear." I have the heavier clothes still in my bag on the side of the course. But it looks like it will be an easy weather day.

The runners spread out as expected. We had three hour marathoners, four and five hour marathoners, six and seven hour marathoners as well. Last year they had five runners do all seven marathons in less than three hours! This year there is only one who hovers around three hours. The last and only standalone marathon I've done was the Air Force marathon three years ago I finished in just less than five hours. I have no idea what to expect on this one.

It isn't like training at the beach.

The first loop is fine and I just pace myself for another five hour

Clothing and equipment are so vital to success on your adventures.

marathon. But on loop two the sun starts dipping and the wind begins to pick up. I find myself zipping up my sweater, buttoning up my wind breaker and picking up my outer light weight jacket and putting it on. When I am running into the wind, I put my gloves back on. Later, when I am running with the wind at my back, I unzip stuff and take my gloves off. But as I start loop three, it is becoming colder. Like really cold.

By now the faster runners are on their last loop and I am on loop three. Progressively, the wind picks up and I am colder now than ever. My head is full of voices arguing. Some voices tell me not to stop and forage through my stuff to find warmer gloves and a jacket. Then another voice says I am fine. I can handle this weather with the clothes I have on. That voice wins out. My brain tells me not to stop and freeze while searching through the piles of backpacks laying in the snow near the start location. I pretty well remember where I strategically placed it, but it is a hassle to go over there and find it. All the backpacks were black it seemed. This voice tells me to just plow on into the wind. I feel like I can just press through. I just want to get through this moment and get OFF THE COURSE!

I have been running the last five hours pretty much alone and talking to myself the whole way. I had to get ready for this last six mile loop now in twilight as the sun has really dipped. It still is summer and a 24 hour sun is there, but barely. I now choose to pull my hands in my gloves inside the sleeves of my outer jacket and pull a cap way down over my right side of my face. My face feels hard, blue and numb. As I run by the jets for the last time on the front side of the loop, the people in front of me have shorter strides like me with their heads down. They are fighting the cold and wind as well. I am close enough to two people in front of me now to see their feet disappear into the sideways blowing wind and snow. It looks like a Sahara or Gobi Desert sandstorm but it is snow. We are all plowing through this thing that should have a CNN reporter giving commentary like in a hurricane.

I get to that curve of the loop and turn left into the wind and say, "Oh my God this is cold!" My face is stinging. My hands hurt. My fingers are numb and frozen stiff. My snot is a hard icicle under my nose. My running shoes were blue, but now they are encased in a white block of snow.

And wonderfully, my nine 3 x 5" encouragement cards that I put in the pocket of my pants for this race are speaking to me as I hoped they would.

These thoughts were gleaned from all those podcasts I listened to, and the books I'd read, leading up to the 777:
1. There CAN BE NO DOUBT!
2. I am stronger than this moment!
3. Kokoro: 50 HOURS. This is a piece of cake!
4. Easy Day. Fun Day. Good Day, Epic Day. Unbelievable Day.
5. Only six hours of work!
6. Just BREATHE. REFOCUS.

7. This is an EPIC moment. Live Legendary!
8. This moment and stage is not too big for you! Just Press THROUGH.
9. Remember: Pain is for a moment. Glory for a lifetime.

I said these over and over the last two laps. Self-talk was huge. I turned that last left turn and onto the last three mile stretch and ran into the wind. All I could think of was, "If stop, I could freeze to death." The weather was just getting colder and windier. There were seemingly only a few of us still out there which made the run more desolate. There were five and six hour marathoners in front of me. Repeatedly I had made it a game to see if I could catch them but it never seemed to happen. Now I felt alone. Like really alone. Like the alone I'd thought about on those training runs. I just put my head down and started counting my left foot steps. Just get to 100 then walk 50 then run 100 then walk 50. Over and over. My hands were frozen and repeatedly my cap (which was almost useless) was trying to escape from me. The wind was blowing almost

The first marathon was on Antarctica. Pretty neat to run alongside our Boeing 757 jet on the frozen continent.

horizontally, and the falling snow was making the run that much more miserable. It was one of those gut check moments that I had anticipated in my training. But I kept up my self-talk and micro-goals, as I visualized crossing the finish line.

I got to the point where I had taken off my jacket on the first lap and had left it on the side of the course in the snow. I just chuckled and laughed a little thinking how the weather had changed in that short period of time. I had been so naive. I had lived in Alaska and

**Running marathons for me is a mostly alone experience.
The weather was changing and dropping 30 degrees as the sun set.**

remembered all my cold weather training and experiences. If only I had put on my other clothes on the last lap. I just hadn't wanted to stop, plus my hands were frozen and I wouldn't be able to zip up my jacket. But being there encouraged me that I was almost at the last left turn on the curve. I put my head down and continued counting my steps.

I set visual markers in front of me and played my game. Finally I believed I could make it to the beginning of the curve stake in the ground, in 200 steps. I counted them and made it 186 steps. I won!

Sweet! I was getting better at this. I beat my projections!

As I made the curve to my left, the wind was now at my back which was wonderful. I had my momentary reprieve. I walked and gathered myself, as in a few moments, I would have that side wind again. I was maybe a half mile from the finish. The sky was dark blue and gray. I could see a long way. The snow at that end of the course had stopped blowing so it was just a minus something degree side wind. I started counting my steps. The first 100, then the second 100, then the third 100. I could see the flags representing the different countries represented blowing sideways in the distance and finally I saw two guys come out from somewhere and wave and yell out to me, "Come on Robert! You're almost here!" Then they grabbed the finish line banner and stretched it out to make the finish line. My thought was where is everyone else? I wondered, "How did these guys get stuck to come out of some warmer place to take pictures, officially record my time, and stretch this banner for my finish?" There wasn't a crowd, just two frozen looking guys. I lifted my hands and tried to smile because my face felt frozen. But I ran through. I had finished the Antarctic marathon! Tremendous! The adventure was over!

They said, "Go in that building over there. Runners are in there getting warm." I was worried for these two guys but then stopped worrying about them. They must know what they are doing. I walked quickly to my bag with my unused winter clothing and stuff and walked with the wind at my back toward the one metal building out of maybe ten that was a Russian cafeteria. It seemed like a long walk. We had been pulled by a snow mobile in a sled cart to the start hours ago. Now this walk on hard packed crunchy snow was another event. It wasn't probably very long thinking back, but at the time, it seemed like a trek. It must have been about 11 p.m. We had been up since 4 a.m. Cape Town time.

I found this hut/temporary building and opened the door. Inside were a number of our runners warming up as well as some Russian and

Completing my first marathon on Antarctica.

Argentinian workers sitting at four tables on the left and four on the right. If you walked up the aisle between them, in the back was a Russian cook with a small kitchen area. He had long, skinny, hot dogs, some cabbage, and mashed potatoes. That was it. Then there was some hot water for tea or instant coffee. He was the cook, dishwasher and waiter. Off to the right was a sink full of dishes and the area looked dirty. I shook my head as this was the meal promised to us at the end of the marathon. It brought back memories of my 15 trips to Russia and the old Soviet Union starting in 1990 through 2005. Nothing appealing.

I found the instant coffee and went and found an open seat at the back table by the door by a wall mounted TV. The TV was showing a Russian game show that looked like it was from the 1970's. It was profoundly weird. No one was paying attention. I guess it served as white noise for the shack.

Everyone was sharing their stories. My feet began to warm which now made them wet for the first time. This was not good. They had been in their warm cocoons for hours. Somehow my shoes and socks had done their job. But now the ice and snow had melted into my shoes. They were getting really cold as I was warming. Amazing...

We sat in there for an hour. Then another hour. The flight crew needed eight or twelve hours of down time before they were allowed to fly again, and it took a while to get the plane turned on and warm. So we just sat around with the Russians and Argentinians.

Finally, sometime after 1 a.m. someone stuck their head in the door and said we were finally loading.

Somehow, some of the locals took a liking to us or the aircrew and staff. When we went outside, there was a snowmobile with the open trailer bed outside. The planes were about a 5-10 minute walk away so they told us to get on the trailer bed, sit down and get situated. About 15 of us climbed in with our gear and then it took off towards the plane. It was one of those moments I'll never forget. Everything in front of us was white and going on forever except two large jets. The air was cold and the sky was clear. I believe the wind had died down so it was somewhat still. I don't remember seeing any sun and I believe it was twilight gray.

We all just hung on as this skidoo taxi trailer transported us over the hard packed snow back to the jets. We all were quiet and looked around or covered our faces. Then they got us to the stairs at the base of the forward doors.

You may say, "How do you vaguely remember and not clearly not remember?" I was physically tired. It was really cold and I kept my head down a lot as the moving air came across my face. Many people didn't look up at all. You had to want to take in the situation or else you would shield your face. Plus, many were focused on just hanging on. I went for a corner open spot on the trailer bed to try to not get squashed by all the people trying to find a place.

I just remember looking around as we crossed the snow and ice, thinking "This is a once in a lifetime moment. I've finished an Antarctic marathon! And I am escaping from a lousy Russian cafeteria with stupid TV shows and bad coffee and hotdogs and cabbage. These planes look amazing out here in the middle of nowhere. We all made it! I can't wait to get back on that plane, be warm and get out of here."

Then we unloaded and waited politely for our turn to go up the stairs. Many were talking and laughing about their experiences. The fast runners had been waiting a long time. They must have really been antsy to get out of there. I just thought, "These flight attendants are out in the cold standing at the top of the stairs welcoming us." They looked way cold as well. That plane must have been really cold when they opened it up after being shut down for 11 hours on the snow.

When we got to the top of the stairs, they welcomed and congratulated us with big smiles. We got in and found our seats that we flew in on, and talked with all our new friends who were sitting around us. The plane had its auxiliary power units going which allowed us to have much appreciated heat.

Now to Cape Town. It was going to be one of our shorter flights. It's only five and a half hours from Antarctica to Cape Town, which is a shorter flight than Los Angeles to Hawaii. We would run again soon after we landed, which meant we were doing the first two marathons within 24 hours. I don't think I slept on the way over; I had been awake for about 24 hours. If I didn't get any sleep on this return flight, I'd have been up about 30 hours and then have to run the second one. And there wasn't a shower planned beforehand.

The obvious question is "Why would they schedule two marathons within 24 hours?"

It is because there was a pretty tight schedule. We have seven twenty four periods to get all seven marathons completed. There are records for lowest accumulative marathon times that have been set and one of our runners was shooting to beat. Last year there were five runners that ran sub-three hour marathons for all seven days. Ryan Hall, our U.S.

Marathon Olympian at the Brazil Games was one of those. He finished fifth last year. So they knock two out quickly which gives the organizers wiggle room for any unexpected situations that might come up with our travel.

As we found out, immigration into or out of the different countries, can be very slow. Also issues with the plane may come up. Every year is different.

The seven runs had to be completed within 168 hours to be an official seven day event.

All that is to say we got on the plane, changed out of our winter clothes and watched as the plane taxied away from the desolate set of buildings in the middle of nowhere. The 757's windows were full of runners staring one last time at a place that most would never see, or want to see, again. It had been quite an experience.

The plane taxied back down our marathon course and then turned around. The pilot said a few things and he gunned the engines. The plane shook as if we were on some rough concrete. Finally, a sense of peace and accomplishment filled me. I was satisfied. What an experience that was. A few of my fingers were still numb and the tips of my toes were still without feeling but I had done it! I had finished and survived those last two laps.

We sped down the runway until the nose lifted off and within one minute we were over water again. Antarctica was behind us. What a barren, desolate and beautiful place it was. The other Russian cargo jet with the staff would follow us a few minutes later.

What a relief! I settled back into my chair and let out a sigh of relief. It was behind us and me. My seat mate was the 67 year old Frenchman. He looked tired and relieved as well. We couldn't talk but we read each other's facial expressions and congratulated each other.

Our bags were in front of us and partially under the business class seat in front of us. We had enough luggage to put our feet on if we didn't raise our foot rests. There aren't any FAA rules on these flights, so we could put our bags of clothes pretty much where we wanted. It was a nice way to travel.

Everyone started to take off their wet clothes by their seats. I got my wet clothes off and put on dry socks and a set of slippers. I am not a big slipper guy but they worked great for the situation. My running shoes were wet, so I put them in a bag along with the socks. My feet were clammy and blue. The skin had all the wrinkles that long term wet feet get.

The flight attendant served us something hot like coffee. We had an open bar, but none of us used it much for any of the flights. Then they served us a hot dinner and we tried to go to sleep. We now had four hours before we had to get off and run again in Cape Town. I think I slept for three and a half hours before the announcement came from overhead, "Good morning everyone. We will be landing in about 30 minutes."

Then Richard the Race Director got on the microphone and said, "We will be landing, going through immigration, then bussed to a hotel, where you will change into your running gear, and leave your bags there. Then you will be bussed to the Cape Town course where we will be hosted by the Cape Town Marathon Club. You will get a shower after the marathon.

The race will start hopefully at 12 noon. And it looks like it will be about 90 degrees. Bring your sunscreen and electrolytes. We will be landing at 8:30 a.m. When this one is done, then you will have a nice long flight to Perth. Things will get easier after today!"

We all just looked at ourselves and some said, "This is going to be a hot day! We have to start this thing in the hottest part of the day?"

We were stiff and tired. Thank goodness I managed a little sleep. Hopefully the others did too.

Wednesday: Cape Town

We landed and taxied in. It was weird to be back in less than 24 hours. We had gone to Antarctica, run a marathon and come back! It dazzled my head, but just for a moment. Mainly, I was tired and focused on finding our bus. Cape Town immigration is like home to me, I've come through it so many times. It was nice to go through it. I still hadn't talked to most of the runners so it was an inner experience. You know how you smile at people and listen off to the side of people's conversations but you don't know them? I think I had four solid conversations so far. The French guy I sat with the whole way didn't speak English so that gave me 10 hours of nice silence. I mention this because in these types of events it is a solo experience. Everyone is pretty focused on getting through the runs. There is talk, but it is small talk. We weren't there to make friends. We were there to do the runs within our timeframes and finish. A few people even seemed unfriendly. They just wanted to finish.

We found the busses, got our roller bags stowed underneath and left the airport. About 40 minutes later our bus driver couldn't find the hotel where we were to change. It was comical. He was on the phone going over instructions and trying to figure out how to find this little winding road in the Sea Point section of Cape Town. Finally he figured it out and somehow got our bus through narrow winding streets to our hotel.

We were told we had 30 minutes to get our stuff to our storage area, get changed and get back to the busses. We weren't getting rooms, but just going to change. It was a 'one of a kind' situation. Our bags were to be rolled or carried to a storage area and 50 runners were to open them up and change. It was quite chaotic. Bathrooms were elsewhere, one bathroom for 35 men, and one for the 15 women next door. Most of us thought it was not very well planned out and with so many being tired there were many comments like "What the hell? Who thought this up? This is fucking stupid."

Thirty minutes turned into sixty minutes before we all made it back to the busses and on our way to the starting area. Richard wasn't pleased that we were behind schedule and many weren't thrilled with Richard's logistics. We went about five minutes down to the boardwalk by the ocean in Sea Point and got off.

He gathered us together at the finish area. Gave us some instructions and then walked us to the starting point about 100 yards away. He had a picture taken, talked to us again then blew the air horn.

It was beautiful and picturesque. However it was also really hot. I hadn't expected this level of heat.

I ran alone again. I just wanted to focus on the joy of accomplishing this thing. I also wanted to space out and do my thing. I was sweating like the others and fortunately had brought different pairs of socks and shoes in case my feet blew up. They did.

I changed my shoes after the first loop as they were again both swollen from the flying. I was fortunate to never have one blister the whole week. It was a miracle!

The run along the water was wonderful. The waves at times crashed powerfully into the seawall. Sometimes, we were running along the seawall and the water splashed up onto where we were running. That was great! I'd be dodging splashes while watching a guy surf. It was so nice to have something distract me from running. The water was sparkling. The sky was blue. There were a few cargo freighters offshore and it was a glorious day. Except I was hot, tired and just wanting to finish.

One of the guys I met was Terry Harker from Cabo San Lucas in Baja, California. He made the Antarctic marathon but today he looked terrible. He looked pale and was sweating profusely. By the end of the afternoon, he was wobbly and looked semi-delirious. He was sick. I remember talking to him when we crossed each other going out or coming back towards the start and finish area. "You OK Terry?" And he'd mumble something back. But the guy was determined to finish.

By three o'clock, the late afternoon sun was burning me up. The sun's dipping angle was now below the bill of my cap and I felt my face and neck just cooking. I had sunscreen on but it seemed worthless. The sun was baking my face and neck. Many of the runners were now walking. It was just so hot and they had ever increasing blisters. I stopped to talk to one guy named Nick from the UK because the Chaplain side of me came out. His feet were a mess. I decided to walk with him and try to encourage him. We finished the race walking and he made it. And somehow, Terry also crossed the finish line.

We took seven hours to complete this marathon, due to the walking. We didn't care. There were many behind us as they were hobbling.

You may say six, seven or eight hours? That isn't a marathon time. That is a walk. And you are somewhat right. However, if you've never run with blisters getting bigger with each step on multiple spots on your feet, you won't get it. You need to take into account that we were going from the Antarctic at below zero temperatures, and getting off a plane and running in 90 plus degree weather less than 12 hours. It was a different experience; hard to imagine, even harder to train for.

Plus, it was two marathons within 24 hours. Don't scoff at it until you try it. It will test your mind as much as your body. I was amazed at the grit and perseverance of all the runners.

By the grace of God, I didn't have one blister the whole seven marathons, but some runners were now into their own personal sufferfests. They were miserable. Terry staggered to the end. He was glassy eyed and sick.

When we finished there was to be a shuttle bus to carry the runners back to the hotel. Our shuttle wasn't there when we were done, so we sat around and just waited. Our finish was also sub-glorious. Nick and I jogged through the finish line then went and sat down.

A race staff member told us our time. They pointed and said, "That way over there was supposed to be the shuttle bus." But it didn't show up. It was maddening. All Nick and I wanted to do was get out of there and get to showers. Feeling normal was a long time ago. Two marathons and a lot of traveling had transpired since our last showers. We just sat there frustrated. We didn't talk much waiting for a non-existent shuttle. We knew that others were in the showers and changing clothes as we sat. I asked twice "You sure the van is making the rounds and is coming back?" And each time a guy under the tent said, "Oh ya. He'll be back."

Finally, it came back around and we got in. Sarcastically, I said "Where have you been?" But the driver didn't react at all, like he didn't understand English.

He drove us back to the hotel and we shuffled down a flight of stairs to the storage room for our bags. It was a chaotic scene. There were two showers with no towels. Men and women were going anywhere and everywhere trying to find or steal towels. Most seem to find them by the pool area. The word came to us that we were to be upstairs in 30 minutes and we all laughed. The line to the showers was three deep. Screw that. We will get there when we get there.

This was the lousiest logistical situation someone could put together. Someone should have been fired for arranging this situation. We were climbing over each other, in this small storage space to get our bags and find clean clothes.

Richard is a great guy, but this was stupid.

I finally took a shower, and washed out my shirt, socks and shorts. I couldn't imagine putting these sweaty, salty, wet clothes in a Ziploc bag for the next six days. Can you imagine unzipping that bag in six days?

A hand towel in my small roller suitcase worked as my towel. The small shower area floor was wet and littered with towels just left on the floor. It was a self-centered environment. At least the shower had hot water, and the toilet worked. I felt bad for the guy waiting outside the door for his shower. I hoped he found a towel.

In a few minutes we were all assembled in the hotel lobby and we stood around waiting for the word to get our gear to the busses. There was some mumbling but not much. Most were too tired to carry on a complaint session or a conversation.

At last, the word finally was given and without much conversation we got on.

The ride to the airport was quiet. We were exhausted. It took probably 40 minutes to get there. Then it was back through immigration and down the hallway to a place I always have exited from to fly back to London. I purchased a sandwich and a coke and enjoyed them immensely. I walked by myself as did many. Some had made friends and you might see groups of fours or sixes but most mainly walked alone.

I think distance runners are normally loners and this was a tired group of distance runners. The ages ranged from 23 to 67. I watched the dynamics all week long. We broke into small groupings of personalities, except for the large Florida group. They were always talking and laughing. But mainly, there was little small talk within certain groups who had learned to be comfortable with each other. Many just kept to themselves.

After a little wait, we loaded onto our transit busses and off we went to an area away from the airlines boarding area. Off on its own sat an AirBus 300-400. It was the four engine charter plane we'd fly in the rest of the week. It was awesome and the size of a Boeing 747.

Before we left on this adventure, I'd received a question and answer email from the World Marathon Challenge staff asking me about a number of things. One question I'd been asked is where I'd like to sit on the airplane which was great. I am not sure why they asked that question but I mentioned that I preferred to sit in the front if possible.

Sure enough, they gave me a boarding pass with my seat in the very front. The plane was configured with 100 Business Class seats in a 2-2-2 configuration, I was given a window seat with no one next to me! It was glorious! I made my window seat floor into my drying out area for those wet clothes I'd just washed. No one could see the clothes drying except the flight attendant but she never looked.

I had my own little private area to stash stuff. I didn't have to talk to or sleep near anyone. I was alone with 49 runners around me. I had a sweet lady with short purple hair across the aisle from me by the name of Heather Brien from Oakland California. She was quiet most of the time. Occasionally, she Facetimed her little kids which was fun to watch but otherwise she mainly talked to the Australian next to her.

She turned out to be a Cal Berkeley hedge fund CEO and was always pleasant to come home to for six days. Lastly, we had the same flight attendants for three more days which worked great. They got to know our preferences and we got to know them. My first one was from South Africa and the second one was from Spain.

When we came on, we were tired, hungry and wanting sleep. And this was to be a great flight of 11 hours! Everyone got on and situated themselves. The flight attendants closed up the doors, the plane taxied, and this big plane rumbled down the runway. We were off to Perth, Australia for number #3. Two down and four to go. Really five to go.

For my mental state there were really only five marathons to think on. Here's how I broke seven marathons into doable runs or small measurable goals:

First an adventure: Antarctica.

It was in a league of its own as far as planning and executing. Just grit and bear through it. Who knew what to expect except the few on this plane that had done a North Pole marathon or a different South Pole marathon. It was more of an adventure experience than a marathon for me.

Then there would be five marathons to worry or think about: Cape Town, Perth, Dubai, Lisbon and Cartagena.

The seventh marathon didn't matter. Miami would be all adrenaline and the easiest.

It didn't matter what I did there except finish.

I also had to remember - it doesn't matter what my times are. Just finish. People won't care what my times are. They will just say, "Did you really do seven marathons in seven days on seven continents?"

I had a previous experience in life that informed these perceptions. When I went back to University for the fifth time I worked my butt off to get my best grades ever. I had been a long time C student and this time, on the GI Bill, I was going to do better. I made the best grades of my life since 6th grade with a 3.25, which would have been better, if I hadn't taken Russian and three semesters of German. Notice the .25 at the end. It was a big deal to me.

When I graduated, I wanted the people who knew me to ask me what my grade point was or what my major was or something. But usually they just asked, "Did you go to college? Did you graduate?" That was all. They never asked about my 100 page papers or all kinds of other questions. Just, "Did you graduate?"

With the previous endurance races, most people never asked much except, "Did you do an IRONMAN? Really. Which one?" Then maybe one out of 10 will ask, "How many have you done?" I'd say, "11 and now 12." Most would shake their heads and a conversation might start. But mainly because it was sort of a benchmark question, it would be, "I hear you are an IRONMAN?" They never asked my times.

So I figured that this was going to be the same way. Just finish the 777, and it will be enough.

And it has proven true.

The lesson here is that no one asks for details. Just "Did you finish?" Come in messy, slow, muddy and pained, but come in and you're good.

When we got on the plane, Terry Harker, the sick developer from Cabo, was across from me on the opposite window. He had 10A and I had 10J. He looked terrible. He was really ill. Most of us didn't know how he finished Cape Town. But we do know he stumbled his way to the end delirious. He had a fever plus the heat to deal with. But Terry wouldn't quit. As soon as he got on the plane he went to sleep and didn't move except to eat something, for 11 hours. It was like having a body under the blanket across from me. We were all concerned about if he could go on. His wife was to watch him run in Dubai, but he had to get through Perth first.

I ate everything they gave me and got to know my flight attendant. I thought if I gave her extra kindness, there might me extra food or desserts. It worked!

For many others, the new adventure had just begun. They had blown up their feet with blisters and all kinds of ailments. This was going to be a whole new experience for them. Each day their feet were getting worse. Blisters don't need daily marathons.

Like on the "300 of Sparta" Greece trip the previous May, there was one "physio" guy on board as a medic. He knew how to tape legs, ankles and feet as well as drain blisters but that is about it. If something major happened, you were expected to deal with it or quit and find your own way home.

Now in the back of the plane the line of guys and gals needing foot

It matters more THAT you finish, than the time you finish in, no one ever asks about times. I started in a size 12 shoe and was now running in a 13 1/2 . My feet kept swelling.

and leg care grew. It was really sad. I remembered those blisters. They only got worse each day. And most only had the same size shoes to force their feet back into each day. I was so grateful I had four sizes with me – from size 12 to 14. Lesson learned from Greece, I'd take two pair with me to the start line, plus what I was wearing.

My heart went out to them. They were in pain! And when you are limping, you walk and run differently which means new pressure on different areas. Their bodies were out of whack trying to survive the runs.

The flight itself was wonderful. Long and quiet. I got up once to pee, and eat more food, and then went back to sleep. It became obvious: we were going to land about 2 or 3 p.m. That meant it was going to be a night marathon. Wow. I'd never done one of those before. It played with my head a bit.

Thursday: Perth Australia

Sure enough, we landed, dragged ourselves off the plane, went through immigration and found our two busses. We got on and this time checked into a casino hotel by a beautiful rugby venue which was alongside a river. The thought was that we were going to get a hotel room for the first time in 48 hours. Richard wanted to upgrade this year's experience with more hotel rooms. He wanted the runners to be able to get a little sleep if you could finish with enough time. I knew now that I was a six hour guy, there wouldn't be much sleep.

We got to our rooms, changed and met in the lobby area at dusk. Then we walked out of the casino and down the street a bit to the river walkway. A makeshift start and finish line was set up with the Perth Marathon Club hosting us.

They were much more organized than in Cape Town. They had a variety of nutritious offerings for us on tables well as great music playing. I was really tired and I was about to go run for five or six hours. The real runners just made it look so easy. The three to five hour guys didn't seem to be tired or bothered much at all. But us joggers, and athletes turned runners for this event, looked tired.

We were gathered together again by Richard and told to stay on this running path for eight loops I think. We stretched and I made the decision to take off my shirt. It was very warm again. But not as warm as Cape Town. Why waste a clean dry shirt? Then a few other men took theirs off. I felt bad for the ladies as I wished they could take their shirts off but that wouldn't work. However, a couple of ladies had a sports running top or sports bra thing that worked.

I was really tired until two minutes before the start. We were getting our last minute instructions when my adrenaline kicked in and I was fully engaged. It's always weird how that happens so quickly. All my exhaustion was gone. I was excited and anxious to get this over with. My mental state was again, "I just need to go to work for five to six hours and it will be over! I've prepared for this. No big deal. Live Legendary! Easy Day, Fun Day, Good Day!"

Then the air horn went off!

It was a beautiful night. Some wore head lamps. The quality of the surface was smooth which was quickly noticed by all the runners. In Cape Town we had to run on cracked sidewalks, through construction areas with flagmen holding up traffic, in the streets and up and down curbs. The Sea Point area of Cape Town is beautiful. We just happened to hit it during major road construction. But it was by the ocean. That made it special.

Perth was a different atmosphere. The music here was great all night. The temporary flood lights were good. The calm river was beautiful. The area was peaceful and quiet. The river walk was grassy with lots of trees. It was idyllic.

The Perth Marathon Club members were fun and engaged throughout the run. It made a difference to me. It is nice to have happy, pleasant people helping out and cheering you on.

I began to sweat quickly as most did, and all was good. At one end of the loop, two ladies were seated on folding chairs. They were really nice volunteers. They greeted us, marked off our numbers on a sheet of paper and as we made our U turn they cheered us on. They'd say, "41...You look spectacular! Keep it up!" I'd laugh and say "Thank you very much. You are nice ladies."

Sometimes I'd stop and walk for 30 seconds and ask them if they were having fun and other quick niceties. I looked forward to saying Hi since I had to do it eight times that night. Then back along the quiet river with a full moon out. It couldn't have been prettier or nicer. Richard had done a great job choosing these courses or trusting the Perth Marathon Club's recommendation. They all had something special about them. I ran the whole six hours by myself. Why talk? Just wasted focus. I had work to do.

At the other turn around area was an Australian restaurant with a grassy bar area with tall tables behind a fence along the river walk. It is filled with singles and couples dressed up in evening attire pounding Aussie beers with more blaring music. The guys looked drunk and the ladies looked great in their black and white formal wear. I loved it because I could hear the music for three or four minutes before we could see it. We ran under a bridge and then there was this party area! I noticed a lot of things because all along the courses were sections of quietness or activity. I enjoyed coming and going into each of these areas because it meant a mental break from my monotonous running.

When you run alone it is monotonous. There isn't any joy in it for me. It may be a little fun. But the fun is in winning and putting miles behind you. Every step is a win towards getting to the end. There is only satisfaction in accomplishing mileage and progress. Just get it done. Press on.

There was a guy there marking off our number which seemed like a lonely assignment. He didn't even bring a chair. He must have been a rookie volunteer. He had to be there like the rest of the volunteers until everyone had come by. It was going to be a long, lonely late night for him standing up with his clipboard.

As I did my U turn, I said, "Hi!" and he replied with an enthusiastic "Good job 41!" "Thanks!" Then he was gone and it was back by the partiers again.

Some of the revelers were drunk enough to hang over the fence and cheer us on, or yell something at us. It was about the same. One big, dark haired guy dared me to have a beer with him and asked me where I was from. I told him I was a Yank and he went nuts and spilled his beer. He now dared me to have a beer with him to which I replied, "When I get back, I'll have a beer with you" which surprised the five or ten semi-drunk revelers. I told him I'd see him later and ran away. I had a great time smiling and having fun with them and couldn't wait to get that loop done and be back there. I was thinking, "It was 8:30 p.m. I wondered what they would be like when I got back. Then I thought, "What was I going to do and how much beer would I drink with them?" Those thoughts helped that loop pass pretty quickly.

Along the river was a lot of tall, thick trees and grass. It was like a buffer area from the rugby stadium and its parking lot. The river was on one side and the arena was on the other. Fortunately, it was empty at

Perth, Australia first night marathon.

night but the stadium and the area around it, was lit up. All this came with a full moon.

I ran another loop and when I got back that guy yelled, "Hey Yank!" and lifted a beer towards me. He was in a group of people and they were all laughing and talking. He looked a little more intoxicated than before. I thought this would be a fun moment so I ran up to them and took the beer from him and took a big gulp. They were stunned. I lifted up the glass in victory and said "To Yanks everywhere!" He laughed and they cheered. It was another special moment. Then I said I'd see them on the next loop and ran off. A glorious moment on a long, quiet night. The next loop went the same as the previous ones, but I wanted to get back to the partiers again, so it went fast.

Sure enough, they saw me coming and started yelling, "There is the Yank!" I did my turn around and came back to them again and grabbed the beer. It was way fun. I said something and we all laughed as I downed a big gulp again. I made sure to burp really loud which grossed out the ladies but the guys loved it. I said I'd see them next time but it was getting late. Sure enough, next time I came back all the people were gone and the restaurant was closed. It was fun while it lasted.

The loops weren't as long as the Cape Town loops. They were pretty easy. The darkness, the full moon, the silence, the heat and a slight breeze off the river all made for a peaceful, long night.

The only challenge came later when the homeless began to gather in the shadows of the trees and hang out. Our ladies rightly were nervous. As a guy, it didn't bother me much as I just kept my antennas up as I ran through these areas with these people. Some of the guys made sure to run alongside of the ladies. The Perth Marathon Club sent a guy on a bicycle to patrol the river walk after a woman runner complained about the situation. It was an unforeseen situation that could have been anticipated by the club. Everything worked out, but the security situation was addressed the next day with Richard, and I am sure the club learned something about hosting a night marathon there. I wonder if they had ever done one before.

I remember the later it became, the quieter it was and the louder the voices in my head were. I was very alone in my head. This is where I'd lose my Zen monk state and fight to get it back. I heard my feet hitting the ground and worked on my breathing. I was practicing nose breathing and running with my mouth closed. I tried to exhale every four steps. It kept me focused

I talked to myself and played my running distance perception games mile after mile. I found myself not allowing myself to think on certain topics until I had reached certain milestones during the night. Then I'd reward myself by opening up that drawer in my mind. One thing I thought about was a speech I had to give after I was home. By this third run, I had an outline and thesis statement. This night, after the three hour mark, I developed my first two points with stories accompanying each point.

Some may think "That is bizarre!" But for me, I needed to break down a six hour run into segments, or micro-goals, with milestones and rewards. It started on the Antarctic run and now I was on my third revision. It worked for me.

BEYOND AVERAGE

Terry Harker had willed himself off the airplane and was wobbling all over the place on the course. Finally, staff came and took him off the course. They said he could not keep pressing. He was cooked. It was very sad. He had worked so hard to prepare for these moments. But sickness is indiscriminate. When you get sick, you can get really sick. And he was extremely sick. He went back to his hotel room at the casino, and went to sleep. And later the next day, he slept all the way to Dubai.

I was cooked. No one was home in this picture. This was after Perth at 2 a.m. I ran alone again. Talked to myself the whole way. People tried to talk to me, but I couldn't hear them.

Then he was gone. I never saw him after he woke up. As it turned out, he was sick in Dubai for a week, and for the next two months. Something really bit him in Africa or before. I really liked Terry so I flew to Cabo to see him two months later. He had just finally begun to feel better.

Back in Perth, I finished about 2 a.m. after starting at 8 p.m. It was another six hour run. For the finish, I put on my long sleeve white Pararescue shirt. It went well with my new red running shorts. I thought it was a good looking combo. Number #3 was behind me.

When I went through the finish line it was quiet. Everyone was gone except the photographer and a guy to hold up the ribbon to run through. This was a pattern now. No music at 2 a.m. All the Perth Marathon Club members had gone home. Just silence. Climactic and anti-climactic. I did it, and I celebrated by congratulating myself.

LESSON TIME: Do it for yourself. Don't require outside validation. It'd be nice but it's not necessary. I was happy with myself. I said, "Good job Owens." I congratulated myself out loud all the way back to the hotel room.

I walked for about 10-15 minutes back to my hotel room which seemed like a long way. I showered and wonderfully fell asleep about 3:30 a.m. sitting up on my bed. We had to be downstairs in the hotel lobby at 7:00 a.m. I washed out my clothes again and put on the clothes I was now comfortable to travel in. They were a pair of tan cargo shorts, a black SEALFIT t-shirt, some long black compression socks and my flip flops. The socks with flip flops allowed for some fun comments. One guy said I had to be from California with the way I looked, to which I replied "Yep" with a smile. He said he enjoyed the "camel toe flip flop style" look and I said that I did too!

Honestly, by this time, I didn't care if everyone saw me in the same clothes every day. They were comfortable and they worked. Their opinions weren't important to me as I am sure mine weren't important to them. We all were doing what worked for us. And I was hoping there was some magic in those long to the knee black compression socks that I had purchased at Bed Bath and Beyond. They were the kind that Brett Farve endorsed with the copper in them. I was hoping Brett was right! It was a stab in the dark. Then I always had a lightweight black jacket around my waist in case a hotel lobby, bus or airport was cool. Amazingly, it came in handy a lot. I was colder more than usual. I think it was my body being wigged out from burning all those calories and pushing it so much. I hadn't eaten anything during the marathon but one gue. I wasn't hungry at all.

When we all assembled down in the casino lobby some of us talked and others just stood or sat in silence staring at their phones. This time though, one of the guys I didn't know went and purchased about 20 McDonald's egg and sausage McMuffins. He kindly was passing them out to anyone who thought they might like one. They were all gone in seconds. I don't even like McDonald's egg and sausage sandwiches but this one was great! He was a nice guy that I never got to know.

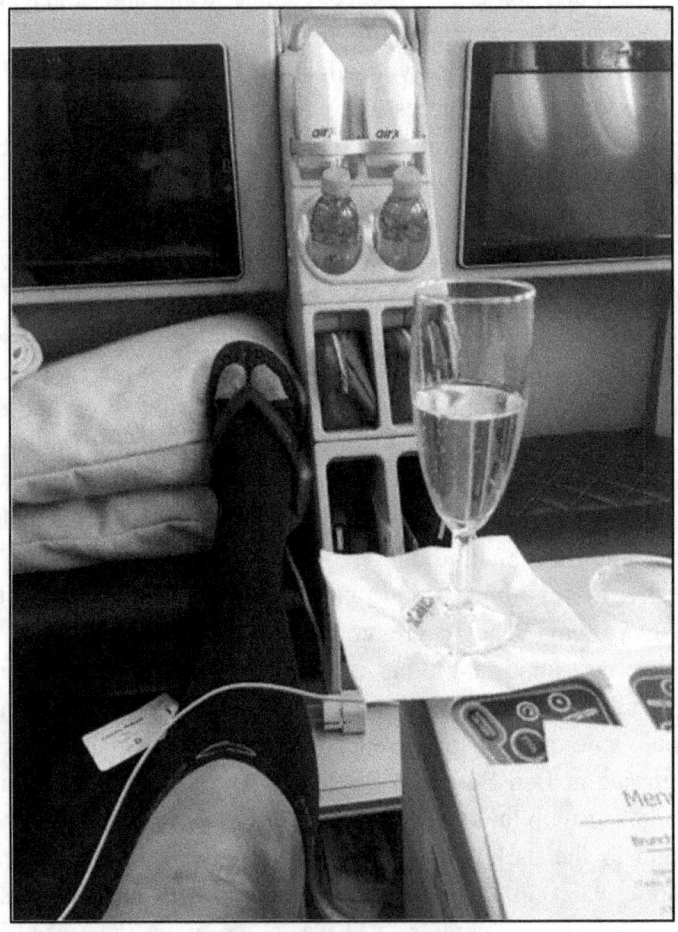

From Perth to Dubai flight. Third champagne for breakfast before our 11 hour flight. My Camel Toe look was quite a sensation.

We all loaded up again and off we went to the airport. Next stop was Dubai.

It was another long nine to ten hour flight. We got through immigration and began the trek to the gate pulling both of my rollers. Finding the gate was a challenge but we found it after a bit of a search.

Sometimes charters and charter airport gates get tucked away in some non-normal areas. I don't like being lost or not understanding things. This stuff should be easy. But international travel isn't always easy. I made it to the gate and bus area with the others. We went down the runway to our charter on the tarmac.

I got on the plane and into my little cubby space and felt happy. Getting on the plane was always a fun experience. Getting off was always non-exciting. I almost dreaded it. But this was fun. I took out my "clean" wet clothes and laid them back on the floor to dry. Clean is a relative term. They are as clean as you can get them in the shower.

Then I thought, three marathons were behind us and I wanted to celebrate. For some reason I was feeling spunky so I asked for some champagne and ended up drinking three glasses at 9:00 a.m.! They went down great! It was a wonderful 30 minutes. I didn't see anyone else imbibing, but I didn't care. I was an adult and didn't need anyone's permission. And that isn't really the point. I just felt like I wanted to celebrate. Everyone could be happy their own way. I was happy that three marathons were behind me and it had been a nice first time ever night run.

Moments like these need to be savored and appreciated. I took a picture of the moment to keep it for reflection later. And I captured my compression sock camel toe look for posterity. Who knows, it might go mainstream someday. My kids might shake their heads with a smile on their faces and say, "Wow Dad, you are cool at 66! Where did you come up with that?"

Then came the eggs and bacon and more eggs and off to sleep I went again. The champagne helped. We slept all day. It is weird to get on a plane about 9 a.m. and pull down the blinds and sleep all day. Terry Harker didn't even wait for breakfast. He crawled under his blankets and didn't move again for nine hours. Poor guy was wrecked. He had a fever and the sweats. He'd be getting off in Dubai for good.

Friday: Dubai

When we opened up our window shades all we saw was brown desert in every direction. Occasionally there would be some small outpost of people, but by in large the area was empty. I thought, "Wow... we are out in the middle of nowhere!" Then out of nowhere there's this huge city on the edge of an ocean.

Actually it is the Persian Gulf. Upon landing, we taxied to a VIP terminal away from the general population terminal. That was nice and an unexpected experience. Inside, it was like being in a future land. Expensive cars and planes were in the lobby for viewing, as well as a lady who would get us any food or drink we wanted. She was a tall, thin, black, statuesque South African and had been working there for 10 years. She loved it she said. We lounged around there for an hour as our papers were being processed then we were bussed to our opulent hotel.

The downtown is designed to make a statement. They want to be known for the biggest everything: from the world's tallest building, to huge lobbies in hotels. It reminded me a lot of the Las Vegas strip.

This time I had a roommate from Washington DC who was a real runner. Somehow my extra money to have a room by myself didn't work in Dubai. I walked into my private room to a guy all unpacked on his double bed. It didn't really matter I thought, because I didn't get much time in my Perth room anyway.

We dressed and headed downstairs to see all these Arab men in their elegant, white, flowing robes everywhere. The ladies were dressed in different levels of Muslim and non-Muslim dress. It was fascinating to see the variety. The guys basically looked the same, but the women had freedom to do as they pleased. I'd say most had stylish scarves on and black robes but not all. In this five star hotel were Arab women in burqas, and ladies in tight pants and heels. I looked at one lady with a burqa on, where I could only see her eyes. She had eyeliner and mascara on and was strikingly attractive. I just wondered what her smile looked like. It was fun to stare. And they stared back at us in our shorts and running attire.

One of our lady runners, Sarah Reinertsen, who was sponsored by Nike, decided to run with a scarf on to honor the Muslim women. It was a great move I thought. She only has one leg, so to see this woman with one cheetah foot and in shorts wearing a headscarf, caused some interesting looks from lots of locals.

We bussed to the start area and it would be another night run. We started about 7:30 p.m. again which meant another unique run. It was challenging.

On the bus to the race start, I fell asleep. I might not have been the only one to do so either. We got off the bus and walked in the dark to an area they were transforming into a start and finish area. It was damp and I was a little cold which I hadn't anticipated for Dubai. I kept my running windbreaker on and knew I'd be starting with it on. I stashed my extra socks, shoes and Vaseline in my runner's bag in a designated area and all of a sudden came alive.

As in Perth, with about a minute to go before the start, my adrenaline kicked into gear and I was amped to begin. I thought, "Let's go and get this thing over with. It is time to go to work!"

This course was six loops. We were dropped off in the dark next to a super smooth, concrete beach walk. The concrete was lime green which was unique, but also a little slippery. The Persian Gulf wet dew had settled on the concrete making it fun to run on. I could almost slide on it which made the foot plant dangerous. It felt like I was on ice skates. The night air was about 60 something degrees and cool. I didn't know they had mild weather ever. Within five minutes of starting the jacket came off and I tied it around my waist until I could get back to the starting point.

The air horn went off with a camera man standing in front of us videoing us as we ran by him. This Argentine cameraman Francisco was enjoying shooting us. He had a lot of life in him and was around a lot on the first three runs. He was always smiling and laughing. In Dubai, he spent a lot of time on his skateboard alongside us shooting different angles. He was a happy, fun character.

We started the race next to a big parking lot like an open air nightclub. It was full of cars and beyond the lot was a street with shops and bars facing us and the ocean. That night, the parking lot was full of young Arab men and women doing what all kids do. They were drinking, with loud, western music blaring from their open car doors and driving around checking each other out. It was like a Friday night football game at home, with all the kids hanging out. Except these kids were screeching tires and racing around in Ferraris, Land Rovers, Mercedes,

Lamborghinis and Porsches. It was quite a scene with all these white robed, and bearded guys and the girls in their elegant attire. It was like in the lobby of our hotel, the girls were in burqas or black robes with scarfs or regular western clothing. But to see these 20 to 30 year-olds with beers in their hands and smoking cigarettes was unexpected. Kids were just being kids.

I couldn't help myself from watching. I was intrigued. As Richard blew the air horn to start, I was watching these kids. I was running by car after car of partiers and feeling spunky so I said to the cameraman, "Hey...follow me!" With his big eyes he said, "What are you going to do?" I replied, "Let's go meet these kids!" His eyes got wide and he said, "No, we can't go over there" but I said "Come on, let's go!" and I pulled off the sidewalk and went up to this group of Arab kids who had really loud music blasting from their car. There were girls and guys hanging out, and this one Arab kid in his white robe and head scarf was dancing by himself just messing around. I ran up to him and just started dancing with him to his amazement. He had this thin stick in one of his hands and was pantomiming like a maestro with an orchestra so I smiled at him and took it from him and tried to do what he was doing. He was stunned.

Fortunately, he and the group just smiled and laughed. My cameraman thought this thing could go either way. He was nervous with his camera filming away. A couple of the Arab guys had beers and one asked me "Hey, where you from?" To which I replied, "US.... California." They all smiled and laughed. One said, "It figures." To which I asked while dancing around, "You go to school in the US?" And they all nodded in agreement, "John Hopkins" in perfect English.

I really started laughing then. Here were these Arab kids drinking beers, smoking cigarettes with their loud U.S. music in their desert sheik robes. The girls spoke English as well. All U.S. educated and now back home partying in a parking lot. Kids are the same all over!

The cameraman was now a bit more relaxed and filming all this with a big smile on his face. We had crashed the party and lived to tell about it.

They asked me what all of us were doing at 7:30 that night and I mentioned we were starting a marathon to which a guy said "What.....

that is stupid! Why?" I laughed and agreed. Then I said "Nice to meet you! Have a great night. I got to run now. See Ya!" And they laughed and said "Bye."

But I told the cameraman to stay and do some more filming and interviewing. It would make great "B roll" for his video. He smiled and stayed with the young Arab men and women. He gave me one of those "this is unbelievable" looks and I took off back to the beach boardwalk and the run. I couldn't help but laugh all the way. We had done it. We had crashed an Arab street party in Dubai and lived to tell about it.

Our cameraman Francisco and me
after the Dubai marathon.

The cameraman Francisco told me later in the evening that he had fun talking to them and getting footage. He said to me, "Dude, you are crazy!" I just laughed and told him "You have to seize the moment sometimes. Life is about fun moments. I may be 66 but there is still a kid in me. You snooze you lose." He just smiled big and laughed. He would have loved the drunk Australian beer guy the night before. He should have filmed that guy.

The next three days, Francisco and I grew close. We had bonded over having fun. He included footage of that in the next day's official World Marathon Challenge video which brought lots of comments.

Richard came up to me the next day and complimented me, saying that I was always happy and had a great attitude. I guess he was having challenges with a number of runners who were complaining. Actually, he said one guy was such a pain in the ass that if the guy gave him any more crap, Richard was going to kick him off the plane. That guy was a rich NYC primadonna. He could be an ass, as could a number of the East Coast rich guys. Some acted like they had always been privileged. Others acted normal.

To me this whole thing was supposed to be fun and an adventure. I thought, roll with the ride. Why be so serious? This is an experience of a lifetime. I wanted to live it and enjoy it as much as I could. Francisco got it and smiled. Others didn't enjoy it as much as me. They were put off by the disorganization.

Running in Dubai was another long, lonely night. The damp air made it comfortable. I had a slight sweat going. The surface was fun as I adjusted the stride to slide a bit on the concrete. I ran a little bit with the Florida Marlins president Mike Hall and his friend, which was fun. We talked a lot about nothing, just to make the time pass. And Heather, the nice hedge fund lady was part of the group for a while.

By this time, we all knew how everyone ran. It was obvious. I was in the six hour range so I knew all the six hour runners. I knew the guys with bad blisters and blown up feet, ankles, hips and knees who were struggling behind us.

My daily running game plan continued to be start out strong for the first three hours and not walk at all. Then reevaluate. Each day so far was different. I wanted to see how long I could be ahead of the six hour people.

In Perth they passed me up about at the 20 to 23 mile point to my disappointment. And they enjoyed passing me too. Not wanting to be caught and passed kept me focused and pushing. One of the guys was just a little older than me and doing great. He was steady and disciplined. And he was always talking and having in depth conversations about something. I tried to not waste my energy by having conversations, so I didn't talk a lot. It wasn't fun to have him pass me.

Honestly, I just wanted to get on the course, and get off the course. It was six hours of work. I loved the accomplishment but it was a daily physical and mental grind. I noticed how I wasn't eating anything on any of these runs nor was I drinking a lot. It was weird. I didn't seem to need it. I just got in a zone where I'd try not to sweat much, focus my thinking and just motor along. In the Antarctic we froze. In Cape Town and Perth we sweated. Here we were wet from the dew.

I want to thank Richard for his course selection. Each one was unique and pretty in its own way. I couldn't be happier doing those marathons. If I had to do seven marathons, these courses were fine for me. My brain and senses were stimulated by each location.

The last loop in all of these were lonely experiences. They could eat you up emotionally or cause you to lose focus. Most everybody of the 50 were off the course by around five hours so there were long stretches of quiet aloneness in the dark. Most had discarded their head lamps by the end of Perth as they really weren't needed and I didn't see them again at night. The dark was clear and bright with occasional streetlights showing the way. There were maybe 5-10 people still running. And sometimes we said "Hi" to each other and other times we passed each other in silence. It was just a grind.

On this one, as I came close to finishing, I decided to slip into a beach public toilet, take a leak and put some water on my face. Why? I am not sure. Then I ran through the finish area acting like it was a special Olympic moment! It was about 2 a.m.

Someone took pictures and told me my time was 6:10 and I didn't care. It was over. That was all I cared about. I had another one in a few hours in Lisbon.

I grabbed my bag with my extra shoes, socks and light jacket and headed to a shuttle bus.

It wasn't far away as I could see the driver napping through the windows. He took two of us back to the hotel which was quiet by now.

Up to the room and there was my roommate going through his one hour post-race rituals with all the room lights on. He had his motorized compression bags on which massaged and vibrated his legs. It had an irritating noise coming from it. He informed me that he was going to stay up all night and wasn't going to sleep. I said inside, "Crap... Why did I have to have him for a roommate?" I hadn't had one before.

I paid extra for single rooms specifically for no roommates. Not this time. Then he told me that he was an entrepreneur. He had started his tech company, and was doing better than expected. He had lots of employees, and his kid in private school. Overall, he liked to be impressed with himself. He thought I would be too.

I listened for a little bit as I was winding down. I was hoping to shower, and get maybe two hours of sleep. Not a chance. When I was finally done showering and getting my gear packed and ready to go, I just moved a pillow on my queen bed and sat up against the backboard fully dressed and closed my eyes. I so wished I was between the sheets with the lights off. I just longed to be in them even if it was only two hours. I agonized over what I was missing. The guy was a self-absorbed, self-centered asshole. He made lots of noise and had his music on, and never once asked if I wanted the room quiet or dark. Or maybe I was just tired. I had an attitude but it would do no good to get into it with him. So I just shut my eyes.

Somehow the time came to get downstairs and we made it. I never talked to the guy in the room after getting out of the shower, nor the rest the trip. Nor did many others. But he never noticed. He was into himself.

I probably ought to clarify something here: When I talk about this guy like that, I feel a guilty but honest. Let me explain: I am a Christian guy and was a Senior Pastor of a large church for 25 years. I don't know how many personalities are in you, but I have at least two Roberts inside of me.

One is the kind patient guy who goes to the ICU and Pediatric ICU floors in hospitals and visits people, kids and babies who are dying. He has buried over 50 people and done way too many teen suicide or drug overdose funerals. He serves food at rescue centers and has offered street people to come live with him. He's raised over $400,000 for non-profits that have great causes. He tries to be nice and be like Jesus. He has tears come down his cheeks unashamedly often at touching things and almost always at the singing or hearing of the National Anthem. He tries to do what the scriptures say. New Testament Scripture in Galatians 5 says that the Fruit of the Spirit is love, joy, peace, patience, kindness, goodness, faithfulness and self-control. After 47 years, I still have a tough time living them out at different times.

The other Robert thinks people deserve what they get. He isn't very merciful. The Law of the Harvest says, "You Reap What You Sow!" Other religions call it Karma. It says "What goes around comes around." I have other voices in my head that are not so nice or loving. That other guy inside me hoped the proud insensitive ego'd out guy would get dealt with and break a leg. He needed humility and awareness of other people. Those two men inside me battle every day. For me, it can be a challenge to be the nice patient understanding Christian guy around some men.

Here's something to think on: In our last class of Air Force Special Ops candidates, we had 50 to make it out of eight weeks of training called BA (Basic Airman) Prep. It used to be called INDOC it is where you do everything possible to still be there at the end of your eight weeks of training and graduate BA Prep. Then if you are fortunate you go to "The Selection Process" - eighteen straight days of testing. It is a more intensified BA Prep. Everything gets harder and more stressful. It is where the instructors put pressure on you even more to see who the real you is. It is like the end of Navy SEAL BUDS training.

This last class, 50 candidates made it to "selection" out of probably 100-120 kids.

At the end of selection, 36 kids were picked up to enter one of four Air Force Special Ops Communities. Pararescue being one.

That means 16 Candidates didn't get picked up by any of the four Special Ops Communities. After surviving all that training.

Why ?

Because most often, the four Special Ops communities did not feel that the personality of the kid or young 30 year old guy would fit in their teams' environment. Meaning, a lot of kids didn't learn the most basic lesson of the eight weeks of training: look out for your teammates. Instead they were selfish, self-centered and not good team players. At the end of the selection process, the 52 candidates do an assessment on their 51 other classmates. They are asked, who were the best guys in the class in certain things, and who were the worst guys in the class in other things. They were asked who they did not want to be deployed with. It is like in business getting a "360 Review".

If you ranked at the bottom as being a jerk or where no one wanted to be your teammate you most likely were not picked up by any of the four Special Ops Communities. To me that's really sad. The Special Ops candidate never learned in eight weeks about being a good teammate. Probably still to their surprise was the fact that their teammates didn't want to be around him if they didn't have too. Those who didn't get selected probably still think they got screwed and got a bad deal. They are now back in the regular Air Force.

There are people like that. They are whiners and complainers. They are selfish and self-centered. There are cocky and know-it- alls. They think they're hot when they're not. They don't know that their so-called friends really are not their friends and don't like them. It never occurs to them that is a possibility.

In combat we have something called friendly fire. Friendly fire is where one of your teammates gets shot and killed somehow. And it wasn't by the enemy. Nobody misses that guy. He was not a good teammate and he was a pain in the ass. He was draining and maybe a potential hazard to the team. He was eliminated.

I am a Christian guy and try to be a Christian guy. However I am not a "Praise the Lord" church guy. I don't like or appreciate certain types of men. I hang out with real men who are good, kind, sensitive men. It doesn't matter to me if they go to church or not. I like humble men who know who they are. They are the kind of men who are quiet and confident. They don't need to talk a lot or draw attention to themselves. They are aware of others. Probably, you don't want to mess with them. Guys like him are the opposite. It wouldn't surprise me if guys like him run into a friendly fire situation in their lives. Like getting fired. One guy came to my church after a divorce with his 4th wife and still blames all of them for not getting and appreciating him.

He was an unteachable jerk and didn't last long with us. I occasionally told some men to find a different church. The pastor side of me wasn't always patient or long suffering. Somebody else would be happy to have a warm body in their church pews. I want men who want to be good strong polite men.

I am a father of three girls and two boys. My girls taught me a lot about being sensitive. My boys taught me a lot about fathering stuff. I am grateful to them and my wife for helping me grow.

I've talked to secular and Christian men in over 30 nations about becoming better men. Some guys liked to hear me speak and asked me back yearly. Some didn't.

This roommate of mine stirred all this up in me. A lot! But I was tired. I'd just finished my fourth marathon in four days and my second night marathon in the last two days. I was a little edgy leaning against the wall of my bed with the room lights on with his music playing at 3 a.m. I didn't like the compressor sound of his leg massage machine making its rhythmic whooshing sound every 15 seconds. Lastly, he liked his singing to his music! I developed an attitude.

We got down to the lobby at sun up. No one talked much. Sarah had run with her headscarf and had some local Muslim girls start running with her and was elated. They wanted to be runners too, but girls didn't run in public much there. I thought she was having a Lawrence of Arabia moment.

Then I asked Dave McGillivray if he wanted to have a picture together with the world's tallest building in the background. He did and it was a fun way to close up Dubai.

In Perth, Dorn, the México Walmart executive came up to me and said excitedly, "Robert, you've got to meet Dave. You both did IRONMAN year three together in 1980 in Honolulu!"

I said "Really. Who is Dave?"

And he took me over an introduced me to David McGillivray, a quiet 63 year old guy. He was the long time race director of the Boston Marathon.

We reminisced some and laughed a bit. He was 23 and I was 27 back in 1980. Now I was 66 and he was 63. We enjoyed knowing that after all these years of endurance sports, we were still in the game. Here we were in year four of this crazy new event like we had been in year three of IRONMAN. I guess, if it was new and crazy, we were attracted to it.

Dave had finished 140 something marathons and is always the last runner each year in the Boston Marathon. He called himself the sweeper. Someone told him about this crazy thing and paid his way. So he did it.

Then somewhere in our conversation he mentioned that he NEVER WALKS any marathon he does. NEVER. It was his code or something. I

**Me and Dave McGillivray at the Burj Khalifa.
It's not easy to get a selfie and the world's tallest
building in a photo!**

mentioned that I did and that he was The Man! I was just a poser. He laughed but you could tell he was a long time hard core marathoner. He is a nice, warm, smart, professional man who was focused, intense, and mostly quiet. The rest of the trip we spoke occasionally but not a lot. I think he didn't have much to say and neither did I. We just wanted this thing to be over. However, it was fun to be the two senior endurance guys on this trip. We had 38 years of stuff like this. The rest were just kids.

We took the bus back to the VIP Terminal and then waited and waited again. Finally the tarmac bus came to take us out to our plane and board. Up the steps again and back to our homey beds. No champagne this time. I just wanted to get to sleep.

I laid my wet stuff out again to dry on the floor. It was about 8:30 a.m. and about 75 degrees. We had landed yesterday about 3:30 p.m. It was a quick stay. The flight attendants said they had gone to their hotel, had dinner and slept. They were tired too. They had served us since leaving for the Antarctic. In Lisbon, they'd be rotating off. They were looking forward to that.

We finally rumbled down the runway. It was a relief. Dubai was in the books. I pulled down the shades and stuck in my earplugs and crashed. I mentioned that I could be woken up for breakfast. Then I was out. We all needed a quick sleep as the flight was only going to be five and a half hours today. That meant with takeoff, landing and eating, we could possibly get four and a half hours of sleep. It was a short sleep and it had been a long night. The next marathon would start in 10 hours

Saturday: Lisbon Portugal

We landed in Lisbon at about 4:30 p.m. to a typical European winter day. I never tried to get the time changes down. All we knew was that no matter what time it was, when we landed, we would be running shortly. Lisbon was cold, damp and overcast. It had been raining on and off for some time.

After the Lisbon immigration process it was to our busses and then a short ride to our hotel. This small corner downtown boutique hotel was our home for 10 hours. We again were told we were running behind a bit. "So hurry. Get checked in, changed and downstairs in 30 minutes." That was impossible. Check in was slow for 50 people with two receptionists.

The elevators were slow and small two to three person European elevators. I was on the sixth floor so I wasn't about to walk those steps. I waited and waited for an elevator with the others. After about 30 minutes

I finally made it to my room, changed and got back downstairs. I grabbed a coffee as we waited in the lobby for directions.

Going on at the same time with us, was a black tie event for some company. There were lots of young men and women everywhere going to their formal event. Guys were getting tuned up and drunk. Ladies were looking to have a good time in their formal black dresses and new hairdos. I saw attire that I hadn't ever seen before, probably because I am not stylish, and I'm old. But one guy had a black top hat and cane and looked very Churchillian. I complimented him as did his friends.

We were in running clothes with windbreakers and they were in formal attire which made for a fun time in the lobby. But all of us had to go outside into the rain.

We left about the same time. A big guy name Jack who had done the 777 back in 2016 met us at the hotel and greeted us. He was a big, fun, opera singer who had done the 777 on a challenge. He didn't train a day for it and made it! He must have been 6'2" and 230 pounds. He was a 777 celebrity! He was going with Richard and the staff to the starting line. He was dressed all in hot pink. He was a trip, a great fun happy guy that worked in a private boarding school.

We all walked in the rain about four blocks until we arrived at a waterfront area. That road was cobblestone walkways and plazas. I thought, "They wouldn't have us run on uneven cobblestones would they?" Sure enough, part of the course and loops were on these slick and uneven slippery cobblestones.

The course was six loops along a waterfront area which ran past a large bridge and back to the cobblestone area.

The rest of the course was on wooden planks, then on asphalt and concrete walking paths. It was cold and you could see your breath. It started finally at about 7 p.m. It took longer than anticipated to set up the start and finish areas so we just stood in the rain. I wore my light jacket with my baseball cap.

The small horn went off and it was just a grind; not much sleep, in the rain, and cold. The one thing I could say was that it was a lovely setting! The bridge and hotel lights made for a beautiful postcard setting. However the cobblestones were slick and jagged. The wood planks were wet and slippery and gave a little as you ran on them. They were laid end to end so you had to be careful where the ends came together. One board could be higher than the other which meant you could catch your toe on a higher end of a board than the previous one and stumble. But it was a great night to be running in Europe along a busy shipping and boating river in the rain!

About the fourth loop, I slipped on the cobblestones and almost went down. As I regained my composure I almost pulled my hamstring again, but survived the near fall without injury. But it woke me up. I didn't want that hamstring injury to flare up again.

Then came the plank section again. The boats were all lit up going both directions on the river. Boat horns were going off. I was so enjoying watching the boats and cars on the bridge above that I forgot to pay attention to the end board planks.

Sure enough, I caught the front of my shoe on a raised end of the plank and tripped. I was heading face first into the wet plank when I turned and landed on my right shoulder and just slid which was sort of cool. I rolled with the fall and was unhurt. I just laid there in the middle of the course. It was about 10 p.m., cold and raining. I opened my eyes and felt the rain falling on my face and just said to myself, "This feels soooo good. Nice fall. I wish I could just lay here for a while and forget the run. How rad is this! Laying in the rain!" I looked up at the black star filled sky and heard the boats passing, their horns honking. It was an exhausting, but memorable moment. I enjoyed the whole thing.

Then another couple of runners ran by and said, "You OK Rob?" To which I replied, "Yep, all good. This is great. You should try it!" They laughed and took off without a word but I could hear them on the planks leaving me. I was having a moment again! You had to love it. I would never have chosen to be down there but it was so comfortable. I was getting soaked so I did the prudent thing and slowly got up and checked myself out. All good. Just wet. I got going quickly, so I wouldn't get cold cold. You get to know your discomfort levels. There is cold and then there is wet to the bone cold. I was just cold. So I started again.

The other eventful moment came when I found myself needing a toilet or a bush. If you are a runner, you always check out the landscape because you never know when you might need a toilet. We were running sometimes through a bar and restaurant section that was pretty lively for a rainy night. All of a sudden I felt like I had diarrhea about to make its debut. It was a small panic. Fortunately, there was this one friendly beer bar and restaurant with red and white plastic tablecloth covered tables outside and normal tables inside. I'd run by it now probably three or four times and it had caught my eye as a good potential pit stop place if I was going to need one.

I was wet with my running bib number on my front and just slowed into the front door. I gave a big smile to the hostess and bartender and asked if they would be so kind as to allow me to use their toilet or loo? They stared at me like I was a little eccentric and finally said yes and pointed to the back of the bar area. Thank goodness for the bib number on. It at least gave me a story for being out there in the rain. I could have looked like the homeless guys I'd been running past.

When they asked, "What am I doing?" I said I was running a marathon outside in the rain. They said "Why?" I asked if I could tell them after I went to the "loo." They said "OK."

I got in and pulled down my pants in this little, tiny toilet area and Wham...I had just made it! Where did that come from? I guess my body was talking to me on my fifth marathon in five days. It was a bit stretched and taxed. Maybe the crash and burn on the planks had shaken things up. Whatever. I was so glad to have made it to that toilet. It could have become a really long, uncomfortable, night.

When I came out they asked again, "It is midnight. What are you doing again?" And I explained, "I was on my fifth marathon in five days on five continents." They just looked at me strangely then saw other runners pass by again outside. "There are 50 of us out there tonight," I mentioned. "I'd love to stay and have a beer and tell you all about it, but I have to finish this run. Thank you for letting me use your loo." They said "No worries", and out the door I went.

I ran until about 1 or 2 a.m. in a light drizzle when I finally finished my six hour run. I ran through the finish area, had my picture taken and headed back to the hotel. It was uneventful as usual. No one was around except the two staff that got stuck staying up. I received a "Good job Rob. Way to go! Go get some sleep." I hugged them and laughed and said, "Thanks you guys. I appreciate you!" Then I walked back towards the hotel alone. It was a moment again. Alone in the rain, exhausted. The walk was therapeutic. I had made another one. Number five was behind me. It was the fifth night congratulating myself – celebrating alone. There's no need for outside validation. It's the opposite of a million in a crowd. It's a unique moment.

There were still five or six men and women hobbling behind me. I felt for them, and wished there was something I could do to ease their journey. They amazed me with their strength in pushing through all the pain they were enduring. Their feet were shot from Cape Town, and some were severely limping.

The most courageous guy was Brett Parker, President of the New York City Bar. At 37 years old he was battling Parkinson's. He was dragging his right leg and right arm now for five days. He said that Parkinson's was not going to steal his life. He was going to live life to the fullest. So he signed up for this thing.

Another guy was an older, pro baseball player. He developed real bad blisters in Cape Town and then had an old baseball hip injury flare about the second day. He was limping and miserable, but would not quit. There were lots of stories out there. But none of the runners would let their conditions knock them out.

One 60 year old or so lady was a real long time distance runner. She had run the North Pole marathon and many others. But day by day, she just slowed down. I didn't ask her much about it but she wouldn't quit. When she ran, she shuffled and just looked at the ground. She had been through this before. And she always had a smile on her face if she looked at you.

I got to the hotel wet, but not too cold. I was just tired. I found a wonderfully empty elevator which took me quickly to my floor and then went quietly down the hall to my room. It was probably 2:30 a.m. It wasn't fair that the fast runners got to sleep a little. We five, six and seven hour runners almost never did.

We had to be downstairs at 7 a.m. I went in and just sat on the end of my bed. I bent over and put my hands on my knees and said "Wow. This is an adventure." I thought to myself again, "Another one. I did it!"

Then I reflected on only using the room a total of 12 hours and me being in it maybe 3 hours. Sort of a waste. It was about time to leave it, hardly using it. It was a nice room. I'd like to stay there a few days and hang out.

I took off my wet clothes and got into the shower. Hopefully there was wasn't further diarrhea damage. There wasn't. I washed my socks and shirt and wrung them out. Then shaved, and got to repacking my stuff. I needed to figure out which Ziploc bags of running stuff I had left to wear in Colombia. Actually, I wanted the one with the Eternity CrossFit t-shirt. Can you imagine...I'd be in Colombia tomorrow! One more to go then Miami!

Amazing!

I threw away the last of the food I brought with me as none of it was, or had been, appealing. Candy wasn't going to cut it, nor the small, boxes of Krispy Kreme Cherry pies I'd brought along. I'd already thrown away some of it in Perth, and this was the remains. Nothing seemed to satisfy my desires. Before I left the States, I had tried to think of special treats that I might like after each run. But now nothing looked good. All that hard work and mental preparation was for naught. I couldn't believe it. I was only eating a breakfast and a dinner on the plane. I ate nothing during the marathons at all. Not one bar, or GU during most of the runs. Nothing seemed to taste right in my mouth or stomach except some basic stuff. Maybe the diarrhea was killing my appetite.

And I felt skinny. Like real skinny. Like diarrhea for days skinny. I wasn't like Louis Zamperini in the movie Unbroken. But I was thin. It was hard to believe looking in the mirror that I had muscle mass back in October at Kokoro. It was all gone. It fell off somewhere on the asphalt during my training, or on the marathons. Now I couldn't do three pull-ups if I tried. I'd lost probably 15 pounds since October. But I felt light. And light is good for doing marathons.

I fell asleep in my sheets for three hours when the alarm on my phone went off. Let's go! It's 6 a.m., have to be downstairs by 7 a.m. so I watched some television and had an in-room coffee.

I brushed my teeth, and rolled my two roller suitcases to the elevator. I made the right choice in the roller suitcase sizes I had brought. What bugged me was that I had all these winter clothes in Ziploc bags that I never wore. But at least they were clean. About nothing else was.

I took the elevator down to find a bunch of tired runners sitting around in the lobby. Some were in the hotel restaurant eating a light breakfast. I went in and got a dark European coffee which was really satisfying for some reason – then I got a second one. It was a nice jolt.

It wasn't raining at the moment. Shortly we rolled our stuff to the busses and loaded it back underneath on a busy street corner. Ted the opera singer, was continuing with us. Richard was fun like that. He said, "If you want to go to Colombia and Miami with us, you are invited" to which Ted said, "Sure." He called his wife and said he'd be back sometime next week and was now part of the staff.

Back to the Lisbon airport and through customs quickly. The tarmac bus took us to our plane where we met our new crew. They'd finish the journey with us. I missed the first crew as they had come to know us, and we them!

Everyone was anxious to get on this flight because it was our last long one. It was 11 hours. We would sleep all day. That was a tremendous thought.

We rumbled down the runway again and off we went to South America. Breakfast was scrambled eggs, bacon, toast, potatoes, 2 cups of coffee, orange juice and a smoothie. I hoped this would plug the diarrhea urges and not give it more fuel. Then I pulled down the shades, got my earplugs to stay in and it was time to sleep.

Sunday: Cartagena Colombia

I never knew airplane flying could be so satisfying. It was comfortable like a bed but not a real bed. Lying down is a wonderful thing. I slept the whole way. We approached Cartagena about 11 a.m.

The airport only has one landing strip going one way. I'd spent so many years flying in and out of Central and South America that it seemed like home. We came in over the ocean, then turned over the jungle, and flew over huts with clean clothes and sheets flying in the breeze in people's backyards.

This time we just came off the plane and walked to the terminal. It reminded me of Managua Nicaragua. Inside, we went through a seemingly 1970's immigration process; old computers, lots of paper checklists and nice people who didn't speak much English. But what they did have, was a bunch of kids holding welcome signs for us as we exited. They were plentiful and so sweet. Someone had organized these elementary and junior high aged kids to come greet us. They smiled with toothless grins and screamed for us. It was picture time and many took moments to be their running stars. It was really a fun welcome to this pretty hot and humid city.

We gathered our bags and were directed to busses in a very crowded parking area and off we went to the hotel. It faced the ocean. Cartagena has an area like Honolulu with tall highrises along a main downtown area on the beach. Our hotel was just outside the downtown to the north. Even though we had a lot of sleep, we were still tired from running five marathons in the last five days.

The ex-president of the Florida Marlins was walking in to the lobby of the hotel and was talking and not looking where he was going. He fell into the indoor fountain pool. I say that not to make fun of him, but it exemplifies how tired we all were. He just walked through the sliding glass doors and right into the water feature pool. He went down face first. Thank goodness he didn't hurt himself. I felt like it could have happened to any of us. He reacted so fast to getting wet that I thought he might have pulled a muscle. It was great comic relief for just a moment. And he was a good sport about it. Everyone had a good laugh and it lightened the mood of exhaustion.

We made our way to our rooms, changed and got back downstairs. Then we waited and waited as arrangements were being organized behind the scenes. About four to five p.m., the busses pulled up and took us to Cartagena's old walled city and fortress. Hundreds of year ago this walled city with cannons facing the ocean was the real deal. Long, high walls face the ocean with buildings behind those military walls. Now the main street runs in front of it along the ocean and into the downtown.

We were bussed to an area in front of the Fort and given directions. We would have a motorcycle police escort through the downtown then turn left into the city and do a big loop back to the old walled city where we would do eight loops around the inside of the old walled city. It would be like running through Honolulu and back to where they dropped us off. It was now dusk and still hot. The sun was setting on the ocean and it was beautiful! Richard had done it again from my point of view. Each race had its own beauty and challenges. Running at sunset along the beach front was great. Lisbon would have been really beautiful if it wasn't for the cobblestones and the rain. But that made it unique and special in its own way.

The challenge here was this third world city had some real poverty attached to it. The road was full of holes and the concrete sidewalk was missing concrete. You had to watch every step or you would twist an ankle or break a leg. I guess that made it fun. It was a broken down Honolulu experience.

The air horn went off and we began. I was excited. Tired but excited. One more to go. Tomorrow morning Miami. I wanted to look at the waves breaking not far from us on my right, but I couldn't see much. Everyone was passing on immediate information like "Hole here", or "Watch this one", or "Watch out here!" until we got in the downtown area. It was an obstacle course. Then we just had to make sure we weren't hit by cars, busses and motorcycles. I really liked it because so much was going on. I found myself running with Sarah and her Cheetah foot. She is sponsored by Nike and is famous for her Cheetah design pads on the bottom of her Cheetah foot. I think she brought seven different rubber pads for different types of terrain. The wet cobblestones gave her challenges as had the snow in Antarctica.

She had problems in the Antarctic because she said she couldn't get a good grip on that snow and ice. This night she was doing great and was, as usual, being stared at by the locals.

These loops were fun, crossing streets, running next to cars and figuring out where to go. The city was alive with cafes, taxis and people. And it was humid and hot.

We made it back to the old walled city after an hour or so and started our interior loops. Richard was having problems with the host race director because the course began to change. One time we were directed to go down one street and then the next time we were routed in another direction. I think it changed three times. We were told the loops weren't long enough for an official marathon and they were trying to get us to run the right distance. I said screw it. They didn't know what they were doing. Two would point to go one way, and another pointed down a different street on my second loop. I took over. I was running the way I knew and not changing. Then it became fun.

I ran in secret as if that was possible. I went down the first loop course with streets that no one else was on and figured out my way around the officials who acted like they didn't know what they were doing. I was going to do my eight loops and not theirs. I think a few of the others were doing the same thing. There was frustration with the runners and the officials and with Richard. He had contracted with some guy to put on this marathon for us. He was pissed. I was having a great time. It was number 6. Enjoy the night! Have fun. Catch me if you can.

By now my shirt was off and stuck in the back of my shorts. I was glazed with sweat. The t-shirt bounced on my butt like a short tail. I had specifically worn my Eternity CrossFit t-shirt for owner and coach Gary Villegas who had another CrossFit Box in Colombia. I thought he'd enjoy me crossing the finish line with his t-shirt on.

And as always, on every loop, I am studying the terrain for potential toilets if I need them. Three things I noticed on the first loop in the Old City:

First: My legs were the freshest they had been for any of the marathons. They felt light and strong. It was such a surprise that it made me smile and want to run faster all the time. But I wasn't going to be lulled into that mistake. Legs can change at any moment as can stomachs. But they sure were fun to feel. Why in the sixth marathon I'd have the best legs of the week is beyond me.

Second: there was a row of restaurant bars on this one main street we ran down that all seemingly had large screen TVs with soccer games playing. But the last bar had the Super Bowl on! The Patriots and The Eagles were just starting to play. Can you believe it?! I would be able to see the score if I ran slowly by the big window in front.

Third: There was one nice restaurant bar owner standing in front of his restaurant who smiled at me and yelled some encouraging words in Spanish. He was my guy to nurture a relationship with. I may need his toilet later in the evening.

On the second loop, my legs were still fresh and strong and I saw my restaurant owner again having a cigarette outside his front door. I waved at him again and made him smile. He yelled something back at me in Spanish. I was securing my friendship.

From then on, I felt so good that I just kept knocking out the loops. I had decided to not worry about the Super Bowl until the second half and just stay focused on my run.

About the fifth loop I checked out the Super Bowl and it was the beginning of the fourth quarter.

It's the SUPER BOWL! I had to stop and watch the 4th quarter and have this moment. I really look and felt skinny.

I thought to myself, "I have a lot of time to finish and I feel so good that I think I'll shut down my running and watch the game!"

I was sweaty, my shirt was off and my bib number reversed and on my butt as I walked into the restaurant. All the seats were filled with Americans and other locals. It was the Super Bowl in English. Tremendous! I found an open spot near the door, got down on a knee and watched the game. A few people looked or stared at me but most couldn't care less. They were enjoying the game.

This was a Super Bowl moment to remember for sure. Soon I wasn't sweating and it became a nice experience to just relax for a while.

When the Eagles won, the place went crazy. Seems there were more Eagles fans than Patriots. I had hoped Tom Brady would pull a rabbit out of his hat but the last drive didn't produce a score.

When I turned around, there were six more American runners who had stopped to watch the game. Other runners just kept running by, uninterested.

I went outside and we all talked for a minute about the game. It was so fun. We were enjoying ourselves taking in the moment. Then we resumed running. I think I'd taken 40 minutes off, and now I was stiff and felt like an old man. I started jogging and finally began to warm up and break a sweat.

We all scattered and I was alone. It was time to focus.

Running in the streets of Cartagena during my 6th marathon in 6 days.
One more to go! Notice the lady in the background.
The main square was filled with working ladies after dark.
Sort of unique to run 8 loops by 20-40 women soliciting.

I made the rest of the loop when I had to go to the restroom. I knew exactly where to head.

It was now dark and the owner had gone inside. I guess he was tired of looking at the runners. I stopped and he was seated at the bar. I smiled and asked if I could use his toilet. He pointed towards a hallway. I went down and it was a dead end. There a small closet sized room had an accordion door, a toilet and the sink was outside in the hallway. I thought "OK", this will be interesting. Not sure if I could get the accordion door shut with me in there.

I backed in thinking that I may want to sit down as my stomach was talking to me again like yesterday. But when I looked back over my shoulder, there was a big, dark rag in the toilet. How gross. Who would have left their stupid cleaning rag in the toilet?

"What was I going to do?" was my thought. I knew I needed to find a way to win so I stuck my hand down in the toilet pulled out the rag and dropped it on the floor on the side of the toilet. Fortunately, my stomach ended up being OK and I just took a leak. Then I pulled open the accordion door and left. I smiled at the owner and thanked him and went out the front door. It had worked. I had made a friend of the guy and he let me in his restaurant. It always is wise to make friends in these things. I never know when I will need some help.

About half way around in that loop I was startled by this thought, "Where is my T-Shirt?" It wasn't bouncing like a tail as it had been before. It was gone. Then I had a worse thought, "Oh No, that wasn't a big rag in the toilet but my shirt. Crap... No way. It must have fallen in as I was maneuvering around in there." My Eternity CrossFit t-shirt was now soaking wet on the floor by the side of the toilet.

I sped around on that loop and went back in and the owner just looked at me like "What are you doing here again?" I pointed to the toilet area and just said I had to go back there again and didn't wait for his permission. He probably thought I had diarrhea.

I felt awkward and stupid to say the least. There it was. My t-shirt was in a clump on the floor in a puddle of hopefully only water. I picked it up and took it to the sink in the hallway and began to rinse it out over and over. If it had had pee or crap on it, it was gone by now I hoped. Then I squeezed it and rung it out one last time and walked out with it.

I showed the owner who had been drinking for a while by now. He just stared at me like I was bothering him. I smiled again warmly and showed him my wet t-shirt which puzzled him. Then I smiled again and quickly left. When I got back to running, it was now cooling as it was after midnight. I thought what the heck and put the t-shirt back on. It could be gross or could be clean. I didn't care. No one else would either. It kept me cool as I wasn't sweating anymore.

By the end of the race it was dry.

When I ran through the finish line about 2 a.m., I smiled and raised my hands like a winner of something. I made sure the two staffers who

The next to the last run. Finishing in Cartagena with the Eternity Crossfit shirt on, thankfully the toilet water had dried, and this was clean sweat.

were still there took a good picture of me with my nice clean shirt on in an empty public square. I couldn't help but chuckle at my Super Bowl night and where my t-shirt had been earlier in the evening. It was another moment! It was great and I was cooked.

At the finish there were as usual, two guys congratulating me, "Good job Owens!" I said, "Thanks." and went to find the bus.

At the end, I, like the others, was directed to walk outside the Old Walled City to where a shuttle bus was supposed to be. This time it was there. The driver had two of us and we asked him to not wait for a third runner which was selfish on our part. But we really wanted to get back to the hotel like the others. And we didn't know when the next runner would finish behind us. Seems a like a terrible attitude on my part. Looking back I'd probably do it again. We were surviving. Everyone wanted their shuttle to leave when they got to it and get them back to the hotel. We had to be in the hotel lobby again at 6:30 a.m. ready to go. I had a few hours in the hotel before we left for the plane.

In silence, the driver drove us back to the hotel. We got out and went up an elevator to the second lobby. That in itself was strange. Why have a lobby on the second floor where everyone had to go up a small elevator to check in? When the doors opened up, there were probably twenty runners sitting in the lobby talking and eating room service. They had all decided to say "To hell with sleep." They were laughing and having fun and acting like they hadn't just run a marathon, nor that it was 4 a.m. They all smelled that the finish line was close. It is almost over.

It was bizarre to me. It was like a bunch of giddy people throwing sleep to the wind and just enjoying the knowledge that they had made it. Now all of us had to do was show up in Miami and finish.

On top of this, the flight to Miami was only two and half hours long, meaning we wouldn't get any sleep on the plane before the last one. It was not overwhelming anymore. We were beyond tired. We started Cartagena at about 5:30 p.m., I ran until two something and will start the last marathon in Miami by 12:00 p.m. the next day. We will do the last two marathons like the first two: start two marathons within 24 hours. But we will also have been up for twenty four hours when starting number seven.

Most people would think this was crazy but by now it was expected.

As I got off the elevator, a couple runners called me to come to join them but I was exhausted. I wanted to get to my room and get my much anticipated shower. I lied and said I'd be back in a few minutes and just went to the other set of elevators down the hall to get to my room on the sixth floor. If I sat down, I'd never have gotten up.

That picture will stick with me for a long time. In Kokoro, I learned that time could become irrelevant. Here again, we'd run six marathons in six days and these runners said screw sleep. We don't need it. Just get us to the starting line and we will run number seven.

I got to my room, looked out my ocean view window at the beautiful, dark shoreline lit up with all kinds of street lights and just took it in. I'd done it. It was over. Miami would not be an issue. Sandy was already there waiting for me and it would be a fun day. I remembered my memorized self-talk thoughts: Easy day Fun Day, Epic Day, Feel Good – Look Good – Look like Hollywood, There can be no doubt, This moment is not too big for me. Pain for the moment – Glory for a lifetime!

I took my shower, washed my stinky clothes and repacked. We had to set out our running clothes here in Cartagena for the 10:30 a.m. Miami landing because we would go directly to the starting line from the Miami airport. No hotel.

When I was organized, I just sat down on my bed, set my alarm for 6:30 a.m. and closed my eyes while leaning against the wall. I was out quickly. An hour later, my alarm went off and we all met in the lobby to go back to our charter jet for the last time. Sleeping sitting up never felt so good, even though it also felt worthless.

It was humid and warm when we got out of our busses about 8 a.m. Getting through immigration was much easier this time and a tarmac bus took us to our big comfortable AirBus 300-400.

We took off about 8:30. It was my last flight sitting next to Heather. We chatted and enjoyed the moment. We had had some good talks on the flights which were fun. She had adopted kids and I was adopted which led to some rewarding conversations.

The flight went quickly. The runners were excited to get this last marathon behind us. Everyone was tired. Family and friends were flying in for the celebration. We had made it.

We touched down in Miami about 10:30 a.m. and then made our way through immigration again. That took a while. They wanted to know what we had been doing in so my places in a week. I guess it didn't make sense to them. Finally everyone got through.

I asked Richard if I could take an Uber and leave to meet Sandy at our hotel and change there. He agreed.

Precedent had been set for acting individually when one of the Miami hedge fund guys asked if he could leave after the Cartagena race and meet the group in Miami. He wanted his private jet to come pick him, his friend and Sarah up. He was tired of all the immigration hassles. He was allowed to do so and meet everybody at the starting line at 12:00 noon. So I asked for the same. Uber was a little different than a private jet but I wanted Sandy to be informed and taken care of. It all worked out.

I Ubered to South Beach and went to the wrong hotel. Of course! I was tired, sweating, rolling my two rollers and frustrated. I had made plans to stay at that hotel, and then canceled them when I found that it wasn't at the finish line. But I finally found the name of the hotel that I had booked and went there. I felt so inept. How did I mess this thing up. They gave me a key and I went upstairs to change when the runner's busses rolled in across the street. I panicked thinking they would start the marathon without me. I searched for my clean last day running clothes and couldn't find them. I had taken them out in Cartagena but forgot where I had put them. More panic!

I kept looking across the street to see what they were doing. Nothing organized looked like it was happening so I kept scrounging around trying to find my stuff. But then I thought about Sandy: She was looking for me on the bus for sure, but I didn't come off it. I had texted her about my Ubering but I didn't get a response. I now called her, so she wouldn't panic not seeing me with the rest of the runners, but she didn't answer.

I was becoming more concerned for her, what was she thinking?

I found my clothes and put them on in a minor panic. Probably Richard wondered where I was as well. I'd hoped to beat them to the starting line but they got through immigration faster than I anticipated.

Down the elevator and running through the hotel in sort of a OJ Simpson old Hertz car commercial fashion I went. I know that example dates me a bit. Then across the street and to the portable event tents I ran.

All sorts of people from all over the world were there to celebrate the final big day. We had a number of nations represented. It was exhilarating to see everyone and feel the excitement in the area. Pictures were being taken by everyone and there were giggles and laughter everywhere. People were hugging people they knew and didn't know. The media was there and the locals just stared. It was a fun scene. We were celebrities for a few minutes. We had made it, and in a few moments we would start the last one.

After about 10 minutes of searching I found Sandy having a great time with all her new friends. She was laughing and chatting with many excited ladies. All of them were there to celebrate with the 45 husbands or boyfriends running their last marathon. She wasn't even looking for me.

We hugged and kissed, and she could see I was OK to her relief. I had so much adrenaline running in me that I again forgot to be tired. Tired was for later. I was excited! It was almost over!

Richard congratulated us and told us about the course. He apologized to us for starting at 2 p.m. instead of 12 p.m. as scheduled. It was warm for sure, but not a Miami heat deal breaker. Maybe it was 80 degrees.

Then different people said nice, excited things. A final announcement came amongst all the hugging that there was a finisher's victory party paid for by the guy with the private jet. He was a nice guy. We all appreciated his gesture to take care of all us. It was to be at 9 p.m. in the penthouse of a hotel close by. That gave everyone seven hours to finish.

There were pictures taken and then the air horn blew to start the final marathon. There were yells and cheers going on from everyone! Runners and spectators went nuts. It was a tremendously great moment. We didn't care that most of us hadn't slept since the last one. It was our last time running together even though everyone would be finishing at different times. There was a sense of community and goodwill in the air.

And we were off.

I just ran by myself and found my pace. My sweat broke and my lungs were nice and open. Rhythm came easy. I just had to go to work six more hours. It was finally my last six hour work day.

These practiced "self talk" words came quickly:

"Easy Day! Fun Day! Good Day. Epic Day! Legendary Day. Having fun Day. Loving it Day. Crushing it Day. Amazing Day. This is not too big for me day!" They made me smile.

All these thoughts began to fill my senses:

Mark Divine's words from before Kokoro came back to me, "Robert, you will crush it." I didn't crush it, but I did it!

Gary Villegas, my CrossFit coach's words came back as well, "Owens, you are a BEAST!" with that huge smile and those staring eyes. He used to say all the time with a big smile on his face, "Go Boy! Come

At the start of the last marathon in Miami.

on Boy. Let's Go Boy." Thinking of that made me smile again. He would be smiling today. He was half my age and he called me and lots of people "Boy" in his Venezuelan accent.

Roy from Eternity CrossFit would have a fun smile right now as well as Mike, Tom, Frank, Derek and Bruce.

The Neanderthals were alive and well! Michelle and Erik, my other coaches would be beaming!

I relived telling Mark Divine at the end of Kokoro when we were shaking hands, "Thanks Mark. Now I just have to do an IRONMAN and the 777." I remembered him just staring at me. He looked at me like, "How delirious is Owens? What is he talking about?" I smiled back but I wasn't completely delirious. I was delirious and serious. "Not only can I do Greece, and the Quest, I did your Kokoro, and have two more to do. I will do these next two. It will be an experience. I will live in another realm. Kokoro will not define me."

Then I relished the thought. Like a pig rolling around in new mud. I did them all. The SEALFIT guys don't even know about this.

I remembered the 20 mile weight vest runs. I remembered all the stairs with an added 20 pounds. The sprints up the stairs without the weight vest for closers. I remembered almost puking.

I remembered driving to Encinitas all those mornings for the 6 a.m. workouts, and the almost three years of training at Gary's Eternity CrossFit in San Juan Capistrano, and at 24 Hour Fitness. At my gym, no one ever knew what I was doing there. I was just another senior citizen working out who a few people knew does IRONMANs. I loved being anonymous.

I remembered falling asleep so many nights in my chair at 8:00 or 8:30 watching something with Sandy and she saying to me, "What a great partner you are" and shaking her head. Then she'd get me up, I'd brush my teeth and she'd put me to bed. By the time she got around to her side of the bed, I was gone. Like before I hit the pillow gone. I felt bad that I couldn't remember the night before, the next morning. I thought about all that again. Selfishly, it was worth it. But now she deserved my attention.

I thought about the shoulder surgery from the box jump contest. And now my left one was really sore and needing surgery when this was over.

I thought about my torn left hamstring and how glad I was that the marathons were flat. I remembered I had to stop and lift my left foot up a curb in Cape Town because my hamstring was screaming at me.

I thought about all those videos with Tom Bilyeu, with Mark Divine, Tim Grover, and David Goggins. Over and over I had watched them.

I remembered Jon Gruden's ESPN Quarterback Camp interviews. He'd look at a young quarterback and say to him, "There can be no doubt. Got it?" And they would reply, "Got it sir. I had to have no doubt!"

I remembered my Pararescue classmate Garry Lewry reminding me that we were tough back in our twenties in PJ Indoc. I remembered his recent encouragement. It reminded me that there was more in me than I remembered. We had done 15 behind the neck pull-ups in 1974! I was capable. I'd been through tough things before. Suck it up. No excuses. I love being 66! Hooyah!

I remembered Jon Urbanchek telling us, "Hard work can overcome better talent." And him smiling and calling me an "Idgit" in his thick Hungarian accent, mispronouncing idiot, as he flung a kick board at my head!

I remembered so much so quickly. One moment after another came flooding back to me. I was doing it and I had made it: seven marathons in seven days on seven continents with:

1.) No one believing there was even a reason to do it.
2.) No one knowing if I could do it.
3.) No one encouraging me to do it. Most admired my focus but thought doing the five events was insane.
4.) No one except Sandy and Matt, my son, got it. They saw all five. Matt had witnessed all 50 hours of Kokoro. They understood that if you are in shape, go for the gold. Go for as much as you can. I may never have this time or opportunity in my life again.

I knew I wanted to be legendary before I die. To whom you might ask? I don't know, maybe no one. Why? I don't know. But I wanted my Super Bowl moment. I was having it.

I thought, "Why not? Anyone can be average. Anyone can have regrets. Anyone can live vicariously through others instead of living their own adventures. I don't want regrets. I want to plant my flag I want to win at something! And I want to live life richly."

Real life is made up of moments like these. People in the viewing stands enjoy the experience vicariously. I want to run through the tape. I thought, "I feel completely alive! These three years have been worth it!"

All these thoughts are running through my mind in that first mile.

I ran the first four or five loops by myself and just knocked them out. It was fun! No tiredness. Just happiness. Each loop I was closer to ending it.

About the sixth loop Nick from England and I started running and talking together. We had a good talk and reconnection. We had not run together since Cape Town. Sandy was bored so I mentioned that on the last lap I'd walk so as to have Sandy join me. He said great.

We're on the last loop, Nick, Sandy and I started walking together. It

BEYOND AVERAGE

was about 7:30 p.m. The weather was perfect, it was warm, we had a nice breeze and it wasn't too humid. However, it was harder to walk than run, so Nick and I excused ourselves. We said, "San, sit here. Let us go run and get this thing over with. This walking is hard! We will be back in about 20 minutes. Here are three nice ladies. Have fun." She was a little bummed but after trying to walk, we really wanted to just get it over with. Why prolong this thing.

So we ran to the end of the last loop and came back. It worked out great. When we came back, there she was talking to the ladies.

I said to Nick he probably ought to just keep going. I'd walk with Sandy the last bit and finish with her. He said OK and kept running. I've never seen him again.

I ran to the toilet and sent her ahead to set up the camera, and see me run to the finish line. I ran the last 100 yards and I finished. It was a tremendously fun moment and memory for us. People clapped and cheered. There were all kinds of pictures taken and lots of hugs given. It was dark. It was so worth it. I finished it.

I had my LeBron, Kobe, and Tom Brady moment.

We hung around a little while but we had to get ready for the party like everyone else. So we walked across the street to our hotel.

We went up and I just sat for a while. The rush was wearing off. Sandy reminded me that I needed to get in to the shower. I came back out to the living room and sat in my clean clothes. She then took her shower. When she came out she found me passed out on the couch. I was gone and out.

She tried to wake me but couldn't. Finally she got me to bed and that was it.

I woke up about three a.m. and was so bummed that I had missed the party and seeing the runners one last time. This time Sandy was out. I went back into the living room and was starving. She had purchased some things in a brown grocery bag. I went exploring and guess what I found?

A Box of 12 Krispy Kreme Donuts.

A large bag of Cheetos.

A large bottle of Coke.

It was so uncharacteristic of her, but I loved it. Why would she buy this crap?! It wasn't like us. I'll have an occasional Coke and occasionally some Cheetos. But the donuts?

It didn't matter. I was in heaven. I was like a starving man finding a hidden cache of food on a deserted island.

I ate the whole box of donuts. I ate all the Cheetos and washed it all down with the Coke! And I did it mostly with my eyes closed.

That added to the intensity. I was focused.

Glory to God in the Highest. Peace on Earth and Goodwill towards men! I was in heaven.

I may feel like a mess tomorrow, but it was a moment in time.

Then I brushed my teeth and went back to sleep.

> **"Remember Robert,
> It's 80% mental and
> 20% physical.
> Time is irrelevant –
> stay in the moment."
> – Mark Divine**

The final moments of an amazing year!
Five epic endurance events, and I'm still in the Game.

Just changing the oil and rotating the tires for the next 20 years.

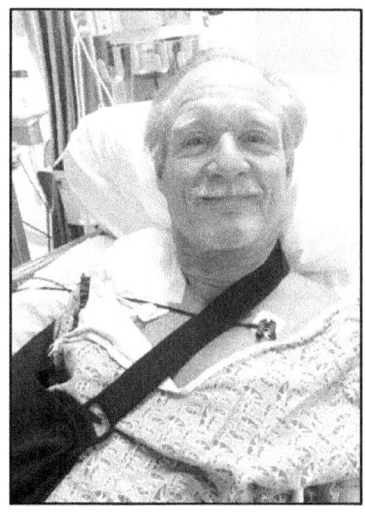

Right shoulder surgery 6/2016.

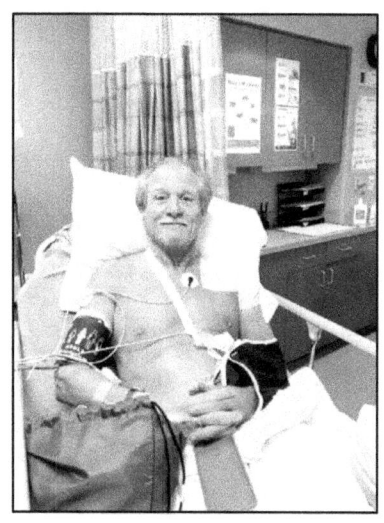

Left shoulder surgery 3/2018

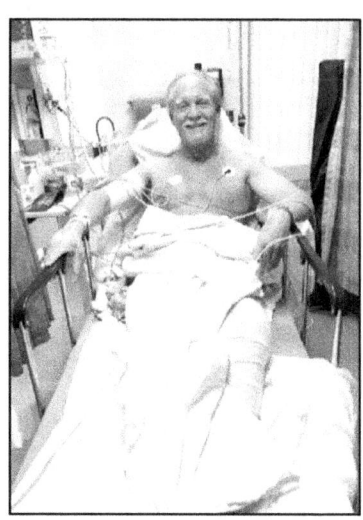

Knee surgery 3/ 2019.

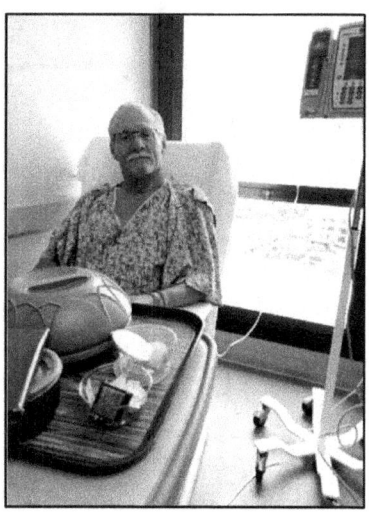

Heart attack 9/3/19 – 3 stents.

BEYOND AVERAGE

Final Thoughts:

I've been asked many times "What was it that you heard when you had that Army Major in a body bag and you were pushing him on a gurney towards his wife and kids that caused you to leave the military?

The voice said "You are always concerned about rescuing people. You rescued people as a beach lifeguard and you helped people during the winter as a ski patrol guy and now as a paramedic and a Pararescueman. This Army Major did not have to die. He was stupid. He made a bad decision to be out there alone and he paid for it. Now his wife and kids are paying for his stupid mistake. I want you to stop putting bandages on the outside of people and start working on people's insides helping them make better decisions so they don't have to die and be dead. I want you to get out of the military and go into the ministry.

I said "Are you kidding me? Please don't make me do that. There's nothing about churches that I like. They are a bunch of losers who don't have a life. They sing stupid songs stand up and sit down all the time and get asked for money. They say hello brother or sister to each other and act like they love each other. Then they go badmouth each other later and gossip about each other. They are hypocrites. I'll do anything God just don't make me go into church work. They should get out of that church and go do something with their lives. I don't want to be associated with them. I want to change the world. I want to do something significant with my life. Please don't make me do church work." (Remember : This is the '60s and early '70s.)Then the voice said, "I want you to go work with young people that are screwed up like you were. Go reach them your way and don't worry about the church. I said, "No. I like it here. I trained my butt off to be here. The Air Force spent over $1 million on me training me. I like being a PJ. I don't want to do it."

A couple weeks later, my Senior Master Sergeant Udo Fischer told all of us the he'd just received notice that there were going to be Post Vietnam budget cuts. Each unit was being asked to downsize 20%. Udo said to us, "Who wants to get out? We need a number of you to leave the military due to budget cuts. All you guys need to think about it because some of you need to get out. I need to know who you are soon. They want a list." I was stunned. I knew God was after me. I remember that I couldn't sleep a lot. I woke up often thinking "Oh God, you're not gonna make me do this are you? Please don't make me do church work."

So I finally said to God, "OK. I told you before in my heart because you are Lord that I would obey you and serve you. I've tried to be obedient to you. I dodged the draft in high school. You told me to make it right and go in. So I did. Now you're asking me to get out. I'll serve you but just don't make me a pastor and have to do church work. I'll work with kids. But, Church work will kill me. It is so boring and worthless. Let me do something fun."

Right after that somehow I came across the book called "God's Smuggler" by Brother Andrew. It was a book about smuggling into the Soviet Union. It was a small paperback and I read it quickly. It had story after story of going in behind the Iron Curtain and serving people. So I wrote to the address that was in the book and told them my story and that I would love to be a smuggler. Could they use a guy like me? And I sent them some money. I never heard back from them.

That Christmas I went home to see my parents. I told them there were budget cuts coming and guys were being asked to consider leaving the military. My parents asked me what I was thinking. I said I didn't know yet. I got home on Tuesday. Then my dad asked me if I'd like to go to Men's Bible Study at 6:30 on a Wednesday morning. Like tomorrow. He said they usually have interesting speakers come once a month and talk to the guys. I said, "Sure."

I didn't like our church but I wanted to spend some time with my dad. I went that morning and the guy speaking was the National Director for Open Doors Ministry which is the smuggling ministry of the book I'd read. I was stunned. What were the chances of that happening? I knew God was still after me. It unnerved me.

After the guy spoke I asked if I could speak to him when he was finished speaking to the other men that had questions. When he was free, I told him that I'd written his organization a letter recently asking if they could use a guy like me. I also mentioned I had never received a reply. He said, "What did you say?" and I told him. He just looked at me and said "What are you doing after this meeting?" and I said "Nothing, I'm just with my dad. I just got in from Alaska yesterday." He said "Come with me to my office" which was 5 miles away. I told my father I was going to go spend some time with this man whose name was Johnny Mitchell. He said ok. Call me later.

Johnny asked me a lot of questions and gave me a personality test. I spent the morning with him and he said, "We could use a guy like you. I can make it happen."

Then he asked me what I thought God was saying to me and I mentioned that I felt he wanted me to get out of the Air Force even though I didn't want to and work with young people. I also wanted adventure and travel and not be working in a church. He said he understood. He said stay in touch and go back and put in for the "early out" the Air Force was offering.

I went back to my Pararescue unit and said I'd be one of the 20%. It was hard to say goodbye to all my relationships there. Within 6 months I was smuggling in Eastern Europe.

I also knew God wanted me to finish my university studies. When I left the Air Force I applied to four different universities but received rejection letters from all four due my previous grades. It didn't surprise me. One of the schools was Oral Roberts University. Why? Because they had some really pretty girls singing on their TV program and it was in the Midwest. I knew I needed to get away from the beach and my old friends. The Midwest seemed boring which would help me with my studies.

In December of 1977, I was with my team of two other guys smuggling in Czechoslovakia, Poland, Romania and Hungary. One night we were on the Hungarian Russian border and praying for guidance and wisdom about meeting a certain underground group. As we were praying, I had that same voice that I heard in Alaska say, "Go home and go to Oral Roberts University this next semester. Start school. They will let you in." I told the two other guys that I had to leave Holland immediately after we returned to get back to the States and go to school.

When we returned to our home office in Holland, I took my backpack and headed to the airport. Somehow I had the money for this impromptu flight and flew to New York then to Tulsa. I caught a bus to the campus and walked to the admissions office. I was wearing a black turtleneck, jeans, clogs, a corduroy coat and my large yellow Jansport backpack and a leather satchel over my shoulder. I must have looked like a hippie, or at least strange. I went in and asked to speak to the Dean of Admissions. The secretary asked if I had an appointment. I said, "No. I just flew in from Amsterdam. But I'd like to speak with him." She just looked at me with that "Who is this guy?" look.

She came back and said he'd come out in a few minutes. In a few minutes, Chuck Ramsey came out and introduced himself and looked me up and down and asked what he could do for me. I told him I was there to start the Spring Semester of school that had started the day before. He asked me if I had applied, to which I said, "Yes."

He left and brought out a file and asked me nicely if I had ever received a letter from the school after I applied. I said, "Yes." Then he looked at me with that kind of interesting look and said, "Did you read it?" I said, "Yes." He said, What did it say?" "It said that I wasn't accepted due to my poor grades." He smiled and said, "Ok. Good. So, why are you here?" I told him that a week ago I was on the Russian border smuggling and I heard a voice that said I was to come and you would let me in. I was to be a Theology Major. And that he could put me on 30 day probation. If I didn't make good grades starting tomorrow, he could tell me to leave. He could do that each month all semester. And I told him I'd be a great student. He leaned back in his chair and just stared at me.

He asked me a few more questions then spoke to some ladies and asked, "Do we have any empty beds this semester?" A lady chimed out, "We have one student who didn't show up in Old Towers on the 4th floor." I said, "That is my bed!"

He stared at me and finally just shook his head and said, "Ok. I'll let you in."

The next year, they made me a Resident Advisor which paid for half my school costs and the GI Bill paid for my other half. The next year they asked me to go to the Athletic Dorm and again be a Resident Advisor with the athletes. I continued to make smuggling trips on my breaks and once in the summer. I graduated with a BA in Theology and a Business Minor two and a half years later without any financial debt.

I've heard that voice occasionally over the last 30 years.

People ask me all the time about the stuff I've done and accomplished in life. I speak a lot to secular and Christian groups and am asked questions about developing mental resilience and mental toughness.

Honestly, this stuff in the book is nothing, compared with trying to be like Jesus every day. It is the hardest thing I've ever attempted to do. Maybe like you, I have a war within me every day. For me, it is between two Roberts. The natural guy who wants to be a normal selfish guy. The other Robert wants to be Christ-like, kind, forgiving, merciful, unselfish and not self-centered. My daily goal is not to be religious but to be a better man. It is a daily struggle. I enjoy the struggle.

Thank you again for reading the book. I hope it encourages you!

Rob

www.ingramcontent.com/pod-product-compliance
Lightning Source LLC
Chambersburg PA
CBHW070526010526
44118CB00012B/1063